Global Outsourcing

Executing an Onshore, Nearshore or Offshore Strategy

Marcia Robinson
Ravi Kalakota
Suresh Sharma

Mivar Press, Inc.

Publisher's Cataloging-in-Publication Data

Robinson, Marcia.
    Global outsourcing : executing an onshore, nearshore or offshore strategy / Marcia
  Robinson, Ravi Kalakota and Suresh Sharma
    p. cm.
    Includes bibliographical references and index.
    ISBN 0-9748270-3-7
    1. Management. 2. Business process outsourcing. 3. Information technology. 4. Re
      engineering—Management. 5. Performance. I. Robinson, Marcia. II. Kalakota, Ravi.
      III. Title.
  HD31.B626 2005
  658—dc21
    2005923304

Mivar Press

Published by Mivar Press, Inc.
4080 McGinnis Ferry Road, Suite 603
Alpharetta, GA 30005

Cover design by Graphix Works.

The publisher offers discounts on this book when ordered in quantity for bulk purchases and
special sales. For more information, please contact Corporate and Government Sales at
Mivar Press at contact@mivarpress.com.

Visit Mivar Press, Inc. on the Web: www.mivarpress.com

Printed in the United States of America.
First Printing 2005

Other Books by the Authors

By Marcia Robinson and Ravi Kalakota

Offshore Outsourcing: Business Models, ROI and Best Practices
Mivar Press, 2005

Services Blueprint: Roadmap for Execution
Addison-Wesley, 2003

M-Business: The Race to Mobility
McGraw-Hill, 2002

e-Business 2.0: Roadmap for Success
Addison-Wesley, 2001

e-Business: Roadmap for Success
Addison-Wesley, 1999

By Ravi Kalakota

Mobilizing SAP: Business Processes, ROI and Best Practices
Mivar Press, 2005

Electronic Commerce: A Manager's Guide
Addison-Wesley, 1997

Readings in Electronic Commerce
Addison-Wesley, 1996

Frontiers of Electronic Commerce
Addison-Wesley, 1995

Contents

Preface

Who Is This Book for?

This book is written foremost for the people who are either tasked with or are carrying out the "heavy lifting" of their companies' ambitious global outsourcing efforts: the project managers, team leaders, and team members assigned to improve, redesign, and create low-cost, high-quality business processes.

In addition, we hope that the business leaders who are guiding global outsourcing projects (often called champions or sponsors) can use the book to gain insights into the tasks, actions, and challenges faced by their teams in the trenches.

Finally, anyone seeking to better understand the details of global outsourcing can learn from the material contained in the ensuing pages.

What Does This Book Cover?

When building something innovative, one needs a clear blueprint. Unfortunately, while there is much general discussion about global outsourcing, almost all of it is either anecdotal or simplistic. In order to help you unlock the value of global outsourcing, we decode some of the core concepts behind this trend.

- **Best practices.** Global outsourcing encompasses a broad array of business skills that are essential ingredients for success. Throughout this book, we use best-practice case studies to show you how to apply the concepts to many different processes and tasks and maximize the impact of your efforts.

- **Business models.** Many different outsourcing business models exist. This book gives you customizable guidelines that take into account your business needs and readiness for change.

- **Creating your roadmap.** Global outsourcing is as much about people, vendor selection, country selection, and project management as it is about cost reduction. Our goal is to show you how to achieve a balance between managing people and improving performance.

It doesn't take a genius to realize that the companies that successfully implement global outsourcing are going to put a lot of pressure on their competitors to follow suit. Obtaining even a small cost advantage in today's brutally competitive marketplace can mean the difference between market leadership and failure.

The Organization of This Book

When we wrote this book we tried to structure it so that a variety of readers, from novices to managers in the midst of outsourcing projects, would find it easy to navigate. While you may prefer to read it cover to cover, the content is organized in four parts to help you learn about global outsourcing at the level of depth you choose. Following is a quick guide to the content.

- Part One of the book provides a thorough overview of the global outsourcing landscape. We begin by defining key concepts and trends (Chapter 1), the business process landscape (Chapter 2), and a step-by-step methodology for executing global outsourcing (Chapter 3).

- Part Two of the book provides a detailed overview of the strategy planning process — what, why, and when you should outsource (Chapter 4) and the different business models for making it happen (Chapter 5).

- Part Three of the book focuses on the how-to of sourcing. We present the steps that companies need to create clear, focused global outsourcing strategies: gathering the intelligence via the RFI and RFP process (Chapter 6), deciding on vendors (Chapter 7), selecting locations (Chapter 8), and negotiating the contract (Chapter 9).

- Part Four of the book focuses on post-contract execution. Formulating the strategy and signing the contracts are only the beginnings of the sourcing effort: Processes have to be transitioned, management structures established, and SLAs monitored. We present the steps that companies need to concentrate on to get results: transition management (Chapter 10), governance (Chapter 11), performance monitoring and management (Chapter 12), and exit strategies if necessary (Final Thoughts).

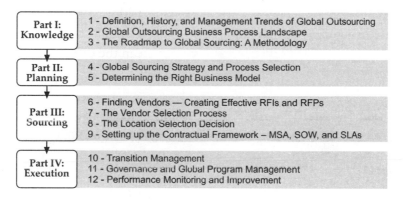

Figure 1: The Organization of *Global Outsourcing*

At the book's end, we hope that readers will return to their organizations with new ideas and an understanding that global outsourcing is a journey, not a one-time event with a quick payoff.

Acknowledgements

We were very fortunate to have the participation of many people who took the time to discuss global outsourcing with us. To each of these people, we would like to express thanks for the ideas, insights, and experiences they shared with us.

In particular, we would like to thank Joe McGrath, Tom Elliott, Shirsh Netke, BVR Mohan Reddy, Deena Harapanahalli, Eric Rongley, V. Bharathwaj, Sudipto Chakravarty, David Burke, Gregg Scoresby, Van Hansen, Janette Everette, Stanley Singh, Srinivas Koneru, Akash Arora, Ismail Al Naqi, Johanna Chapman, Daniel Wittner, Keith Rhodes, Anthony Maeillo, Jim Suciu, Burton Toole, Karl Meyer, Laurent Rotival, Lata Sharma, and Pam Bellamy.

We also would like to thank E-Business Strategies: Jennifer Doty, Tim Geary, and especially Allison Loudermilk for her copy editing expertise and Brandon Doty for his layout and design talent.

Special thanks to Lynn Lorenc, for her encouragement and advice. Finally, thank you to our family and friends who have supported us over the years.

Marcia Robinson

Marcia@ebstrategy.com

Ravi Kalakota

Ravi.kalakota@unisys.com

Suresh Sharma

Suresh1.sharma@gmail.com

Chapter One

Definition, History, and Management Trends of Global Outsourcing

Global outsourcing is reshaping business as we know it. In a handful of best-practice companies, it has migrated from the periphery to the core. Outsourcing has grown so sophisticated that even core functions such as customer care, engineering, R&D, manufacturing, and marketing can be moved either offsite or offshore. The ability to send core functions outside company walls is changing the way businesses think about their processes, cost structures, and competitive positions. This chapter sets the broad stage for the rest of this book. It presents the definition, evolution, theoretical underpinnings, and management challenges related to global outsourcing.

Introduction

More than anything else, the driving force of global outsourcing is customers who want more of everything for less money. If they value low cost, they want it lower. If they value service, convenience, or speed, they want it even easier, faster, and all the time. If they value innovation, they want to see state-of-the-art gadgets and features.

Increasing customer value creation is precisely why companies like Ford, IBM, Siemens, Oracle, United Technologies, SAP, Microsoft, and Unisys are transforming themselves. One or more competitors in their markets are constantly increasing the value offered to customers by improving products, cutting prices, or enhancing service.

For instance, in the IT services sector, Indian firms Wipro, Infosys, and TCS, with their low prices and comparable quality, caused their competitors Accenture, EDS, and IBM to react and move delivery operations offshore. By raising the level of value that customers expect, some leading firms are driving the market and their competition downhill. Companies that cannot cut costs will become a footnote in history.

Most market leaders understand the "more value for less" battle in which they are engaged. They know that customers will not pay higher prices, so they have to reduce their product or service cost structure. This means that they have to drive margin improvement by reducing sales, general, and administrative (SG&A) costs.

Many companies have reached (or are quickly reaching) the limits of traditional cost-cutting methods. These firms realize that to drive even more costs out of their operations they have to adopt a global outsourcing strategy. However, before they can identify and execute outsourcing opportunities that give them operating leverage, three elements are crucial:

- The skills and management practices required to seamlessly integrate both individual projects and large-scale global outsourcing activities into the overall company strategy.

- Leadership that defines and communicates a unifying vision, together with a strategy for achieving it.

- For long-term effectiveness, an organizational culture that encourages and supports global outsourcing.

In this book, we explain how companies can develop and strengthen all three elements, with particular emphasis on the skills, knowledge, and management methods needed to control individual and large-scale business process outsourcing (BPO) and information technology outsourcing (ITO) projects. The focus is how to mold people, processes, and metrics to consistently achieve high performance.

Evidence is mounting that global outsourcing separates the winners from the losers, yet most companies continue to restrict their outsourcing activities to routine operations and cost-control programs. They may require a more thorough understanding of how global outsourcing integrates with strategy and process design to help their organizations compete and grow.

It's Time to Rethink Your Business Strategy

If you are an executive, it's highly likely that you are thinking about this question: How do you lower your cost structure, reorganize high-cost, poorly performing functions, or sustain growth in the fast-changing technology and global business environment?

The answer to this question lies in completing two strategic actions. *Doing sourcing right* will help you extend the life of your current products and business in the short term by keeping costs under control. *Doing sourcing intelligently* will ensure the development of new products and leverage engineering talent globally.

Doing Sourcing Right — Cost-Cutting Strategies

Doing sourcing right lets you compete by lowering the cost of operations. Techniques such as labor arbitrage help sustain you against competitive forces.

What do we mean? Unless you are the lowest-cost provider in the market (or have a tremendous niche or brand), you are constantly fighting against a Wal-Mart equivalent in your industry — a competitor that operates with an "Every Day Low Price" mentality, which forces competitors to keep up or get out. If you do not respond and close the gap between your company and the competing environment it will almost certainly put you out of your business.

Look at what happened to Capgemini, a leading provider of consulting, technology, and outsourcing services, and its relationship with Sony. Although Sony was happy with the services provided by Capgemini, it switched to India's Wipro in 2002. By signing a $5 million contract with Wipro for writing information technology applications for Sony's TV and computer assembly plants in the United States, Sony expects to save 30%. Capgemini could not compete with Wipro's low-priced offshore resources. How do companies like Wipro do more for less? The trick, other than offering low-cost labor, lies in building expertise or economies of scale that a single company cannot match.[1]

Your ability to source and manage global projects is the key to your success. Unfortunately, global project management is still not recognized as a discipline. This book represents one attempt to fill this serious gap.

Although many analysts, experts, and academics have produced good analyses of the outsourcing phenomenon, not much is available in terms of practical know-how that can be used to educate and train professional managers. Clearly, there is a need for rigorous global sourcing project management and execution skills.

Quite a few companies have begun global sourcing but are actually losing money. Many of their initiatives are knee-jerk reactions to the threat posed by lower-cost competition. Doing global sourcing and project management right is indeed a competitive necessity in the short term — enough to sustain your company and then position it for growth as your company innovates with new products or services.

Doing Sourcing Intelligently — Differentiation Strategies

The days of viewing sourcing as strictly an operations function are over. Savvy market leaders consider global sourcing of R&D talent to be their company's lifeline and the best means of driving competitiveness and growth. Significant organic growth in the twenty-first century will come from new products for new markets. Advanced countries and companies must recognize that they need to solve more difficult problems to stay ahead in the growth game.

The Apple iPod, the handheld digital music player, is a great example of intelligent sourcing. Apple handles the iPod design work and sources manufacturing from the Taiwan-based original design manufacturers Asustek and Inventec. Hitachi and Toshiba produce the 1-inch and 1.8-inch hard drives that store the content. Apple has built a multibillion-dollar iPod economy by leveraging global sourcing.

The case of Boeing is representative of intelligent sourcing in software development. For its 787 Dreamliner (formerly known as the 7E7) program, Boeing is taking advantage of the global talent pool across Russia, India, the United Kingdom, Japan, and China. For instance, it has selected HCL Technologies in India as a software development partner. Boeing and HCL signed a multiyear, multimillion-dollar software development agreement under which HCL will provide software services to Boeing, as well as its tier-one systems suppliers for the 787 program.[2]

Doing sourcing intelligently is evident in industries that are rapidly commoditizing, such as textiles. Cheap imports flood the U.S. and

European markets and keep prices down. Global sourcing created a new operating model for textile companies that forced many firms to either adapt to it or exit the industry.

This constant evolution in manufacturing (and even service industries) is called product cycling: when U.S. firms exit labor-intensive commodity products such as textiles, steel, and electronics while lower-cost developing countries move in. This is a natural economic phenomenon that best-practice firms like GE or IBM respond to by adopting a global sourcing strategy.

Global Outsourcing: What Is It? Why Do It?

Every ten years or so there is a surge of interest in cutting operating costs. The previous wave of cost-cutting occurred in the early 1990s under the guise of re-engineering. The side effect of this wave was corporate downsizing. In the early 2000s, after a multiyear economic downturn, we are seeing a similar trend of reshaping business processes with the goal of reducing costs.

The trend is global outsourcing (also referred to as capability sourcing, dynamic sourcing, or strategic sourcing). In this section, we define global outsourcing and provide a variety of examples to illustrate the trend.

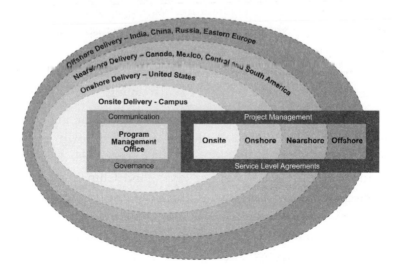

Figure 1.1: Global Outsourcing

What Is Global Outsourcing?

The classic definition of global outsourcing is the delegation of administrative, engineering, development, or technical support processes to a seamless mix of onsite, onshore, nearshore, and offshore resources.

It can also include significant re-architecting of processes. The term "re-architecting" in the context of outsourcing refers to a strategy of developing new process designs and solutions in order to eliminate business performance problems.

Before we delve into the global outsourcing trend, it is important to note that we use the term "global outsourcing" to encapsulate two distinct trends: 1) handing off processes to third-party vendors, and 2) keeping processes in-house but sending them to internal lower-cost locations (insourcing or dedicated captive centers).

Since global outsourcing encompasses onshore, nearshore, and offshore locations, let's distinguish between nearshore and offshore. Technically offshore could include nearshore locations. From a U.S. perspective, offshore would indicate countries such as India, China, and Russia, while nearshore would mean countries such as Canada and Mexico.

The true definitions of offshore and nearshore are based on several variable factors of proximity. These proximity factors include time (time zone), space (ease of access), and culture. Culture is more broadly defined as the reduction of perceived tensions relating to overcoming distance, including differences such as language, accent, and legal barriers. Both terms are defined by the country of origin, referred to as onshore. Nearshore hinges on relative proximity and perceived similarity in culture — your nearshore might be your neighbor's offshore.

With multinational consulting companies out there, many people use the terms offshore and nearshore interchangeably. One of the Big 5 consulting companies we spoke with rejects the very concept of offshore. He stated, "Offshore from whom? When you are in 165 countries, what is offshore?"

As outsourcing gathers speed, the jargon associated with it grows. A few of the newer terms service providers are using follow.

- Best Shore: EDS's terminology for global sourcing, or picking the country that best suits the client's particular situation.

- Rightshore: Capgemini's spin on global sourcing.

- Homeshore: Some people use this term interchangeably with onshore, while others define "homeshoring" as moving work from a higher-cost urban location to a lower-cost rural location in the same country as the company.

Throughout this book we will use the terms global sourcing and global outsourcing to indicate a blend of onshore, nearshore, and offshore outsourcing.

Global Business Process Outsourcing

Outsourcing encompasses manufacturing, IT, and back-office services. Manufacturing outsourcing began in the 1970s and 1980s when U.S. jobs in steel and textiles shifted from the northern states to the southern states. In the 1990s, manufacturing facilities in Mexico, Puerto Rico, Canada, South Korea, and Taiwan began to proliferate and absorb much of the consumer electronics and personal computer production. In the late 1990s, Southeast Asian countries like Malaysia became key areas for manufacturing. In the 2000s, China has become the favored destination with unbeatable labor costs.

Information technology outsourcing (ITO) has followed a similar pattern. In the 1990s, companies began offshoring application development and maintenance, especially Y2K work. With the urgency surrounding Y2K, companies could not find enough IT resources onshore, so they hired offshore firms. The Y2K work soon grew to include mainframe, e-commerce, and ERP programming. In the early 2000s, IT outsourcing expanded to other processes such as help desks and technical support. Originally, companies headed for Ireland, but as Ireland became more costly, they changed course and went to India.

Business process outsourcing (BPO) — call centers, finance and accounting, human resources, and transaction processing — has followed a different pattern. In the 1990s, there was a tremendous movement in corporations to consolidate various fragmented divisional activities and create shared services centers (SSCs). An SSC is essentially a "do-it-yourself" insourcing model in which a large firm sets up its own captive operation. Some of these SSCs began to migrate offshore. The companies that pioneered the offshore SSC model, such as American Express, understood that they could realize more value if they based these centers in foreign countries. Due to their early hard work, we are seeing a steady rise in the number of large corporations establishing back-office processing centers in India, the Philippines, South Africa, and Russia.

The emerging trend of offshoring business processes (or white-collar work) represents a fundamental structural adjustment, not a short-term business cycle phenomenon. The experience of manufacturing illustrates that when it is possible to do things cheaper elsewhere in the world, the work will migrate there. For instance, tough-to-beat labor and overhead costs have made China a top choice for almost all types of manufacturing.

With the relentless pursuit of the lowest global costs, offshoring is becoming institutionalized at many companies. Table 1.1 summarizes some of the drivers for rapid offshore outsourcing growth.

- Continuous cost pressure on U.S. and European companies
- Rapid declines in communication and computing costs
- Dramatic improvements in Internet reliability and functionality
- More offshore suppliers with better capabilities
- High-quality onshore suppliers offering offshore services
- Access to low-cost, high-quality employees, especially for labor-intensive tasks
- A business model for offshoring that has been proven by successful pioneers such GE and American Express

Table 1.1: Drivers for Rapid Offshore Outsourcing Growth

Executing Global Sourcing: The Business Challenge

The complexity and speed with which business dynamics change almost mandate that you follow a robust sourcing methodology rather than be opportunistic. Executing sourcing initiatives effectively is essential for the survival and sustainable growth of your business.

The levels of technology, talent, and business process maturity vary across countries. While a few of the global economies are largely rural, others have reached an industrial era maturity, and still other developed countries have left behind industrial era manufacturing to explore new frontiers of growth. Before we begin discussing and designing the optimal process for successful outsourcing, it is vital to understand that what is right for one industry may not work for others. Cycles of innovation in one market sector and pressures on productivity in another may drive a very unique rhythm for outsourcing. Further, the impact of outsourcing can be visibly seen and felt by others very quickly due to the instant nature of global communications. The tide of modern day outsourcing has swelled to the point that it has become a household topic.

But do not outsource just because others are. You must take the time to understand the gap between the current state of your business and its growth environment. Get to know where you stand. You may be surprised. What appeared may not be supported by your own data. Take the emotion and anecdotal stories out of your strategic planning as much as possible. Assess, measure, and quantify as much as you can about where your business stands today and where you want to take it in the future. Your benefits will become diluted if you are not clear about why you are outsourcing.

The Evolution of Outsourcing — A Brief History

History has shown that societies, countries, and companies that were able to do sourcing right have gained a distinct competitive advantage that brought growth and prosperity to its people.

Let's look at sourcing in the agricultural economy, industrial economy, and the information economy.

Global Sourcing Trends in the Agricultural Economy

Over a few thousand years, the knowledge of agricultural methods, seeds, soil, and tools has evolved and spread over the continents. From the dawn of early modern civilization until the middle of the last millennium (a period of about 4,000 years), China and India posted the highest gross domestic product (GDP) in the world. After all, GDP is a sum of what you produce. The largely agricultural economic output depended upon the number of people in and around the river valleys where most of the early civilizations flourished.

In this agrarian era, the variables in the dynamic relationship between man and his environment were few and changed rather slowly. The same types of seeds and soil were used year after year. Crops depended on weather. Irrigation systems were not well understood or efficiently managed. Demographics remained static too.

The transfer function in this scenario was simple and easy to understand: If you want to grow, either get more people or more property, or move to new, fertile lands. Initially, people did not outsource agricultural produce for growth. They themselves migrated from one region to another to form newer and more prosperous civilizations all over the world. Migration was a means to access more productive agricultural lands. This sounds logical if you remember that the only thing going "technologically" for the early man was his ability to move and migrate. People literally "outsourced" themselves to newer, more productive geographical regions, thus contributing to their economies' and species' growth. The migrations continue today in many parts of the world, although the boundaries, seasons, and skills may not be governed purely by agriculture anymore.

Global Sourcing Trends in the Industrial Economy

New technology enabled new products during the industrial era. Finished products were sold in the colonies while the manufacturers globally sourced vastly needed, cheaper raw materials. Significant advances in materials, manufacturing, engineering, construction, communications, transportation, and management of natural resources changed the GDP equation in a very short time.

Many European countries overtook agricultural societies in the race to economic prosperity. Mechanized farming and modern irrigation systems changed the old coefficients in the transfer function between man and environment. Now a few people in the industrialized world could produce more than an entire country of the old economy. A new order emerged.

Industrialization was such a wide-ranging phenomenon, involving every aspect of the economy and society, that there will always be room for debate about its timing and speed. Most economic historians emphasize the rapidity of British industrialization during 1780–1830. The roots of change ran deep into the past, but during the final quarter of the eighteenth century, industrialization gathered pace. By the time Victoria was crowned Queen in 1837, it had left few lives or institutions unaltered.

The Industrial Revolution took global sourcing to another level and revolutionized the world's supply chain forever. The dynamic impact of the industrial environment was easily perceived. The relationship between man and his new industrial growth environment changed in a few hundred years compared to a few thousand years. As we will see via the following examples, global sourcing started happening within decades rather than hundreds of years.

Sir James Watt and the Steam Engine

In 1784, James Watt, a Scottish instrument maker, invented the steam engine, which revolutionized the railroad industry and contributed to the momentum of the Industrial Revolution. Similar inventions were in advanced stages of development in other European countries. In 1801, Oliver Evans built a similar engine in Philadelphia. Over the nineteenth century, multiple industrialized countries improved on the design of steam locomotives and built their own variations.

Today, more than 100 countries can produce steam locomotives, but most of the technologically advanced nations choose not to. They outsource a large part of the manufacturing of diesel engines and electric locomotives to countries where it can be done at a lower cost. A technology and product that were "once space age in the nineteenth century" have become commodities.

The Textile and Cotton Mills of Manchester and Lancashire

Great Britain generated much of its nineteenth-century wealth through the English mill towns of Manchester and Lancashire. Cotton raw materials were brought from the labor-abundant British colonies like India and from the farms of the southern United States at a low cost, while processed textiles were shipped out. The northeastern United States was the first area to pick up the textile technology in the Americas, but the region suffered from a shortage of manufacturing labor. Later, more textiles mills opened in the southern United States for the same reasons. The southern farm labor gradually transitioned to factories.

Similar mill towns sprang up in many parts of the globe, especially in the British colonies. Gradually, textile technology and manufacturing completely transitioned to lower-cost countries. Surat, a city in western

India, is still considered the textile capital of South Asia. Most of the U.S. and European textile mills have since closed, and now import cloth instead.

More than 200 countries have since acquired expertise in the textile technology. These trends are unstoppable. What took hundreds of years to transition earlier was now taking only a few decades.

The Aircraft Industry

Soon after the Wright brothers made the first controlled flight in an airplane in 1903, about ten countries were engineering and building flight machines that improved on the brothers' design. Today about 30 countries have that capability. Several countries can also design jet engines. As a result Boeing, the leading commercial airplane maker of the twentieth century, has seen its market share plummet from 90% in the 1970s to about 60% today. In order to compete and penetrate new markets, Boeing is leveraging engineering skills available in several of those 30 countries.

Once again, knowledge and technology that took a hundred years to diffuse to other countries during the industrial era was now changing hands within decades or less.

The Race to Space

Space technologies are fast maturing to a threshold that several countries are now able to cross. In addition to Russia and the United States, a select few countries can already design, engineer, build, and successfully launch satellites and long-range rockets, and plan to put a man on the moon in the near future.

Man's ability to figure out what has been done before and improve upon it is amazing. Just as technology is developing in advanced countries, so is the ability of other countries and companies to learn about it and do it better in perhaps less time. The gap is ever shrinking between innovation and competition.

Industrial Era Technologies Have Lost Their Competitive Edge

The previous examples illustrate that many of the industrial era technologies have lost their competitive advantage for growth. It is no wonder then that countries such as South Korea, Taiwan, and Japan have become major economic powerhouses. China and India are also growing rapidly by taking advantage of the commoditization and standardization trends. If their current GDP growth rates are any indication, they will rank second and third in the world in terms of GDP by 2012. Already, their economic power in terms of PPP (purchasing power parity) exceeds that of France and Germany.

The gap between advanced and developing countries has narrowed significantly. As the gap has closed, companies have moved en masse to developed countries to leverage sourcing at a lower cost and enter their growing markets. The exodus of manufacturing and some services and IT work to developing countries like China, India, and Mexico shouldn't come as a surprise.

Nobody has a monopoly on good people. Many new outsourcing destinations are bound to spring up in the near future. Several Eastern European and South American countries are bidding for a piece of the action already. This tide cannot be stopped. It is history repeating itself at a different pace. Once again, the key is not to try to stop global sourcing but to learn to do it right.

Global Sourcing and the Information Economy

With the Internet, a talent pool ten times the size of the U.S. workforce has come online in the last few years with an average wage advantage of 70%–80% versus the first-world countries.

The Internet broke many other barriers of global connectivity to information access and transfer. Computers brought home the reality of sourcing in real time. Before the information economy, it could take time, perhaps decades, before global sourcing affected workforces; thus, the next generation did not feel firsthand the pain of job transition.

In the information economy, global sourcing can occur at lightning speed. Lower costs elsewhere in the world have forced many U.S. and U.K. workers to look for survival options. Skills and experience learned in college and on the job can quickly turn into a commodity.

The Economic Theory Behind Global Outsourcing

Why have onshore, nearshore, and offshore outsourcing become more prevalent? Why now? Is it the ability of nations to focus on and specialize in certain functions (such as India in software development, China in manufacturing, or the Philippines in call centers)? Or is it the reduced transaction costs associated with finding vendors, monitoring their work, and sending work overseas? Actually, it's a mix of both. The first partial explanation is based on Ricardo's theory of comparative advantage while the second stems from Coase's theory of transaction costs.

David Ricardo's Principle of Comparative Advantage

The case for global outsourcing is based on British economist David Ricardo's principle of comparative advantage, that is, the idea that each nation should specialize in what it does best and trade with other nations for other needs.

In his 1817 book *The Principles of Political Economy and Taxation*, Ricardo illustrated the benefits of specialization and trade by using the example of England and Portugal trading clothing and wine. Ricardo famously argued that even though Portugal had an absolute advantage over Britain in producing both wine and textiles, it would most likely veer to producing and exporting its more profitable wine and importing its less profitable textiles.

Ricardo's fundamental argument was that total output would increase if people and nations engage in those activities for which their advantages over others are significant or their disadvantages are the smallest.

Ronald Coase's Theory of Transaction Cost Economics

The roots of global outsourcing can also be traced to Ronald Coase, a Nobel Prize winning economist. In 1932, Coase gave a lecture to students at the School of Economics and Commerce in Dundee, Scotland. He explained why businesses exist as they do — why, for instance, they choose to produce some goods themselves and contract with outside companies to provide the rest.

In 1937, Coase turned the lecture into a paper in the journal *Economica* titled "The Nature of the Firm." Coase's insights, considered by many to be the foundation of modern outsourcing, were not widely accepted until the 1970s when the transaction cost economics school of thought emerged.[3] In 1991, nearly 60 years after he gave his famous lecture, Coase was awarded the Nobel Memorial Prize in Economic Sciences for his seminal work.

Transaction cost theory helps managers think about things such as whether to buy, build, or partner. At the core of transaction cost theory is this notion: When a company tries to determine whether to outsource or to produce goods or services on its own, market prices are not the sole factor. Rather, there are significant transaction, search, contracting, and coordination costs. Those costs, Coase theorized, frequently determine whether a company uses internal or external resources for products or services. This is the essence of the make-versus-buy decision.

At the time Coase wrote his theory, transaction costs were very high. Because information flowed at a glacial pace and supplies moved only slightly faster, companies strove to manage the entire chain of production within the walls of their own corporations. For instance, the Ford Motor Company, a shining example of the vertically integrated corporation of the early 1900s, bought a rubber plantation rather than cede control of that part of tire manufacturing. At that time, Ford's River Rouge plant made steel, glass, and tires, and then assembled the parts all at one site. River Rouge absorbed the industries around it or recreated them under its own roof.

Ford is a classic example of insourcing, or when a company keeps all of its processing in-house. Over time, insourcing has given way to outsourcing. For instance, independent, tier-one suppliers now manufacture many parts that carmakers once made internally. Vertical integration has led to horizontal integration across firms, facilitated by lower transaction costs.

As transaction costs plunge, thanks to the Internet, and as barriers between firms are breached, information is moving offshore at the speed of a broadband connection. With literally a desk and an Internet connection, employees all over the world can process transactions or write code.

With diminishing transaction costs and continued globalization, global sourcing will grow steadily. We anticipate that with lower nearshore and offshore transaction costs, companies will be able to focus on narrow product slivers or business activities and have external parties complete the rest.

Types of Companies Practicing Global Outsourcing

If global outsourcing is a business model innovation, how will it spread throughout the economic ecosystem? Figure 1.2 illustrates the typical categorization of firms in an ecosystem. Based on revenue, we categorized these companies as Global 1000, large, mid-market, small business, and small office/home office.

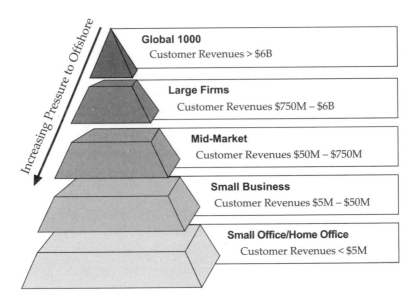

Figure 1.2: Market Segmentation

For the last two decades, the Global 1000 or the big manufacturing multinationals adopted outsourcing. These firms have learned from their many years of offshore manufacturing experience. Now, many years after they ventured into outsourcing, these corporate giants are seeing rising productivity. They are making many more goods with fewer workers.

For proof, look at the numbers. According to the Federal Reserve Bank of Chicago, in the early 1950s the size of the workforce engaged in manufacturing was 35% in the United States. By 2001, that figure had dwindled to 12% relative to overall U.S. employment. Automation is one of the big reasons productivity increased (manufacturing output grew almost 600%). The same trend is evident in agriculture. Only 2.4% of the total workforce is devoted to farming. Technology slowly but surely replaced labor in both agriculture and manufacturing. In contrast, the service sector grew more than fivefold to almost 80% during this period, averaging 2.6% growth per year since 1947.[4]

Over time, the managers of some leading multinationals realized that whatever productivity improvements they achieved in manufacturing they could replicate in back-office processing work, a sizable chunk of the services industry. As a result, the game plan for services offshoring is looking more like the one being played out in manufacturing: automate the processes with technology and offshore the parts that require human touch to low-cost locales like China.

The Global 1000 are putting tremendous pressure on their competitors and suppliers. The reason for this pressure is simple: If one company has a 10%–15% cost advantage in any industry, the other players have to follow suit. This "follow the market leader" phenomenon was quite apparent in IT and manufacturing outsourcing in the late 1990s. Currently, a similar pattern is evident in services outsourcing, which is migrating to encompass the large and mid-market segments.

However, not all of the Global 1000 companies are outsourcing. Even in this segment we are seeing the classic pattern of technology adoption:[5]

- **Innovators.** These are firms like GE and American Express that pioneered the global outsourcing model and are sophisticated in exploiting the economics. Based on a normal statistical distribution, less than 2.5% of the Global 1000 make up this segment.[6]

- **Early adopters.** These are firms like Siemens and Deutsche Bank that followed the innovators in order to compete against the cost advantage the innovators achieved through global outsourcing. Only 13.5% of the Global 1000 make up this segment.

- **Early majority.** These companies are more cautious. They are pragmatists that want proof from the market leaders in their industries before they outsource. Their modus operandi is to make incremental steps to remain competitive. Less than 34% of the Global 1000 are designated early majority.

- **Late majority.** These conservative firms do not like any form of risk — the "if it ain't broke, don't fix it" mind-set. They are more bound by tradition than led by innovation. Less than 34% of the Global 1000 are categorized late majority.

- **Laggards.** Last are the skeptics. Despite the pressure to jump on the global sourcing bandwagon, these firms are staying put. They are perfectly happy being bystanders rather than changing the way they do things. About 16% of the Global 1000 fall in this segment.

The different groups are distinguished from each other based on their ability to absorb risk. The innovators are very entrepreneurial in their ability to adopt new ways of conducting business. Their willingness to tolerate glitches and change the status quo differentiates them.

The innovators tend to view global outsourcing as a continuous process rather than a single project or event. This distinction is critical for successful execution. What, precisely, does the outsourcing process consist of? The basic steps are universal: A global outsourcing opportunity must be identified; evaluated; a solution must be found; resources must be acquired or transitioned; managed; and outcomes measured. When viewed as a process with several stages, it becomes abundantly clear that you don't wake up one day, lay off everyone, and send it all to a low-cost supplier. Management has to gradually get comfortable with global outsourcing, find the right partners, and evolve in a way that makes sense for the overall business.

We expect the early adopters and early majority to increasingly implement the global sourcing model in the next three years. In the case of IT nearshore or offshore outsourcing, companies such as IBM, Oracle, and Microsoft have helped to prove the model, which quickly is becoming mainstream. This implies that the early majority is beginning to embrace the offshore model.

The separation between the best-practice firms and the followers will grow. The ability to reduce operating costs and pass gains to customers is the new competitive game. The impact of global outsourcing is rippling through the entire industrial economy, upsetting not only how business processes are done but also where they are done.

Unforeseen Issues in Managing Global Outsourcing

George Bernard Shaw once defined success as the ability to take the path of maximum advantage rather than the path of least resistance. When pursuing a global outsourcing strategy, you will encounter unexpected management problems not found in any textbook or codified in any Harvard Business School case study.

Nearshore and offshore outsourcing can be a risky business. No matter how carefully you conduct vendor due diligence or how stringently you monitor your vendor relationship, unforeseen issues will arise. Several interesting cases follow to give you a feel for some of the emerging management challenges you could face as you prepare to globally source.

Call Center Disruption — The Process Hackers

Consider the following scenario: Process hackers phone a call center pretending to have a legitimate question or request for a product. They end the call abruptly either by hanging up or by talking rudely to reps. Their behavior clogs the phone lines and affects the service for legitimate customers. If a substantial number of prank callers phone the offshore call center regularly, it can severely tarnish the center's quality.

This type of behavior was brought to light when a Clear Channel radio disc jockey based in Philadelphia called an outsourced call center pretending to be shopping for hair beads he saw in an infomercial. After reaching an operator in India, the disc jockey proceeded to insult the rep, claiming outrage at the outsourcing of American jobs.

What would you do if your company's nearshore and offshore call centers began receiving more abusive phone calls than ever before? What if the volume of calls were so great that it delayed (or even denied) service availability to genuine customers? Would you a) tell your agents to be cordial in the face of adversity, b) tell your agents to hang up if they perceived the call to be less than legitimate; c) notify the authorities; or d) shift the call center back onshore?

One response would be to train agents to deal with this situation, monitoring the call volumes and service levels to ensure this is not affecting real customers. If it is, then you may need to change the process so that reps are not wasting time on these calls. If you are taking orders for products, you could start by asking for the credit card first, which could perhaps shorten the time of the call.

Training reps to be able to handle these types of calls is also essential. Although hopefully this will be a short-lived risk, by educating the call center reps about the potential, they will be better armed to handle the calls if they do come in.

IP Protection — Stolen Source Code

Information is the lifeline of companies. The last thing organizations want are for copies of their source code, product designs, financial statements, or marketing plans to be stolen.

This was precisely why Shekhar Verma was fired from his job at Geometric Software Solutions Ltd. (GSSL), an outsourcer based in Bombay. GSSL was debugging software for client SolidWorks, a software company headquartered in Massachusetts. Verma contacted a number of SolidWorks' competitors, offering to sell them the source code for SolidWorks Plus's 3-D computer-aided design package. India's Central Bureau of Intelligence (CBI), in conjunction with the FBI's Boston Cybercrime Unit, arrested Verma. The arrest led to the first prosecutorial filing for outsourcing-related intellectual property (IP) theft in India.[7]

In the United States laws like the Industrial Espionage Act of 1996 deem it a criminal offense to steal trade secrets. This law, however, does not apply to non-U.S. citizens acting outside U.S. borders. Doing business with an established global firm is helpful in this context. Many of the larger outsourcing firms like Infosys and Wipro are incorporated in the United States and can be sued in the United States.

So which countries have the best IP protection? India is a member of the World Trade Organization and adheres to its intellectual property add-on agreement called TRIPS (trade-related aspects of intellectual property rights). But TRIPS protections still must be enforced locally, and no countries prominent in software outsourcing have local laws covering theft of trade secrets.

If the country has signed the TRIPS agreement but the country's culture does not respect intellectual property, the courts are unlikely to enforce the laws. Countries such as India have a much better cultural and legal climate for IP protection than many other countries. China or Russia have been accused of being more lenient towards intellectual property theft. Examples cited are piracy of shrink-wrapped software and of copyrighted content such as movies and music.

Too few companies that outsource worry about IP theft. So what do you do to prevent this from happening to you? First, make sure to spend ample time on due diligence (see Chapter 8 for more information). Insist on indemnification agreements with the outsourcing vendor and ensure that the provider has substantial assets in the United States. Your company could also get insurance on IP such as source code, in case it is stolen.

The vendor should have established procedures for IP protection. Many service providers do not allow employees to work from home or to take source code home to work on it. Your company should be aware of security levels for each vendor employee and know the access codes for confidential data. Many vendors also have paperless offices and do not allow employees to print any customer information.

Customer Backlash — Listening to the Customer

The backlash against companies offshoring is still an intense debate in the United States. Some customers are refusing to do business with companies that have located services such as call centers offshore.

Dell is an example of one such occurrence. Dell expanded its round the-clock technical support center in India to handle calls from its U.S. corporate customers after success with outsourcing in the customer segment. Corporate customers complained that the Indian technical support representatives were difficult to communicate with because of thick accents and scripted responses.

Since corporate customers account for about 85% of business, Dell moved tech support for some corporate customers back to call centers in Texas, Idaho, and Tennessee.[8]

So what do you do? Accent neutralization training is key for call center reps. If the customer is unable to understand the rep when they need help, their frustration escalates. The other alternative is to offer customers a choice. If they would prefer to speak to a U.S. rep, they have that option, but it will cost them more.

Delta Air Lines, currently has two call centers located in India. The airline appears to be giving the offshoring issue serious thought, as evidenced by the online survey that it sent to frequent fliers asking whether they would be willing to pay a fee to speak to a U.S.-based agent rather than one in India.

Cost is not the only factor that could make customers change their mind about where their service is performed. In the mortgage industry, timing is important. E-Loan, an Internet-based lending company offers borrowers the choice of having their loans processed in the United States or India. According to the company, many of the borrowers select India once they realize their home equity loan will be processed two days faster than it would be in the United States. By giving customers options, companies are empowering them to have a voice in whether the service is outsourced offshore or not.

Disaster Planning

Disaster recovery planning is an important issue for any company operating in the United States. It becomes more essential as outsourcing enters the picture. Unexpected global events can wreak havoc on businesses.

The Severe Acute Respiratory Syndrome (SARS) outbreak that first occurred in February 2003 is a case in point. By July 2003, total SARS cases climbed to more than 6,000, with over 400 deaths. China was the hardest hit, but 24 countries were affected. For months, the World Health Organization (WHO) recommended that people postpone nonessential travel to regions infected with the virus.

Concerns about SARS led computer maker Sun Microsystems to cancel a portion of a massive product launch it had scheduled in April 2002 and to postpone a major conference in Shanghai. Intel and Hewlett-Packard told employees in Hong Kong to work from home when possible.

In May 2003, Dell closed its Taiwan development center and international procurement office after learning that one of its employees was suspected of having SARS. In an effort to avoid disrupting the global supply chain, the company instructed employees to continue their work from home and asked its suppliers to increase their inventory for two weeks from one week previously.

In December 2004, a tsunami hit Southeast Asia and devastated Indonesia, Sri Lanka, the Maldives, Myanmar, Somalia, Thailand, and Yemen, killing over 285,000 people. Cities in India such as Chennai, a major outsourcing hub on India's eastern coast, were hit by the deadly tidal waves.

SARS, earthquakes, and tsunamis are just a few examples of how unexpected events can seriously affect normal operations. What can you do? Establish a disaster recovery plan to ensure your operations will be safe. Most vendors employ either tape or disk backup for their data protection. However, an essential component of any fail-safe disaster recovery or business continuity plan is having an effective, secure offsite backup and recovery solution. Tapes become useless if they are left onsite and an earthquake or fire burns down the building.

Mirroring is the process of copying server data in real time using a common, linked controller to another server. It provides data protection in the case of failure because data is constantly updated to designated servers. Online backup or electronic vaulting entails backing up the server data onsite and then sending the encrypted data over the Internet to secure offsite storage vaults.

Checking to make sure your data is safe at your outsourcing vendor's site is a crucial matter to investigate during due diligence. Question every minute detail of the vendor's backup and recovery plan because a failure could be detrimental to your company.

Most companies that have been affected by a disaster such as the tsunami or September 11 did not have the plans or technology in place to promptly recover. So before you set out to choose an outsourcing vendor envision the worst, plan for it, and guarantee that your vendor has a plan so that your data is safe.

Summary

In the quest for low-cost, high-quality designs, gut-wrenching changes are taking place in corporations as global outsourcing becomes a viable alternative. Smart companies realize that if they don't keep hunting for breakthrough cost innovations, some other organization will.

Advances in global outsourcing are upending the competitive balance across the corporate spectrum and forcing companies to re-examine their basic ways of doing business. The results are impressive: Firms like GE, Dell, Toyota, Samsung, and others that took advantage of outsourcing are reducing their costs in ways that provide competitive advantage.

We strongly believe organizations that realize the full potential of globalization will see dramatic revenue growth; those that can't will lose market share. Embarking on a global outsourcing initiative begins with a decision to change — to embrace methods that can boost the performance of your organization.

The starting point of global outsourcing is verifying that you're ready to learn and to adapt to changes by asking: "Can we change the way we do business?" To succeed, CEOs and senior management need to understand the organizational implications of global outsourcing.

Our research indicates that many firms that fail at global outsourcing do so because they are:

- Vague about their goals, which results in strategic changes after investments have been made.

- Don't understand how to determine the level of partnership that is most productive and how to structure new alliances.

- Insufficient in their due diligence in choosing the right partners, locations, or expansion plans.

- Unable to foster alignment by rewarding all players for maximizing the overall performance.

- Ignorant of the strategies available to mitigate the inherent risk in a significant offshore strategy.

Doing global sourcing and related project management right is a competitive advantage to sustain your business in the short term and a core competency to grow organically through innovations in the long term. It's a global economy with local impact in real time. Businesses need to educate and train their people at all levels in all aspects of doing global outsourcing right. It must be recognized as a new discipline to survive and achieve sustainable growth.

Chapter Two

Global Outsourcing Business Process Landscape

What business processes should your company outsource? This chapter builds on the foundation of the previous chapter and breaks down the term "business process" into its constituent parts — IT, customer care, finance and accounting, high-volume transaction processing, supply chain and logistics, manufacturing, and R&D. The rationale for the breakdown? In order to create strategic value you must have a clear understanding of your core business processes so you can address the question of what to outsource.

Introduction

You might expect British Petroleum (BP) to do its own accounting. And it might, if it weren't cheaper to source accounting services from an external vendor. That external vendor is IBM Global Services, which agreed to handle BP's accounting for 10 years. In the first two years of the deal, BP saved about $52 million. Over the next eight years, the company anticipates saving another $200 million.[1] As part of its contract, BP expects IBM to relentlessly drive down costs by using a global sourcing delivery model.

Now consider this example: CompuCredit, a leading credit card issuer, hired Patni Computer Systems to handle data entry for credit card applications. Patni re-engineered the business process, including mailroom functions, scanning, data entry, and reporting, to take complete ownership of it. During the transition phase, Patni migrated the process offshore in three weeks to prevent any business disruption to CompuCredit. After the transition, the two companies improved process quality through Six Sigma initiatives that helped boost accuracy to 99%. Through training and automation, productivity improved too: staff went from entering 28 credit card applications per hour to inputting 50 applications per hour, and the turnaround time dropped from three days to same day.[2]

Business process outsourcing is becoming the transformation tool of choice to foster earnings growth, alongside alternative strategies such as mergers or acquisitions. Increasingly, corporate strategists located all over the world are taking a closer look of global outsourcing. They are moving from a pure offshore bias to a more integrated global sourcing perspective. But what is still not clear is how to redesign a business process so that it can be completed onshore, nearshore, and offshore. How do you integrate the outputs into a cohesive stream?

This chapter examines the range of tasks that companies are outsourcing. We specifically explore high-potential process groups for global sourcing — information technology, customer care, finance and accounting, human resources, and transaction processing — and set the stage for the rest of the book. To better understand the core versus noncore dynamics of outsourcing processes, we also study two best-practice companies, Dell and American Express.

Business Process Outsourcing

Which processes are being outsourced? Which processes are heading offshore? According to Richard Swanson, director of BPO services at Patni Computer Systems, a global consulting and IT services provider, "The services that are working best offshore are those that are labor intensive, well structured, repeatable, nonproprietary, and low risk to the business. These are the kind of processes that can be moved offshore the easiest."[3]

In order to define the opportunities for your company, we will first break down global outsourcing into the eight broad, value-added categories that follow (shown in Figure 2.1).

1. Finance and accounting (F&A): accounts payable, accounts receivable, risk management, and general accounting.

2. Customer care: customer selection (marketing campaigns), acquisition (telemarketing and telesales), retention (service and support), and extension (cross-sell and up-sell).

3. Human resources (HR): employee support, payroll, recruiting, performance management, benefits administration, and training.

4. Transaction processing: billing and payment services, indirect procurement, and administration services such as tax processing, claims, and policy processing.

5. Information technology (IT): software and application development, systems maintenance, packaged software implementation and integration, and architectural design services.

6. Supply chain management: transportation and logistics, direct procurement, and warehouse and inventory management.

7. Manufacturing: contract manufacturing (which currently accounts for more than 50% of the outsourcing market) and research and development.

8. Research and development: product research, computer aided design (CAD), and clinical trials data analysis and management.

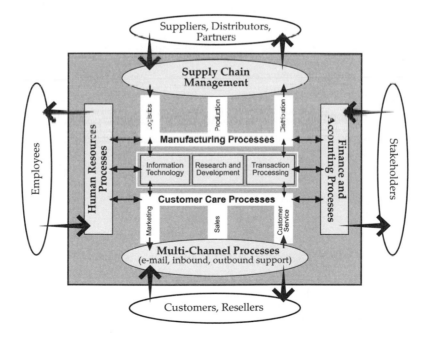

Figure 2.1: Business Process Categories

Initially, outsourcing companies concentrated their efforts on manufacturing and IT application development and maintenance. In the last three years, their focus has broadened to include other processes such as customer care and back-office transaction processing. We think nearshore or offshore outsourcing is feasible for processes that are standardized, easily measured (in terms of service levels), relatively centralized, and, in many cases, high-volume.

The broad spectrum of processes being outsourced means that service providers can specialize in one category or even a subcategory, based on the complexity of the process. This specialization has been critical to the growth of the outsourcing market.

To understand the nuances of the different processes, it is useful to look at how Dell is approaching outsourcing, specifically offshore. Dell's uniqueness lies in its sophisticated use of offshoring to drive down cost.

Best-Practice Case Study: Dell

Outsourcing has been the cornerstone of Dell's direct-to-customer business model. In fact, outsourcing is one of the reasons Dell has been able to grow from a company that reported $18 billion in revenues in fiscal 1999 to one that reported $49 billion in revenues in fiscal 2005.

Dell is concentrating on big-picture issues, such as how to continue reporting year-over-year increases in sales and how to penetrate new markets. The soft economy and the decline in corporate technology spending forced Dell in 2002 to get creative in finding new revenue sources. Along with cutting costs through offshoring, the company is entering new markets, such as printers, storage, and handhelds.

The business requirement to support these new customers at a low cost also is fueling the offshore outsourcing trend at Dell. To maintain its position as a low-cost leader, Dell is migrating to a global delivery model. This case study outlines the different Dell offshoring initiatives under way in Ireland, India, Russia, and Taiwan.

Offshore Call Centers in Ireland

Established in December 1992, Dell Bray was one of the first call centers to land on Ireland's shores and was followed by Dell Cherrywood in

August 2000. The two centers are charged with providing sales and support to Ireland, as well as to small and midsize U.K. customers.

Dell chose Ireland for several reasons: 1) Europe is a key market; 2) the country has a lower-cost business environment; 3) the labor pool is educated, IT savvy, and English-speaking; 4) several government subsidies exist; and 5) the telecom infrastructure is robust.

Companies also cite the overlap in the U.K. and U.S. business days, the compatible cultures, Ireland's proximity, and the lower attrition rates when asked why they picked Ireland for offshoring.

Offshore Help Desk and Technical Support in India

In June 2001, the computer maker announced the formation of Dell International Services, a division of Dell Computer India Pvt. Ltd. It established the division to provide technical support to U.S. home and small business customers mainly through call centers located in India.

According to Dell, the Indian support center's objectives were threefold:

1. To push Dell closer to its goal of providing service worldwide and enabling its philosophy of "call anywhere, resolution anywhere."

2. To expand service for customers in the consumer segment, beginning with the United States and extending to other countries in the future.

3. To support the growing customer base in India.

Dell listed many of the same reasons its competitors have given for setting up in India — the ability to provide a 24x7 or "follow-the-sun" model of service, a favorable cost structure, and access to a vast, skilled, English-speaking workforce.[4]

In 2001, the technical support center had 200 seats; as of March 2003, the number of employees had jumped to 2,000. The center has also added Australia, New Zealand, and Ireland to the countries it services from India. In addition to providing users e-mail- and telephone-based technical support, Dell International Services has added software development and hardware product design to its responsibilities.[5]

Dell's Offshore Failure

After successful trials with the consumer segment, Dell expanded its round-the-clock technical support center in India to handle calls from its U.S. corporate customers. This plan, however, ran into problems. There was an onslaught of complaints from the very same customers the center sought to support. Customers were not satisfied with the level of support they were receiving and complained that the Indian technical support representatives were difficult to communicate with because of thick accents and scripted responses.

Since corporate customers account for about 85% of business, Dell had to bow to customer pressure.[6] It moved tech support for some corporate customers back to call centers in Texas, Idaho, and Tennessee. However, calls from home PC owners continue to be handled by the technical support center in Bangalore, India.

Dell clearly has to adjust its strategy by providing more accent neutralization, employee training, and service quality management at the Indian technical support center, but a few dissatisfied customers won't force Dell to retreat from India. The economics are just too overwhelming.

Offshore Software Development in Russia

Dell, like Boeing, Motorola, Citibank, and Intel, has traveled to Russia to outsource software development. Although India is regarded as the big fish in the offshore software development pond, Russia is climbing the charts with its huge pool of low-cost engineering talent.

One of the leading offshore providers in Russia is LUXOFT, with whom Dell decided to collaborate in mid-2002. The outcome of the partnership was a dedicated software engineering center located in Moscow.

The best-of-breed engineers were hired according to criteria that Dell set to ensure that the employees had the experience, domain knowledge, and education that it sought. The Moscow-based center follows Dell's practices, methodologies, and culture and complements Dell's European IT centers located in Great Britain, France, and Ireland.

The center supports Dell's internal IT requirements for its constantly changing Web site and e-commerce portal, and develops enterprise and system software for the global market. The Russian center allows Dell's IT departments to concentrate on more critical, value-added technology tasks, while churning out IT deliverables at a pace that accelerates Dell's sales machine and supports a market capture strategy.[7]

Offshore Production in Taiwan

In manufacturing, Dell's executives faced the interesting challenge of devising new solutions in an industry that refuses to stand still. The dynamics of the PC industry change virtually every month: Product lifecycles shorten, and demands for reliability, flexibility, speed, and quality escalate. To keep pace, Dell undertook a wholesale revamping of its business processes, from design and forecasting, to raw materials acquisition, production, distribution, and customer follow-up.

One outcome of Dell's revamping was a decision to offshore more production to partners in Taiwan and China. Taiwan is not new to offshore manufacturing. In fact, many high-tech companies have been outsourcing some part of their manufacturing process to Taiwan for almost two decades. However, most of their outsourcing has been at interim Stages 1 or 2 (see Table 2.1). These companies have not yet taken full advantage of the outsourcing model, which can further reduce the cost of goods sold, decrease overhead expenses, and help businesses bring new products to the global market faster.

Offshore Manufacturing Stage	Characteristics
Stage 1: Noncore components	Convenience, flexibility, and alternative source of supply
Stage 2: Commodity but core components and assemblies	Offshore most of printed-circuit-board assemblies
Stage 3: Offshore manufacturing of entire product lines	Reconsider entire manufacturing strategy, examine whether current contractors are the best fit, and minimize management costs. Dell does the design and the partners do the rest.

Table 2.1: Stages of Offshore High-Tech Manufacturing at Dell

Dell has migrated from Stage 2 to Stage 3. For instance, in November 2002, Dell disclosed that it offshored production of its handhelds to

Wistron, a provider of both original design and manufacturing (ODM) and contract electronic manufacturing (CEM) services. Wistron proved it was the one company that could meet Dell's extremely low contract price of $170 per unit. With such low margins per unit, the only way Wistron could afford to take the contract was if it was guaranteed a large order. By selecting Wistron to produce its handheld, Dell has been able to pass its savings on to the customer.[8]

As Dell has learned, offshore outsourcing also raises unique challenges that cannot be anticipated. For instance, Taiwan lies in an earthquake zone. In September 1999, an earthquake hit the country and dramatically affected daily life. One of its effects was to halt manufacturing at an industrial park for PC components nearby to Dell. Due to its lean inventory model, Dell had to slow production and could not take advantage of the PC price hike because it had a limited buffer inventory.

The Bottom Line

Dell is evolving into a true multinational. By 2007, the company hopes to double sales to $60 billion, with 50% derived from non-PC business, in contrast to the 19% of total sales non-PC business contributed in early 2000.[9] Dell won't achieve those numbers through U.S. sales alone, which brings us to back to India, and, to a much lesser extent, Russia and the other countries to which it offshores work. Not only do these countries represent a chance to cut costs through offshoring and a way for Dell to diversify its offshoring portfolio, they, India and China in particular, represent an untapped market for Dell's products.

What is intriguing about Dell's offshore strategy is its evolution. It initially focused on reducing transaction costs and progressed to maximizing cost savings. To achieve those savings, the company needed to make process improvements that fueled productivity gains, so it turned to automation. To realize more savings, it turned to process reconfiguration. Dell is systematically moving up the value chain and sending more complex business functions offshore.

Segmenting the Business Process Landscape

As the case study of Dell illustrates, the offshore BPO landscape is complex and varied. Dell is unique because it is not taking a piecemeal approach to offshoring by outsourcing one task at a time. Instead, it has chosen the more risky approach of outsourcing entire processes.

After analyzing best-practice companies such as GE and Dell, it is clear that there are five main categories of business processes that companies are outsourcing: information technology, customer care, finance and accounting, human resources, and transaction processing (see Figure 2.2). In this chapter, we look at these five categories. We do not cover manufacturing, supply chain management, or R&D.

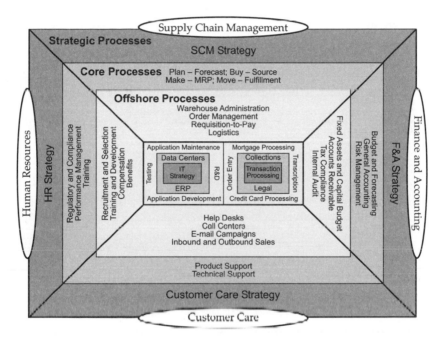

Figure 2.2: Outsourced Process Landscape

When evaluating whether or not to outsource any of these business processes, your company needs to answer three questions:

1. Can you outsource the process without losing your competitive advantage?

2. If you outsource the process, will it generate incremental value to justify the effort?

3. Can you outsource the identified process without losing control?

Information Technology Processes

Information technology (IT) companies were among the first to utilize outsourcing. In the mid-1980s, companies hired offshore labor for low-end, low-cost work such as language localization, device and printer drivers, and motherboard production.

As the outsourcing phenomenon took off, Fortune 1000 companies started contracting with offshore companies for other types of work, like Y2K remediation. The focus gradually shifted to application maintenance, support of existing products, and, eventually, new application development.

Tesco, one of the top five retailers in the world, was among the Fortune 1000 companies that started contracting with offshore companies, and is now considered a best-practice company in leveraging global outsourcing. One of its key outsourcing centers is the Hindustan Service Center (HSC) in Bangalore. It was built to accommodate 770 employees, including 400 software professionals, by December 2005.

The primary focus of the HSC is the "Tesco in a box" program that aims to standardize software across 2,400 stores in the world. In addition to application development, the HSC is also capable of providing strategic shared services including infrastructure support and transaction processing services to its parent company in the United Kingdom and to the wider international group.[10]

The range of IT processes that companies like Tesco outsource includes:

- **Application development**, which spans designing, developing, and installing software for a variety of IT systems. Applications range from single-platform, single-site systems to multiplatform, multisite systems. A project may involve the development of new applications based on .NET or J2EE or new functions for existing software applications. Each development project typically involves all aspects of the software development process, including definition, prototyping, design, pilots, programming, testing, installation, and maintenance.

- **Application maintenance**, which is usually for large software systems that need modifications, enhancements, and product support. It includes migrating to new technologies while extending the useful life of existing systems. Projects may involve re-engineering software to migrate applications from mainframe to client/server architectures or porting existing operating systems to Unix or Linux. For companies with extensive proprietary software applications, implementing such technologies may require rewriting and testing millions of lines of software code.

- **Application testing**, which focuses on critical aspects such as quality assurance, building automated test suites, performance metrics, capacity planning for peak business demands, validation testing, test automation, execution, defect tracking, and reporting.

- **Support services** for constantly changing applications and technology that span help desks, scheduled maintenance, security issues, remote diagnostics, and documentation development.

- **Implementation services**, which are end-to-end application hosting services that allow customers to transfer the responsibility of maintaining, enhancing, and managing custom and packaged applications to the vendor. They also include product lifecycle management, prototype development, technology evaluation, proof of concept, application hosting, and training.

- **New product engineering services**, which encompass Web Services design, product and process analysis, and simulations, and range from basic changes to complex designs. In addition, they may involve customizing the latest object-oriented design, modeling, and engineering software to specific user requirements.

Figure 2.3 shows the different outsourced IT categories.

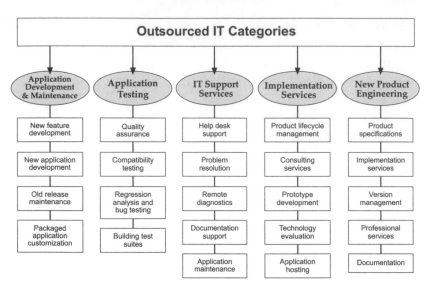

Figure 2.3: Outsourced IT Processes

Customer Care Processes

Customers of today differ greatly from their predecessors. The Internet created a new customer who is armed with more intelligence about prices and greater service expectations and is driving companies to focus efforts and money on customer care.

Within the process category of customer care, there are many subcategories ripe for outsourcing.

- **Support** includes responding to the customer's initial inquiry, product question, and status update and to the invoice query and the order confirmation. Most of these issues are handled through contact centers via voice-based phone support, e-mail, or live chat.

- **Marketing** provides comprehensive marketing functionality such as direct mail marketing campaigns, telemarketing, telesales, lead qualification, lead tracking, and customer surveys.

- **Sales** supports cross-selling and up-selling opportunities, inbound and outbound sales, acquisition programs, campaign management, and retention programs.

- **Technical support** assists customers with resolving product or service problems.

- **Customer analytics** provides content and applications to measure, predict, plan, and optimize customer relationships.

Figure 2.4 shows the different outsourced customer care process categories.

The number of companies outsourcing their contact centers offshore or nearshore is rising steadily. Procter & Gamble, or P&G, which is outsourcing its customer relations to Sykes Enterprises, is a good example. Using a blended onshore-offshore model, Sykes and P&G will work together to handle the more than 6 million customer service inquiries P&G receives annually through multiple channels including telephone, e-mail, postal mail, and fax on its 300 brands worldwide. Sykes manages P&G's global fulfillment services, which include product information mailings, coupons, and other items.[11] P&G intends to utilize Sykes's global network of support centers throughout the United States, Latin America, Europe, Africa, and Asia.

P&G's actions are representative of the global sourcing trend. High-touch customer care is the focal point of many firms. Vendors are expanding rapidly to meet the outsourcing demand. Convergys, the world's largest call center operator, is planning to double its employees in India by year-end 2005 from the current head count of 10,000. The Cincinnati-based global leader in integrated billing, employee care, and customer care service employs over 60,000 employees in 53 countries. Convergys began its Indian operations in 2000 and has grown rapidly in the first-tier cities. Now, the company is looking at expanding into second-tier cities for economic reasons.

Technical support is often the first customer care process to be sent offshore, but providing this service is not as easy as it appears, as Dell illustrated. Lehman Brothers faced similar problems. In December 2003, Lehman stopped using Wipro Spectramind for its internal IT help desk. Lehman wasn't satisfied with the level of service it received and brought the help desk function back in-house. Offshoring technical support, while attractive, can be fraught with pitfalls if not planned carefully.

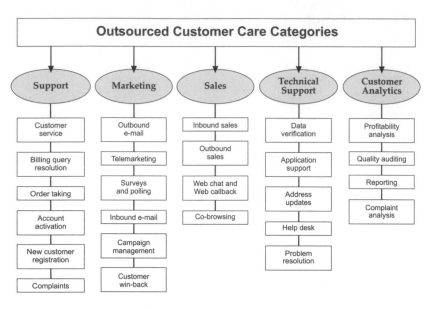

Figure 2.4: Outsourced Customer Care Processes

Finance and Accounting Processes

From accounting to travel management, firms need to analyze voluminous data sets to understand, report, and generate value. Within this process category, many subcategories can potentially be outsourced.

- **Transaction processing** enables enterprises and their business networks to handle customer- and supply chain-related financial processes. Accounts payable, accounts receivable, credit management, bill presentment and payment, in-house account management, cash and liquidity management, and dispute management are typical transaction processing subprocesses.

- **General accounting** records quantities and values from financially relevant transactions and maintains a consistent, reconciled, and auditable set of books for statutory reporting, management support, and use as a source for analytic applications. Subprocesses include general ledgers, bookkeeping, and project accounting.

- **Financial management** encompasses financial statements, revenue and cost accounting, and product and service costing.

- **Financial reporting** supports greater transparency in financial reporting, performance monitoring, integrated strategic planning, business consolidation, and effective stakeholder communication. Typical subprocesses include financial reporting, sales tax filing, shareholder services, and budgeting and forecasting.

- **Tax related processing** is dependent on the general ledger, which is a collection of all balance sheets, income, and expense accounts. General ledger reports, local and federal tax returns, W-2 forms, and unemployment tax returns are the subprocesses housed under tax processing.

Procter & Gamble was one of the early adopters of offshore tax processing. The corporation has approximately 650 employees in Manila, Philippines, who help prepare P&G's tax returns around the world. All the processing can be done in the Philippines, with just the final return submitted locally to the various tax authorities.

Accounting firms like Ernst & Young are exploring sending U.S. corporate tax returns to India. Even the smaller CPA firms are getting into the act. In March 2003, Boston-based CPA firm Rucci, Bardaro & Barrett (RBB) contracted Outsource Partners International (OPI), a provider of tax solutions, to handle up to 70% of its tax returns processing. Under the arrangement, OPI utilizes its offshore processing center in India to provide RBB with completed tax returns, as well as Web-enabled digitized document management.

Figure 2.5 shows the different outsourced F&A process categories.

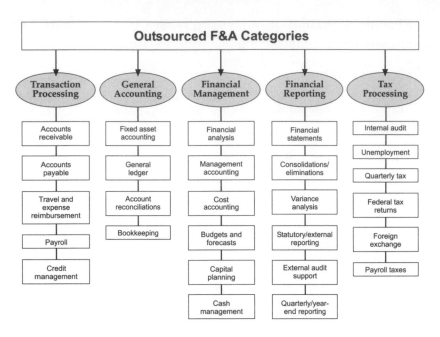

Figure 2.5: Outsourced Finance and Accounting Processes

Human Resources Processes

Human resources (HR) outsourcing continues to be one of the hottest areas. In February 2005, Delta Air Lines announced it was outsourcing a broad range of HR functions including compensation and benefits administration, payroll, call center, and information services to Affiliated Computer Services under a seven-year, $120 million deal. Also in February 2005, Marriott International hired Hewitt Associates to handle its HR for the next seven years.

Human resources is a complex business function that covers a range of processes, from recruitment and retirement, to basic transactions and workforce development.

The initial targets for HR outsourcing are the HR departments of the Global 500 companies. According to *Fortune*'s Global 500 list for 2002, large corporations employed more than 47 million people, and the median number of employees for these corporations was approximately 63,000, in multiple locations and countries. An employee base of this magnitude presents enormous complexities: Multiple HR groups for different business units exist, and corporations lack central information repositories or integrated HR technology infrastructures. Simplifying this complex organizational structure and lowering the cost of providing employee services is the primary driver of HR outsourcing.

The HR process category contains many subcategories that can be outsourced.

- **Compensation services** involve managing deferred compensation, stock options, and long-term performance; analyzing payroll data; keeping track of attendance; recording and paying payroll taxes; and issuing payments to employees.

- **Benefits management** spans a broad range of services that include managing health, medical, 401(k), pension, and life insurance plans; overseeing eligibility and vacation schedules; tracking leave; maintaining retirement earning histories; and supervising the enrollment and termination of benefits.

- **Employee relations** is based on companies' efforts to promote and maintain effective relationships with all employees. This includes capabilities that enable employees through a variety of channels (help desk, Web portal, and voice) to conduct day-to-day transactions. Specific tasks include employee development, employee record management, employee communication, labor management, local compliance issues, training needs identification, training administration, and specialized training requirements.

- **Workforce management** covers the creation of strategies that help to effectively deploy and measure human capital. It also includes developing candidate pools, assessing and selecting candidates, and managing recruiting. For large multinationals, recruiting and workforce planning involves establishing and administering expatriate and domestic relocation policies and programs, addressing and managing the special needs of the expatriate employees, and handling employee repatriation.

Figure 2.6 shows the different outsourced HR process categories.

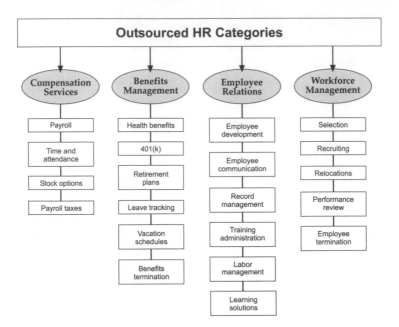

Figure 2.6: Outsourced HR Processes

Transaction Processing

While back-office transaction processing may be boring, the accuracy and timeliness of the information it delivers are the legs upon which today's companies stand.

As the BPO market matures, back-office services are becoming more specialized and vertical-specific. For instance, in the mortgage industry, companies are outsourcing loan processing. In healthcare, companies are outsourcing medical transcription and record administration. In insurance, companies are outsourcing claims processing and policy administration. Figure 2.7 shows the different outsourced transaction processing categories.

Life insurers like Aviva, one of the top five European life insurance companies, were some of the first to embrace offshore outsourcing. According to its offshore plan, the insurer is sending 2,350 jobs (350 call center staff and 2,000 back-office administration and IT roles) that service its general insurance and life insurance businesses to India. Aviva also plans to transfer to India 150 administration roles that support its general insurance business in Canada.[12]

Global reinsurer Swiss Re created a captive center in Bangalore, India. It is offshoring various administrative activities, including technical reinsurance accounting, contract administration, claims settlement, current account management, and the development of special business reports for external and internal needs.

Unisys, the global IT services company, has entered the rapidly growing field of insurance claims outsourcing services. In 2005, it signed a three-year agreement with healthcare giant Blue Cross Blue Shield Association to supply the BCBS companies with claims administration services. Unisys will handle claims processing tasks such as claims entry, document management, member eligibility verification and benefit adjudication, provider verification, and payment processing. Signifying its intent to become a major player in this sector, Unisys developed the Health Payer Administration Solution, which can cut costs and raise the speed and quality of administrative services.[13]

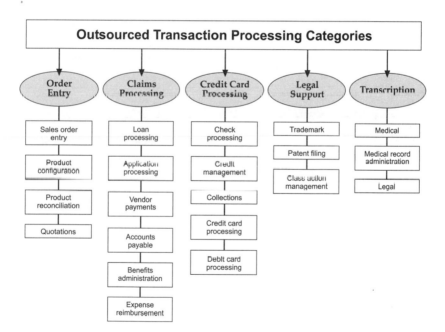

Figure 2.7: Outsourced Transaction Processing Categories

To better understand transaction processing it is useful to look at a case study. In offshore transaction processing, American Express stands out as a best practice. By moving transaction processing offshore, the company has created tremendous efficiencies in its internal back-office services. American Express's offshore presence also gives it the ability to manage membership growth and still keep operating costs in check.

Best-Practice Case Study: American Express

American Express (Amex) started global sourcing of transaction related support operations in the early 1990s. It's widely regarded as a pioneer that helped to prove the viability of the global captive center business model. The company continues to build on its lead and expand its global delivery capabilities to support more transaction processing and customer support processes.

American Express is a mature organization that employs a hybrid of the onshore, offshore, and insourcing delivery models. It has entered into several strategic relationships with BPO providers in Gurgaon, New Delhi, Mumbai, and Bangalore in India. In addition, it has set up a proprietary American Express Global Service Center in New Delhi to offer voice- and data-based customer services, fraud and risk modeling, and financial processing to customers worldwide.

Company Overview

Founded in 1850, Amex is engaged in the business of providing travel-related, financial advisory, and international banking services to customers throughout the world.

- Through Travel Related Services (TRS), Amex offers travel-related products and services including its flagship Gold, Platinum, Optima, and corporate charge cards; card member lending products; travelers checks; and corporate travel services.

- With the aid of its financial advisory services and products division, the company markets its real-estate brokerage, financial planning, and investment advisory services, as well as products such as insurance, annuities, and mutual funds.

- The American Express Bank concentrates on private financial institution and corporate banking, as well as personal financial services and global trading.

Amex's growth strategy has three major components: 1) expanding its international presence, 2) strengthening its charge card network, and 3) broadening its financial services offerings. Amex reported revenues and net income of $29.1 billion and $3.5 billion, respectively, in 2004. The company's long-term internal targets include 8% annual revenue growth, 12%–15% earnings growth, and an 18%–20% return on equity. To achieve these goals, a strategy to improve overall business performance was put in place.

Amex's Offshore Strategy

Amex incorporated its offshore strategy into its overall plan to improve business performance. Following 2001, one of the most difficult years in its recent history, Amex was even more determined to build a sustainable platform for long-term growth. The company is strengthening its business model and the underlying economics by improving its risk profile and investing in business-building activities.

All these activities are clustered around three corporate initiatives: Six Sigma quality, e-business, and global shared services.

Amex has turned to Six Sigma to enhance quality and productivity in key business processes and to eliminate costly errors. Six Sigma is a performance improvement technique for fine-tuning processes. Amex is also applying Six Sigma principles to product design and development in order to build in quality from the customer perspective.

Amex's e-business initiative centers on leveraging the Internet to lower costs. Amex has made a number of its services available to customers online. For example, according to Amex's 2002 annual report, within the United States, 80% of its card servicing transactions are now online. In fact, it conducts more online interactions with customers than it does by telephone or in person. The Internet also serves as an important product development and customer acquisition channel. In addition, the company is moving more internal processes to its intranet.

Amex is transforming traditional processes with insourcing, outsourcing, and offshore captive shared services centers. Amex expanded its global servicing network (insourced) by leveraging educated workforces around the world, outsourced its data operations to IBM, and signed offshore outsourcing agreements with providers such as Wipro Spectramind to deliver customer service from India and the Philippines. It also opened a captive service center in India to complement its existing network.

Of all the outsourcing strategies Amex has adopted, the shared services center approach focused on transaction processing captivates us the most. The history of shared services in Amex dates back to 1993 when the company used a global shared services strategy to implement organizational and cultural change initiatives.

Operational Efficiency Through Captive Centers

In the early 1990s, Amex Travel Related Services (TRS) had more than 46 transaction processing sites, each employing 20–40 employees. These sites performed various tasks related to the processing of credit card records, account activity, or transactions. They sprawled across North America, Latin America, EMEA (Europe, Middle East, and Africa), and APA (Asia Pacific and Australia). They were internally focused, geographically fragmented, inflexible, and legacy bound. Duplications and inconsistencies made these sites inefficient and costly.

Amex devised a shared services strategy to cut costs. The corporation consolidated the 46 sites into three financial resource centers (see Table 2.2). These three shared services centers handle credit card authorization, accounts payable, general ledger, and other administrative services at one location that serves a geographical area. They were designed to reduce costs, standardize business processes, leverage enabling technology, and produce economies of scale in transaction processing. They operate as cost centers with costs charged across the different business units. By treating it as a cost center rather than a profit center, there are significant tax advantages.

To distribute the workload, Amex selected Phoenix, Arizona, as the location to serve the Americas and Brighton, United Kingdom, as the location to serve Europe. After some review, Amex picked India as the location for the third center dedicated to handling Japan and APA

(J/APA). This center, called the Financial Center East (FCE), was established in Gurgaon, India, in 1994.

Before Amex Implemented Shared Services Centers	After Amex Implemented Shared Services Centers
▪ 46 transaction processing sites each with 20-40 employees ▪ Geographically fragmented ▪ Process duplications and inconsistencies ▪ Lack of customer focus ▪ Operating on inflexible, legacy applications	▪ Transaction processing at three sites (Phoenix, Brighton, and Gurgaon) ▪ Consolidated operations ▪ Standardized processes ▪ Customer-focused ▪ Leveraging technology and skills expertise

Table 2.2: American Express's Migration to Shared Services Centers

Why India? Amex had considerable operating experience in India before opening the shared services center. The decision to locate in India has its genesis in 1993 when Amex launched its Indian rupee-denominated card. The Indian operations began to resemble other units in terms of servicing, number, and complexity of transactions. However, its cost per transaction was lower by 40%–50%. In addition, the quality of the output — throughput, errors, and rework — was superior.

The FCE's labor pool is also high quality: It comprises a mix of MBAs, engineers, chartered accountants (certified public accountants), and other graduates. With more qualified and better-educated staff, the number of first call resolutions of customer problems was higher, and issues were resolved more easily. The lower cost per transaction and superior quality caught the attention of management, which picked India as the location for the third shared services center.

In the early days, the FCE processed transactions that supported the Amex card business and serviced local geographies of J/APA. Since then, the FCE has grown by leaps and bounds to service all Amex's businesses and become a global service provider. It has evolved to provide accounts payable, cash applications, general ledger, and forecasting services to divisions in Asia, Europe, North America, and Latin America. Approximately 58% of the work completed at the FCE is for the J/APA operations, 20% for European operations, 24% for U.S. and Canadian operations, and 8% for Latin American operations.[14]

The evolution of the FCE's capabilities has been steady. In 1995, Amex sent the first process to the center. In 1997, it became a business unit servicing all geographies. In 1998, the FCE streamlined its processes through a major process improvement and re-engineering exercise. In 1999, it began performing high-end activities such as financial analysis and forecasting. By 2001, the FCE had turned into a global back-office processor with end-to-end capture-to-reporting capabilities and employed more than 3,000 employees working three shifts. Encouraged by its success with the FCE, Amex began a pilot in 2003 to look at the viability of servicing customers in the United Kingdom, Australia, and Canada by English-speaking telephone representatives based in India.[15]

Back-Office Transaction Processing

To better understand how the FCE adds value, let's go behind the scenes of an Amex card purchase. Amex credit and charge cards allow card members to charge purchases around the world and online at establishments that have agreed to accept them and to access cash through ATMs at more than 500,000 locations worldwide.

The FCE's Role in Processing Card Transactions

Approximately 35.4 million Americans carry an American Express card, and the total cards in circulation reached 60.5 million by year-end 2002. The company reported charge volume of $352 billion in 2002.

A significant amount of accounting reconciliation and processing has to happen daily to guarantee that the correct people are charged and the appropriate vendors are paid on time. Processing, checking, and posting customers' payments to their credit cards also have to be carried out promptly. Behind the completion of all of these tasks is the FCE.

The FCE's Role in Dispute Resolution

Where did this charge on my credit card come from? Frequently customers dispute charges made to their cards. Processing these disputes requires human intervention, which means it is expensive and time-consuming. This is another scenario in which the FCE has a starring role and adds value with its low-cost, high-quality staff.

Dispute resolution begins when customers call Amex customer service to assert that a merchant charged them for a purchase that they did not make. The customer service representative sets up a dispute case in the system that is routed to the FCE, which initiates a chargeback process to reverse the transaction presented by the merchant. The FCE withdraws the amount from the merchant account and deposits it back into the customer's account. An investigation is conducted.

If the merchant refutes the dispute, then the FCE works with the cardholder to provide documentation to support the chargeback claim. This must be done within a certain period or customer rights are lost. A second chargeback occurs. The merchant has a certain length of time to respond. At this point, the merchant can accept the second chargeback and reimburse the disputed amount or ask for arbitration.

Clearly, there are many steps involved in the dispute process, which can take several months, but the FCE has reduced the turnaround time in the dispute resolution process.

The Return on Investment

As Amex moves into new markets, lower costs and better quality become enormous competitive advantages. Processing transactions out of India costs about a quarter of what it does in the United States mainly due to the differences in labor costs. Labor costs in India are very attractive for Amex. For instance, chartered accountants typically receive a salary of $7,000 per year, while CPAs in the United States require an annual salary of $40,000.[16] Beyond lower labor costs, the most significant benefit the FCE offers Amex is the flexibility to delegate common tasks to the FCE.

Amex's ROI also came in unexpected ways, such as incremental discounts from vendors for prompt settlement. By reducing the turnaround time of invoice payment, the discounts were quite substantial. In an interview, Raman Roy, CEO of Wipro Spectramind, said that the incremental discounts that Amex received were more than the salary bill in India.[17]

Summary

Outsourcing has come a long way in a short time. Corporations largely understand traditional IT outsourcing and are beginning to get comfortable with more complex process outsourcing.

When we began studying outsourcing, we were surprised to find so many different players in the market, each with its own unique niche. We have attempted to simplify this complicated space by dividing the many processes into several broad categories.

In general, firms are organizing their outsourcing activities around some or all of the following five core areas: information technology, customer care, finance and accounting, human resources, and transaction processing.

Chapter Three

The Roadmap to Global Sourcing: A Methodology

Five years into the millennium, it's becoming clear what type of organizations may be best positioned to thrive in the coming decade. Evidence is emerging that winning companies are structurally able to refocus and redirect resources as necessary. They fixate on the core competencies needed to excel and outsource processes that are not core competencies to shared services centers or external service providers that specialize in that type of work. Nearly all high-performance businesses are global outsourcing experts: They understand that tight relationships with low-cost business partners can increase their own uniqueness and render their market positions less assailable. This chapter presents a roadmap for the journey to global outsourcing.

The Global Sourcing Journey: Where Do You Begin?

Is your company being forced to do more with less money and fewer resources? Are your service levels below the industry median? Are your competitors' products cheaper partly due to their outsourcing strategies? Do you want access to new technology and capabilities without increasing your budget? If you answered yes to any of these questions, then your company may be a candidate for outsourcing.

Many executives and managers have either contemplated or begun outsourcing projects. Those that have taken the plunge often make the same discovery: The outsourcing savings envisioned and the savings achieved in reality are not aligned. Despite the enticing tales of software engineers who will work for $15 an hour and vendors that promise Six Sigma process quality or CMM Level 5 software development skills, the risks of outsourcing projects deserve serious consideration.

Still interested, but wondering what you should do? A disciplined methodology will improve your chances for success. The outcome of a global outsourcing project depends not only on the strategy a company selects but also on the discipline with which the strategy is implemented. The experiences of the many early adopters and fast followers shows that outsourcing projects achieve better results if upfront planning is in place, project management methodologies are used, and team members understand their roles and responsibilities. Poor outsourcing implementations are typically the result of the "let's do something quickly" mentality. The ensuing rush to execute tends to complicate matters rather than help them.

Overnight success is rare in any field, and outsourcing is no exception. In this chapter, we walk you through the key steps of executing a global outsourcing strategy.

Creating a Global Sourcing Strategy

Let's say your firm has decided to outsource a single business process or some elements of information technology. What are the steps that will help your endeavor to meet with success?

To create an effective global sourcing strategy, there are four main steps:

1. **Knowledge:** understanding the trends shaping the general marketplace, your industry, and even your own company. Don't do it because it's a fad; do it because it works.

2. **Planning:** analyzing your goals and setting the strategy to establish your reasons for outsourcing and what value you expect to receive, as well as determining the best business model and assessing the make-versus-buy choice.

3. **Sourcing:** deciding on vendors and locations and negotiating the outsourcing contract that specifies the general, financial, and legal framework of the relationship.

4. **Execution:** managing the transition and knowledge transfer, communicating the right message, prioritizing relationship management to make the link between the vendor and your company

friction free, and implementing nonstop service quality measurements and audits to show that customer needs are being met and steady progress in terms of quality is being made.

The first step, gaining knowledge, is straightforward. The other steps are part of executing a global outsourcing strategy.

All four steps are interrelated and critical. According to Phaneesh Murthy, CEO of iGATE Global Solutions, "Companies often make three mistakes when they go offshore. The number-one mistake is not enough upfront planning and analysis to try to figure out what are the right processes to offshore, and how to do it well. The upfront analysis is key because C-level management is concerned with risk management. The risks increase if you pick the wrong set of processes. Two, not paying enough attention to the whole process of transition management: How do you control risk during transition management? The third mistake is when companies go offshore for the wrong reasons. You're going offshore because your neighbor went offshore, not necessarily because it benefits your business. Therefore, you make decisions that are not necessarily the right ones."[1]

Figure 3.1 summarizes the three execution steps of planning, sourcing, and executing. To learn more about each step, read on.

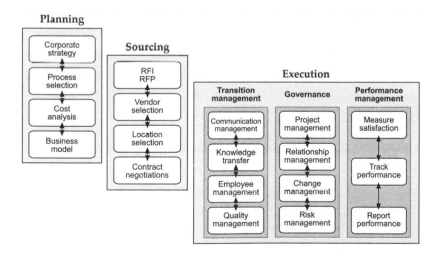

Figure 3.1: The Methodology for Creating a Global Sourcing Strategy

Step 1: Planning

The first step of your journey is defining the objective, scope, and time frame you have in mind for your outsource initiative. Without a clear understanding of the strategic goals for outsourcing, your hard work could be wasted. Many firms have started outsourcing projects with hazy strategies and unclear ROI expectations. In order to avoid that scenario, your company needs to address several issues upfront.

Setting Strategy: To Outsource or Not to Outsource?

Is outsourcing right for your organization? Which processes or functions? The truth is that cutting costs is the preferred route to profits for most firms. Most costs are related to labor or technology. The ability to cut costs through conventional means — productivity improvements and layoffs — is reaching its limits. Outsourcing, and particularly offshoring, is viewed as a viable approach for reaching the next level of sustainable cost reduction.

Every global outsourcing initiative begins with a decision to change, to either reach certain cost milestones or enable changes in the business model. As a result, it is critical to evaluate the advantages and disadvantages of keeping a business process or IT function in-house or sending it to a vendor. The importance of the "why outsource" question cannot be overemphasized. If you are unable to fully answer this question, then you are bound to run into problems downstream.

Companies frequently outsource for the wrong reasons. Sanjay Kumar, founder and CEO of vCustomer, a provider of customer contact and back-office processing solutions, states, "In customer service, the challenge today is that most offshore decisions are driven by tactical rather than strategic issues. If nobody takes a strategic interest in outsourcing, then it's driven by a budget. What happens is the CFO will come and say, 'I heard XYZ company cut its costs by 40% in customer service by offshoring to India. Why can't you guys do it?' So then the pressure is on to achieve 50% savings, enabling the manager to look good for his CFO. The decision turns out to be not as strategic as it could be since the focus becomes cost not quality."[2]

After you determine why you are outsourcing and what your organization hopes to accomplish, analyze your current costs and prioritize areas or functions that could be a match for outsourcing. For each opportunity, clearly state your objectives. What benefits would you like to achieve? What improvements are needed and why? How would outsourcing affect operations? How would it affect your customers?

Once you have decided that your business can benefit from outsourcing, it is time to evaluate the scope of the process selected and the ROI. Before you invest time and money developing an RFP, choosing a vendor, and negotiating a contract, you need to be certain that the business case for outsourcing is airtight. Chapter 4 further discusses how to set your outsourcing strategy.

Process Selection

Begin with the end state in mind. Which divisions, functions, or processes of your organization should be involved in your initial outsourcing scope? Outsourcing has its fair share of success stories, but it's important to realize that some functions or processes should never be outsourced. For instance, pharmaceutical companies should not send their research offshore if they are worried about intellectual property (IP) issues.

Keeping your culture, customers, and employees in mind, determine which processes you want to send offshore. Inbound calls or outbound calls? Telemarketing? Catalog sales? Technical assistance? Early-stage payment delinquency? Processes should be selected based on savings potential, labor attributes, interdependencies, and regulatory constraints.

Every outsourcing project needs careful financial justification as part of the business case. Because so much of the benefit of outsourcing projects lies in the future, it is hard to know when or if they are going to pay off. This creates enormous stresses in the resource and budget allocation process. Developing a well-researched financial model with assumptions plainly stated is a mandatory step.

Part of every financial model is a cost-benefit analysis. Outsourcing cost-benefit analysis takes each task of a business process and defines its value and the basis for measuring its benefits or effectiveness. Chapter 4 also discusses process selection and ROI.

Determining the Right Business Model

What business and delivery model will help you accomplish your stated objectives? Will you build your own operation (insourced or captive centers), buy into an existing one (joint venture), or create a sourcing relationship (outsource to a third party)? Building your own location enables you to maintain quality control and ensure culture transfer, but joining forces with an existing operation — either through a joint venture or an external service provider — will save you a number of headaches, from clearing bureaucratic hurdles to having to learn the nuances of conducting business in a specific country (see Figure 3.2).

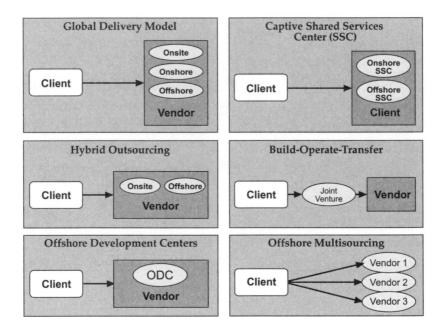

Figure 3.2: Offshore Business Models

Raja Gopalakrishnan, head of U.S. operations for ICICI OneSource, one of the largest third-party BPO services companies in India, predicts, "We can expect to see more hybrid operating models combining both captive and third-party resources, as well as an increase in offshore deals involving insourcing, where after two or three years into a contract, the outsourcing company will have the option of taking over the offshore operations from the third-party provider."[3]

Another factor that affects the relationship decision is your company's level of experience. If you have no prior experience with outsourcing, start with a well-documented process that requires little day-to-day interaction like data entry. Gradually move to higher value-added processes. Our advice would be to wait on more complex models such as captive centers, joint ventures, or build-operate-transfers. Chapter 5 further discusses selecting a business model.

At the end of step 1, you should have a clear picture of what you want to achieve through outsourcing. You should understand the scope of processes to be outsourced and avoid the classic trap of rushing into outsourcing without understanding the current and future state. Why is this important? Without knowing how your current processes are performing, how will you be able to set up metrics for the service provider? How will you know when customer satisfaction improves? Planning is a step that is often rushed and overlooked. We devote Chapters 4 and 5 to making sure your planning efforts go well.

Step 2: Sourcing

By focusing attention on the people, processes, and policies needed to support the sourcing and contracting activities of global outsourcing, enterprises can significantly mitigate the deployment risks and reap substantial benefits. The first step of the outsourcing process is creating an effective RFP that ensure that you are buying the right solution from the right people.

Creating an Effective RFP

Once you have decided on which processes to outsource, it is a good idea to prepare a request for information (RFI) and, subsequently, a more detailed request for proposal (RFP). An RFP spells out your requirements in detail — relevant skill sets, language skills, IP protection, infrastructure, and quality certifications — and gives prospective vendors the information they need to prepare a bid. A good RFP includes sections on four elements: company, people, process, and technology (also see Chapter 6).

The Vendor Decision

Selecting a vendor is like diving into a swimming pool: Once your feet leave the diving board, you are fully committed. Before you dive in, make sure that the water is more than a few inches deep. According to Richard Swanson, director of BPO services at Patni Computer Systems, "There are a lot of pure player providers who haven't been doing it very long. There are a lot of vendors that have just four walls, some lights, some desktops, and some fancy brochureware, and they're in the offshore outsourcing business. So due diligence is really critical."[4]

During vendor selection make sure that you are not the first (or the beta test). Obviously, there must be a first customer for every new service. It is preferable, however, that some other organization be that first customer. The biggest disappointments in using external providers have come from the sale of unproven and even undeveloped capabilities. Successful relationships grow from using experienced "been there, done that" vendors. During site visits and reference validation, it is imperative that your company verifies the vendor has similar industry and process experience.

Given the immaturity of the offshore outsourcing industry, actually selecting a vendor can be quite tricky. Thousands of companies have sprung up in India, South Africa, and Ireland to provide IT and business process outsourcing services. Due to the sheer amount of work involved in picking the right global outsourcing vendor, we devote a separate chapter (Chapter 7) to this topic.

The Location Decision

A critical aspect of any business model decision is the location. Many firms tend to outsource for cost but stay for process improvement and quality. In order to limit their exposure to outsourcing risks, such as inadequate vendor infrastructure and geopolitical instability, many businesses take a multivendor, multisite, or multicountry approach. That way, if there is trouble wherever their operations are based, companies can transfer their processing or programming work to another location within that country or to another destination altogether.

Managing location risk may require multiple vendors. Guardian Life Insurance, which outsources application development and maintenance, thought so. Guardian contracted with three vendors: Patni Computer Systems, NIIT Technologies, and Covansys. As Shelley McIntyre, vice president of technology services at Guardian, said, "We didn't want to put all our eggs in one basket. We went to three to lessen risk."[5]

Every location has a certain risk profile. Evaluate the country based on distance, time zone differences, cultural differences, language barriers, quality of suppliers, legal framework, and geopolitical stability. When U.S. companies think about offshore outsourcing, India often comes to mind, but they should also consider less risky nearshore options such as Canada, Costa Rica, and Mexico.

Johnny Vega, CEO of IsThmus, finds, "The advantages of a nearshore vendor, such as a highly skilled workforce, parallel time zones, accessibility, and country stability, are drawing companies to countries such as Costa Rica."[6]

Selecting a country can be an intimidating task, so we dedicated an entire (Chapter 8) to this subject.

Contract Negotiations

Once you select the delivery model and the vendor, the contract negotiations begin. Negotiations lay out a rational framework that specifics the general, financial, and legal aspects of the outsourcing relationship. Contract negotiations are an important step in avoiding problems downstream. All services and costs must be clearly defined so that both parties have the same expectations about what services will and will not be included in the contract.

Alignment of expectations with vendor capabilities is vital. Nothing will create distrust and dissatisfaction faster than misalignment between what you expect the vendor to perform and what the vendor is actually providing. Several key issues that warrant extra attention follow.

Forging the right master services agreement is critical. When negotiating, you should have a strategic view of what you want to achieve and the goals that are important to you. Think about the incentives and rewards for both your company and the vendor. Make sure that anything that is important to you (meeting deadlines or getting your outsourced project operational as soon as possible) is part of the contract.

You also must try to understand what is important to the vendor. When both companies understand each other's goals, they have the basis for a sound relationship.

At the end of step 2, you should have negotiated a general master services agreement, pricing, and other financial details, as well as the overarching legal framework. You should have worked with legal counsel to negotiate and structure the contract. These actions will help you avoid the mistake of drafting contracts too quickly and encountering problems arising from a relationship that was not well thought out before the deal closed.

Contract negotiations and service level agreements are two extremely important parts of outsourcing. Chapter 9 discusses what documents you will need to have to make sure your company is protected when you decide to outsource.

Step 3: Execution

Are you comfortable managing an outsourcing operation? Despite rigorous due diligence, vendor reviews, and test projects, the real work begins once the contract is signed. Smooth execution is the next issue to tackle, a critical success factor of an outsourced initiative.

Tim Lavin, senior vice president for operations at Ambergris Solutions, a Philippine-based provider of customer care solutions, explains, "Once the contract is signed and it's time to move the business over to the operation, it's important that you have an operations team who is experienced in the implementation of new accounts, specifically in the implementation of new accounts offshore. That's the biggest pitfall. If you do have a resource that has the expertise and attention for detail and project implementation, your rifts and worries are minimized."[7]

Post-contract execution is perhaps the most complicated part of outsourcing. It includes transition management, governance, and performance monitoring.

Transition Management

Transition management is defined as the detailed, desk-level knowledge transfer and documentation of all relevant tasks, technologies, workflows, people, and functions. The transition period is perhaps the most difficult stage of an outsourcing endeavor, taking anywhere from three months to a year to complete. There are many issues to consider when moving to the new vendor. For example, current employees must be a willing part of the process. This takes some effort if employees' positions are at risk, so communication is critical.

Transition management key elements include: employee management, communication management, knowledge transfer, and quality management.

Employee management is the process of assessing employees' skills and determining which positions need to remain in-house and which positions are best outsourced. Communication management describes the processes required to enable appropriate and timely generation, collection, and dissemination of outsourcing information. Knowledge transfer refers to the task of bringing the vendor's employees up to speed on your procedures and processes. Quality management encompasses the processes required for making sure that the contract is fulfilling the business objectives for which it was undertaken.

To minimize chaos, spend some time beforehand creating a transition plan that maps out the processes and includes project management, communication, and education plans, as well as metrics. From people to processes, all aspects of your transition process should be well thought out, documented, and, most important, communicated. Chapter 10 delves into transition management.

Governance

After you begin the transition process, it's time to turn your skills to governing the relationship in the context of the business model — captive center, joint venture, or external vendor. Governance goes beyond the mere monitoring of contractual obligations. It denotes the proactive, collaborative management of the relationship, the evolution of services provided, ongoing communication processes, performance review standards, and overall project management.

Governance has four key elements: project management, relationship management, change management, and risk management.

Even if you outsource processes or IT services to a third-party vendor, you still have to communicate with, collaborate with, and monitor the vendor. In offshore outsourcing engagements, project management becomes even more important to ensure deadlines are being met and reporting is accurate and prompt. Your outsourced project may require new organizational processes to manage the ongoing relationship between team members. Relationship management is necessary to compensate for the loss of direct interaction between stakeholders, managers, and team members.

Another key activity for project offices or managers is change management since every outsourcing relationship exists within the world of perpetual change; new technologies, new competitors, different objectives, new services, redefined services, new management — all are likely to arise during the lifetime of the contract. The goal of change management is to ensure that standardized procedures are used for efficient, prompt handling of all changes.

As circumstances change, the risk profile increases or decreases accordingly. Risk management describes the processes concerned with identifying, analyzing, and responding to outsourcing partnership risks. It consists of ongoing risk assessment, impact analysis, and risk mitigation mechanisms.

Governance establishes a framework to overcome the misconception that once vendors are chosen and the transition is complete, it is smooth sailing. For more information on governance, refer to Chapter 11.

Performance Monitoring and Improvement

Performance measurement is necessary for achieving improvement goals. As outsourcing becomes viable for more business processes, the types and complexity of contracts and sourcing alliances are bound to explode. It's a constant challenge for companies to coordinate interactions, oversee performance, audit contract terms, and track financial metrics.

Performance monitoring is especially important in situations where companies have justified their outsourcing strategies based on inflated savings estimates and assumptions that outsourced processes will suddenly become world-class. In such scenarios, the expectations at the outset tend to be unreasonably high. The external service provider often makes promises that it can't keep during the contracting phase just to get the business. Making the relationship work requires tremendous effort on both sides.

Don't wait until the project is well under way before measuring the output. By then it might be too late. Performance monitoring gives you a learning framework to put in place for continuously improving the overall strategy. Chapter 12 discusses the ways your company can track and report performance.

Summary

The watch word of the twenty-first century is speed. The pace of business has picked up, causing a radical restructuring of old practices. Global outsourcing is one strategy for restructuring that aims to save time and money, but only if companies execute it in a disciplined manner. Many managers become excited as they uncover the potential benefits of going global and, shortly thereafter, discouraged once they consider the practical difficulties of shifting traditional in-house operations either to another location or to an external service provider.

In this book, we do not minimize the difficulties you will encounter during the outsourcing journey. Nonetheless, we strongly think that any company can overcome the obstacles if three crucial ingredients are present: careful planning, sourcing, and execution.

Firms that jump on the outsourcing bandwagon without paying attention to external planning — strategy development, process selection, and ROI justification — will struggle with their projects. Similarly, firms that don't pay attention to sourcing — vendor selection, due diligence, and negotiations — will also struggle to benefit from their outsourcing strategies. Prudent execution allows you to address the issues that invariably arise as a result of cultural differences, lack of communication, inadequate management of projects, and differences in the way projects are structured.

Outsourcing at its core is a change project. Change is always hard. Table 3.1 lists the top ten reasons why outsourcing projects sometimes fail to produce the desired change. Make sure that you address these issues in your global outsourcing venture.

1. Misaligned client and vendor expectations regarding scope of work
2. Bargain shopping — vendor selected on the sole basis of cost
3. Undefined service level agreements
4. Shoddy day-to-day project management
5. Vague accountability — too many cooks in the kitchen
6. Low or ambiguous performance guarantees
7. Badly managed project time lines or budgets
8. The absence of a change management process for change requests
9. Vendor is unable to understand its client's industry or unique processes
10. Very little or nonexistent buy-in from employees and middle management

Table 3.1: Top Ten Mistakes

We have reached the end of the first section of this book, which presented the why, what, and how of outsourcing business processes critical to company performance.

To recap, Chapter 1 focused on the "why" of outsourcing. Chapter 2 examined the business processes that are candidates for outsourcing, or the "what" of outsourcing. Chapter 3 presented the methodology for undertaking your outsourcing initiative, or the "how" of outsourcing.

Our objective in the second section of the book, Planning, Chapters 4 and 5, is to help readers conquer some of the "what to outsource" complexity by exploring the tasks of setting a strategy, selecting processes, and finding the right business model.

Chapter Four

Global Sourcing Strategy and Process Selection

Credit Suisse First Boston estimates that it has saved $115 million since 1994 by outsourcing most of its transactional HR functions. Ultimately, the decision to outsource should fit with your company's overall strategic plan and corporate objectives. This chapter outlines the steps involved in creating a global outsourcing strategy. In the face of disruption, succeeding in global outsourcing requires not just management and planning discipline but also excellence in business process modeling, selection, and re-engineering. Companies that underestimate the organizational disruption caused by global outsourcing do so at their peril. Before jumping on the bandwagon, you must ensure that global outsourcing is consistent with your longer-term or tactical strategic plans.

Is Global Outsourcing Right for You?

Different firms have different motives for outsourcing. According to Somshankar Das, CEO and president of e4e, a global outsourcing service provider, "Different people have different perspectives and reasons for global sourcing. CFOs are trying to figure out how they can reduce fixed costs, make the costs more variable, [and] how they can achieve some of these things without having volatility in the earnings. From the perspective of the VP of engineering, he's less interested in the cost reduction, but more interested in the availability of skills and the pool of engineering talent. From the CEO's perspective, it is about strategic point of view because they are trying to see how offshoring can help them get a better position in the marketplace."[1]

Are you clear on your reasons for implementing a global outsourcing strategy? Do you see opportunities where others don't? If you do, how do you pick a process or function to focus on? Management may choose to outsource operations for a variety of reasons:

- Reduce the operational cost structure;

- Increase the focus on core competencies;

- Accelerate the time to market or delivery of products or services through new delivery channels;

- Increase the ability to acquire and support emerging technologies;

- Refocus limited internal resources on critical functions; and

- Change or restructure the company's business model.

Let's evaluate the various reasons for outsourcing. As you read, think about your own situation to find which "outsourcing need" profile fits you best.

Cutting Costs or Eliminating Overhead

Cost management, by far, is the predominant reason for pursuing a global outsourcing strategy. Companies that try to do everything in-house tend to incur high overhead, all of which must be passed on to the customer. Utilizing a third-party vendor or offshore resources may provide a lower-cost structure, which may be leveraged to create a better competitive market position.

In the financial services industry, for example, products tend to get commoditized rapidly, which creates a nonstop focus on cost management in areas like customer service and back-office administration. HSBC, one of the world's largest banks, announced in October 2003 that it would move 4,000 jobs in five U.K. service centers mainly in data processing and call center roles to India, Malaysia, and China in January 2004. HSBC's chief executive said that global outsourcing was "essential" to remaining efficient and competitive.

Another process that has come under the cost-cutting microscope is finance and accounting (F&A). Consider a typical accounts payable (AP) scenario: A multinational firm wanted to reduce its overall operating costs. It sought a vendor that could provide quality back-office services for its AP process at service levels similar to its in-house capability but at a reduced cost. The firm's internal staff could not handle the process volumes and maintain quality due to ongoing workforce attrition. It wanted the vendor to manage volumes at better service levels, achieve a 30% reduction in overall costs, provide output with a negligible defect rate, supply daily reports, and meet its information security requirements.

Back-office document management and processing activities are also undergoing increasing scrutiny as candidates for global outsourcing. One of the largest commercial mortgage companies decided to offshore financial statement analysis to TransWorks, a BPO company. The mortgage company received the physical financial statements customers sent and then grouped, scanned, and forwarded them to TransWorks via FTP. The scanned statements were uploaded into the TransWorks workflow application and then reviewed and recast into standard templates based on the mortgage type. TransWorks analyzed the recast statements to evaluate the loan servicing capability of the business and uploaded its analysis to the FTP site for the client to review. By offshoring financial statement analysis to TransWorks, the mortgage company reduced data processing costs by 55%, decreased turnaround time by ten days, and managed peaks in volume that occurred during the quarterly financial reporting period.[2]

Focusing More on Core Competencies

Many companies that want to focus on their core competencies decide to outsource IT, HR, F&A, or customer support. When vendors assume operational functions, companies can concentrate on what's important to them. The cereal maker Kellogg reported that outsourcing reduced the time it took to fill employee vacancies from 67 days in 2000 to 39 days in 2001. Over the same period, the cost per hire was cut in half, from $7,905 to $3,784.[3]

Coors Brewing Company, the third-largest brewer in the United States, had limited time to dedicate to its core competencies after it doubled in size in a decade's time. Managing that growth became problematic. Coors wanted to retain the technologies related to producing and selling beer but was open to outsourcing other commodity IT work that was not considered its core competency.

In 1991, Coors decided to outsource strategic infrastructure, desktop support, SAP application support, and network management services to Electronic Data Systems (EDS) in a five-year agreement. By utilizing

EDS and its global delivery model, Coors was able to reduce the cost of application management by as much as 40%.[4]

The choice between keeping the core competency and outsourcing the rest for cost reasons is a difficult one, as LexisNexis knows. With more than 1.6 million subscribers worldwide, the company ranks as the largest provider of online information. It supplies digitized information to professionals globally in the legal, corporate, government, and academic markets. LexisNexis's core competency is organizing information and offering fast access to more than 3 billion documents culled from thousands of newspapers, magazines, trade journals, industry newsletters, and public records. It adds from more than 9.5 million documents weekly to the existing online collection.[5]

As Google provides free access to more and more raw documents, LexisNexis finds itself in a precarious position. Unless it moves up the value chain, customers will lean toward the equivalent free service. Well aware of this, LexisNexis started introducing value-added services for busy customers while lowering the cost of the commodity processes — paper to electronic document conversion and transformation. To keep document conversion costs low, it outsources substantial conversion and data-transformation work offshore to several vendors in China and India. For instance in India, LexisNexis works with Datamatics, a Mumbai IT company, to analyze and convert the documents before they are loaded onto the mainframe systems.

The LexisNexis example shows that core competencies (in this case, document conversion) can become commodities quickly. For LexisNexis, outsourcing offers one way to respond to the threat Google poses. Competition can often trigger the need for a global outsourcing strategy.

Achieving a Faster Time to Market

With ever-changing customer requests, the breakneck speed of technology, and growing competition, it's difficult for companies, especially technology firms, to stay ahead in the marketplace. Companies have only a small window of opportunity in which to deliver new products to the market.

San Francisco–based Embarcadero Technologies, a leading provider of database and application lifecycle management solutions, relied on Aztec

Software to help it take a new product, Embarcadero DT/Studio, through the entire product lifecycle. Aztec's contribution to the DT/Studio tool helped Embarcadero establish a competitive market position for the product more quickly. Early entrants into a market space adept at leveraging external service providers, as Aztec is, often reap significant rewards and grab the dominant market share.

Tapping Abundant Talent Resources

For many companies, especially those specializing in R&D, talent represents a competitive differentiator and a reason to pursue an outsourcing strategy. Google, for example, opened its first offshore engineering R&D center in Bangalore, India. The company wanted to expand the resource pool of computer science and engineering candidates from which it hires. According to Wayne Rosing, Google's vice president of engineering, "We just want more really great engineers. It's clear there are a significant number of really talented computer scientists in India."[6]

Google isn't unique. There is a growing push to adopt a global outsourcing strategy among R&D companies. Talent pools in statistics, mathematics, biochemistry, engineering, and other core sciences are large and relatively untapped in many offshore countries.

Many vendors are striving to differentiate their companies amid the rapidly expanding BPO and IT services sectors by extensively investing in technology, methodologies, and people. Experienced staff that have worked with many companies facing similar challenges act as an additional bonus. So instead of building a deep talent bench organically, one method is to take advantage of the vendor's investments. This strategy allows your company to avoid some of the upfront costs involved in keeping up with leading technology and incurring slow ramp-ups in specialized training.

Supplementing Sales and Service

The growing cost of serving online customers has forced many companies to adopt a global outsourcing strategy. Predictably, organizations have responded by moving e-mail customer support offshore. For example, Amazon.com depends on an e-mail contact center in India operated by Daksh, a New Delhi–based call center vendor acquired by IBM in 2004.

Keeping the cost of customer churn manageable is another driver of outsourcing. Take SBC Communications, which hired ChaseCom to manage its small business accounts. ChaseCom has call centers in Texas, Chile, and India and offers "win back" services, which involve calling customers who have left SBC to try to get them back, a common occurrence, particularly in the telecommunications industry.

One credit card company enlisted ICICI OneSource, a leading Indian vendor, to manage two outbound campaigns designed to increase its customer base. The first campaign centered on acquiring new, preapproved customers through telemarketing for four different products. The second campaign involved trying to persuade existing cardholders to sign up for add-on programs, such as balance transfers. The truth is that companies often do not have the in-house resources to follow up on the important aspects of customer service and sales, and vendors are more than happy to complete these tasks, for a price.

Peak-and-Valley Resource Management

Outsourcing permits organizations to redirect resources, most often people, from noncore activities to value-added projects that serve the customer. U.S. CPA firms, for instance, constantly look for ways to improve the productivity of their highly skilled personnel and reduce costs during the tax season (January 1 to April 15). Tax return preparation is a highly seasonal and low-margin service. During the season, CPA firms work their permanent tax staffs 80-plus hours each week and employ temporary personnel who often have little or outdated knowledge of current tax law.

Outsourcing can help CPA firms survive this hectic period. The tax preparation process involves three activities: consulting with the client; entering disparate pieces of information and records provided by a client into a tax software system; and reviewing the information for accuracy, completeness, and compliance with the law. Often temporary personnel and overtime-working tax staff perform the second activity. Sending it offshore would free accountants to apply their knowledge more meaningfully, reduce costs, and enable firms to deliver a higher quality of service.

Instead of spending long hours engaged in populating tax returns, staff members could apply the tax laws and their analytical skills, and consult with clients in a less frenzied manner. The quality of offshore work is commensurate with onshore alternatives. Lower labor rates enable double- or triple-checking for errors, so reviewers in the United States can focus on substance instead of correcting data entry errors.

Restructuring the Business Model

Some companies are using outsourcing to radically restructure their businesses, as British Telecom has done. BT has partnered with Accenture HR Services for HR functions; Computacenter for desktop IT; HCL Technologies and Progeon for call center support; Telereal and Monteray for property and facilities management; and Xansa for financial transaction processes.

In 1991, BT had more than 250,000 employees mostly in the United Kingdom organized around 61 geographic areas. HR was a disparate department sprawled across 26 sites. Employing 14,500 employees to serve the needs of BT's staff, HR used 26 separate systems, 30 different help lines and was not only costly to run, but also unable to keep up with the rapid changes happening within the business.

In an attempt to become more effective, BT restructured operations from a geographic focus to customer-centric functional units. The HR business unit followed suit with a similar rationalization of its services to nine sites with a consolidated HR system portfolio.

BT made massive efforts to streamline HR by automating its HR functions in the late 1990s. Its new e-HR portal reduced administrative costs by 45%, increased staff efficiency by 5%, and led to a huge reduction in both paperwork and staff by e-enabling such functions as payroll, annual leave, expenses, and even training.[7]

In 1998, BT decided on a new HR approach: outsourcing its transactional HR functions. In August 2000, the telecom company outsourced its entire HR function to a 50-50 joint venture with Accenture called e-peopleserve. BT transferred 1,000 of its HR people to the joint venture to create a full-scale, end-to-end HR transactional solution that covered the complete employee lifecycle. The e-peopleserve model combined the management of BT assets, systems, and processes related to its HR functions with global solution centers.

Interestingly, the e-peopleserve joint venture was dissolved in 2002, with Accenture buying BT's stake, taking the operation in-house, and rebranding it Accenture HR Services. The Accenture unit continues to serve BT and supports 103,000 employees with just 600 HR staff.[8]

As this example illustrates, dramatic changes are occurring in the business transformation outsourcing landscape. Technology coupled with outsourcing is leading to new, low-cost alternatives for companies hoping to completely restructure their operations.

The Strategic Planning Process

Now that we have discussed why companies outsource, let's look at how to formulate your outsourcing strategy. Global outsourcing is reaching a point where execution is more important than theory (or endless analysis). The execution steps for creating a strategic plan and selecting processes are:

- Set your business growth goals,

- Develop a strategic global outsourcing plan,

- Define or identify objectives,

- Map the as-is process,

- Conduct a gap analysis,

- Benchmark products, technology, people, and tools, and

- Select the processes to be outsourced.

In this section, we take a different perspective on global outsourcing — how to leverage it to grow the business rather than just focusing myopically on cost-cutting. Your global outsourcing strategy and execution must stay in sync with your company's near- and long-term growth goals. A comprehensive review of all your business processes is a must.

Set Your Business Growth Goals

Your company, like most, probably claims to have a plan for business growth, but how robust is it? For how many quarters or years has your business been expanding consistently per the plan? How much has your company deviated from it? Have you instituted any measures to see what worked last year, or how much variation occurred in what you planned versus what you did? How do you convert your strategy for business growth into a tactical action plan? How is the plan tied to your people, productivity, sourcing, and tools? Is the growth organic or through acquisitions?

The chances are that even if you met your targets and everyone was happy, the potential to grow might have been more than what the process set out. Alternately, a bad plan may have allocated resources to less important functions and compromised long-term sustainability of the business even though you met your yearly goals. A good understanding of strategic planning will continuously guide you to decide when, what, and how to optimally outsource globally, including when to exit.

Try answering some of the following questions to get a feel for what is happening in your business today:

- How does your business decide the overall revenue growth targets? Who is involved in the decision? Is there a formal process, or is it driven by a few people in senior management? Does anyone question the rigor of the thought process?

- How are operating margin goals determined? Are they merely gut-instinct growth numbers set by senior management, or are they based on data? If so, what data?

- Has the business measured the process capabilities necessary for supporting growth? Have you looked at data from previous years?

- How does the transition from strategy to action happen?

- Is your growth plan tied to staff development? Does your organization have the right skills?

- How do you engage people in the long-term planning of your company? Do you have a Web site that allows them to input their ideas, or do you conduct town hall meetings, seminars, workshops, or brainstorming sessions?

- When was the last employee idea converted into a product or service at your company? Can you trace innovative ideas and their execution to product and process enhancements in your organization?

If you were unsure how to answer some of the above questions, then you must take a step back and have a methodology for drilling down into your business. The benefits of fixing the growth planning process first will far outweigh any tactical outsourcing advantage you may get in the immediate future.

Develop the Strategic Global Outsourcing Plan

Let's put the pieces of the puzzle together. A solid understanding of strategic growth plans — long-, near-, short-term, and tactical — will lead to a robust outsourcing framework. The different duration plans are defined as:

- Long term: five years or more

- Near term: three years

- Short term: one year

- Tactical: weekly or quarterly

Figure 4.1 offers an overview of three of these plans.

	Market Research 1Q	Long Term (5 years) 2Q	Near Term (1-3 years) 3Q	Short Term (1 year) 4Q
Business owners and reviewers	• Strategic marketing • CEO/chairman • Outside consultants	• P&L GMs • Division heads • Chairman	• P&L GMs • Division heads	• P&L GMs
Activity/ function	• Gather ideas • Landscape shifts • Benchmark • Strategic marketing • Validate ideas	• Strategic view • Identify game changers • Decide sales growth • Decide innovation plan	• Define major programs • Prioritize ROI • Analyze risk • Technology feasibility	• Finalize yearly budget • Set operating plan • Hiring/resources plan • Identify global vendors • Position key resources
Methods and tools used	• Internal – bottom up • Customer feedback • Gap analysis • Risk management	• Brainstorm with marketing • Gather sales feedback • Cross-functional • Cross-business synergy • Payback analysis	• Business case tool • Program definitions tool • New product introduction	• Purchase orders • Financial plans • HR hiring process • New product introduction
Documents created	• New idea database • Technology vision • New initiatives • Technology gaps	• Business vision pitch • High-level strategic plan • Potential game changers	• Strategic pitch • Programs list • Product growth plan • Prioritize game changers	• Product specifications • Communications • Competency analysis • Project costs/ PO list

Figure 4.1: Long-Term, Near-Term, and Short-Term Strategic Growth Plans

Long-Term Plan (Five Years or More)

First, develop an annual schedule for finalizing the plan, such as the first quarter of every year. Identify clear owners to drive the development process. Include ideas that apply to your business as part of the process map. Although company vision and values don't often change, strategic plans may undergo serious revision depending upon the dynamic business environment. Businesses must keep recalibrating and realigning their strategic plans yearly. In the same context, while it may make sense to develop a long-term plan for enabling game-changing products and technologies, a near-term plan may be more suitable for executing sustainable growth targets. Figure 4.2 highlights how to develop a long-term plan.

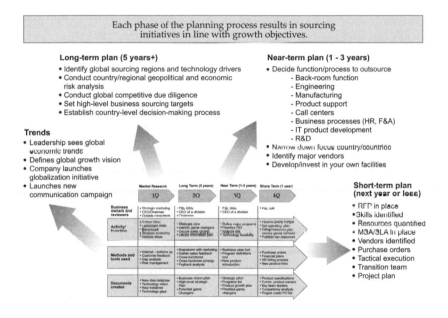

Figure 4.2: Aligning Strategic Plans with Outsourcing Initiatives

Top executives (CEO, CMO, CFO, and CTO) should be the only ones accountable for sustainable growth and the success of the long-term vision. Ideally, their long-term compensation should be tied to their contributions in these areas. In reality, most companies link CEO compensation to yearly, or near-term, performance, which doesn't adequately support the long-term sustainability of a business.

Global outsourcing must be tied to long-term, strategic goals. Companies should not only look at global outsourcing as a means to cut costs in the short term, but also as a way to leverage the international expertise available for product development, local project management, customization, and execution needs.

Near-Term Plan (Three Years)

The fundamental process for creating a near-term plan is identical to the long-term process, except on two points:

1. This plan focuses on actions or goals that can be completed within a window of one to three years with reasonably acceptable risk. The plan should not include high-risk, game-changing technology or long-term R&D necessary for creating innovative products and entering new markets.

2. Accountability for executing and delivering the near-term plan should include second-tier leaders such as vice presidents, general managers, and division leaders, in addition to top-level executives. High turnover within this tier is often the reason why companies cannot explain the deviation from their plans.

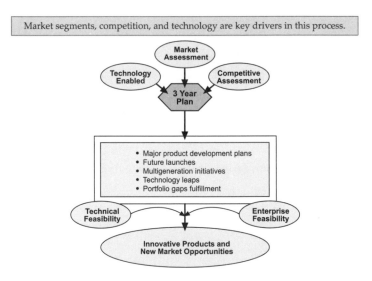

Figure 4.3: Near-Term (Three-Year) Strategic Planning Process

Short-Term Plan (Next Year)

This is where the rubber meets the road. A suitable transition must be made from the three-year plan to next year's specific action plan. Each project in the short-term plan must relate to one of the larger achievements included in the three-year plan. The two have to be in sync with the overall growth strategy.

Time line for planning: If you spent the first quarter making the five-year plan, and the second quarter developing the three-year plan, then the third quarter must be dedicated to the upcoming year's (or short-term) plan. Do not confuse it with a project plan. It is still a business plan but detailed enough to describe all the activities that the business has agreed to undertake.

During this planning process, companies should allocate resources for next year's projects based on suitable ROI models. They should identify new product releases to meet changing market needs and functionality, and designate the corresponding program managers and key team leads. Commercial product-line managers should gather product requirements, sales staff should run sanity checks, and marketing and technology experts should evaluate the commercial and technical risk. In relation to global outsourcing, companies should start assessing competencies, evaluating locations, and selecting major vendors during the short-term planning process.

The responsibility and accountability for this plan drops down one more level of your professional management team   the people who will hands-on manage all that has been planned for next year. The development of the short-term plan must involve all your managers and key team leaders who will be held accountable for its successful execution.

Tactical Project Execution Plan (Weekly or Quarterly)

After the long-term, near-term, and short-term plans are drafted, individual project or program managers must develop their detailed project plans during the fourth quarter. They are charged with identifying technology and skill-set gaps, a task that will help companies ramp up the right resources. Your project managers will live and breathe the tactical project execution plan daily starting January 1.

Upfront knowledge of your requirements and their estimated time line project by project is vital for effective global outsourcing. Equipped with this knowledge, you can recognize the gaps as well as your human resource development, hiring, and training needs. Conducting a cost-benefit analysis of available skills will show you whether you can achieve the set objectives in the approved budget. Common skills sets necessary across all projects can be ascertained and compiled, a process that may help you get volume discounts and choose better vendors free from capacity constraints.

Project managers can take advantage of several off-the-shelf tools to keep them on top of their responsibilities. One Six Sigma analysis tool, FMEA (failure mode and effects analysis), is easy to use and works to detect and counter weak points in the early conception phase of products and processes. FMEA is a methodology for analyzing potential reliability problems early in the cycle when it is easier to take action to overcome these issues, thereby enhancing reliability. FMEA is used to pinpoint potential failure modes, determine their effect on product operation, and identify ways to mitigate the failures. A crucial step is anticipating what might go wrong with a product.

There are several types of FMEA tools; some are used much more often than others:

1. System: focuses on global system functions.

2. Design: deals with components and subsystems.

3. Process: handles manufacturing and assembly processes.

4. Service: centers on service functions.

5. Software: focuses on software functions.

The fishbone, or Ishikawa, diagram is another tool valued by project managers. It helps them orderly categorize the many potential causes of problems or issues and determine root causes. Dr. Kaoru Ishikawa, a Japanese quality control statistician, invented the fishbone diagram as an analysis tool that provides a systematic way of looking at effects and the causes that create or contribute to those effects. The design of the diagram resembles the skeleton of a fish, so it is often referred to as the fishbone diagram.

Top-Down and Bottom-Up Approaches

All ideas must be captured and suitably filtered down to develop long-, near-, and short-term plans. The key to capturing and disseminating ideas is engaging employees only when their input adds value. Strike the right balance in employee involvement. Asking all individuals to participate invites chaos while having only the CEO draft the plan risks one-sidedness.

Both approaches — top-down and bottom-up — are necessary. The flow of ideas must come from both sides. A combined approach empowers your employees and increases the chances of successful execution from day one. A suggested matrix (see Figure 4.4) shows the typical time commitment that may be sufficient to empower your employees while not losing sight of their daily duties.

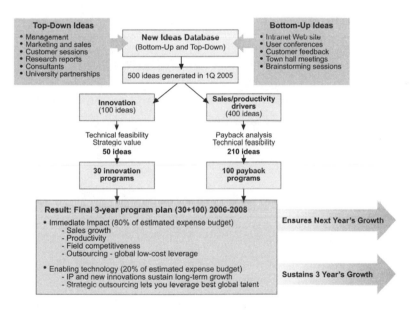

Figure 4.4: Approaches for Gathering and Disseminating Ideas

Efficient processes and tools give each employee the power to contribute to strategic planning without overdoing it. Web-based tools on your company's intranet can be very effective for letting employees input their ideas for growth. They can do it on their own time rather than having face-to-face meetings that could be disruptive to business if held frequently. However, one or two brainstorming sessions are healthy to drive synergy of cross-product innovations. They also generate a sense of participation in the planning process at all levels.

Define or Identify Objectives

Let's assume your company's planning process includes the following specific growth goals:

- Achieve 30% organic growth in five years, with 20% occurring in the next three years.

- Improve the operating margin by 4% over the next three years.

- Increase cash flow by 12% during the next year.

How would these goals affect your project? Let's apply them to a hypothetical project.

The project involves creating a digital asset management library from a mountain of paper records (customer information and their service history records held in the United States for the past 15 years). Most records are typed documents, but some are handwritten notes along with drawings and blueprints. The project aims to:

- Improve customer query response time by 50% (less than 24 hours).

- Reduce facility space occupied by paper storage by 80%.

- Execute the project in less than six months to coincide with the launch of a new CRM (customer relationship management) system.

- Manage the estimated project budget of $100,000, with the condition that it may drop by 50% if the overall company target of a 12% increase in cash flow becomes suspect, thus delaying the launch of the CRM system to the following year.

The productivity benefits from this project are estimated at about $200,000 per year (from reducing office rental space and improving customer response time with fewer resources). Faster customer response was viewed as essential for company growth and would help the company avoid the costs associated with hiring more people to handle the increased volume of customer queries going forward.

This project tells a compelling ROI story. The challenge would be to execute the project in a timely fashion while saving the company as much cash as possible. Another factor critical to the success of the project would be the speed of execution, as any delay could eventually lead to the failure of the whole CRM project.

Other parameters that drive cost and quality would be secondary, such as digital storage technology used, search engine, life and redundancy of hardware, upward compatibility of infrastructure, editing and updating drawings, although they could still achieve the desired response time improvements.

Therefore, the company would have to draw a line between what would drive maximum cash generation and timely completion and what wouldn't. The final answer to the optimal sourcing plan for this scenario would come from completing the next step: mapping out the as-is process of creating a digital asset management library. What would it take if the company completed all the work itself? It may be interesting to note that project scope can change entirely after mapping out the process.

Map As-Is Processes

Measuring where your business stands today is referred to as mapping as-is processes. It's an exercise that your company should be completing because if you can't measure processes, you will have a hard time improving them.

Your functional program or project managers must own the quality of their processes and are the best qualified to map as-is processes. If you do not have a dedicated quality person on your team, leaders can complete the task (and possibly drive a behavior change in your team too).

While mapping the as-is processes, the leaders should encourage the support of all team members. At a minimum, the leader must ensure that you benchmark your company, the vendors, and the competition in following areas: products, technology, employee responsibilities, and the method and tools necessary for the daily work.

Project managers can prepare an accurate as-is process in several ways:

- Baseline the as-is map with what you may have available in your ISO, CMM, PMI, or quality documentation, but remember that companies tend to interpret and implement these standards differently. It is your project, so make it a personal ownership issue. Understand all the steps involved in getting the job done. Your detailed process chart should map out the flow of all identifiable activities so that you can feel the 'touch points' and bucket them suitably for sourcing, if it makes sense.

- Calibrate the baseline with any similar precedent events that have occurred in your business or elsewhere, if available.

- Lastly, hold kick-off process mapping sessions with all possible stakeholders. These sessions could be face-to-face, telecom, Web cast, or any combination thereof. (If your organization is large and complex, surveys may present a better option.) A good first session may last for few hours. This exercise takes different names in different organizations, such as discovery process or workout. The objective of these sessions is to lay out the entire process map in detail, not just discuss it. They must be working sessions; therefore, it may be a good idea to have a trained facilitator for such an exercise. No ideas are bad ideas. However, make sure that certain ground rules are well understood by participants to make the sessions productive.

Incorporating our discussion about mapping as-is processes, let's continue with our hypothetical example of creating a digital management asset library. The project manager launches the project on January 7 with a meeting to discuss the following: who uses the library and how, what the volume of data is, which reports are the most frequently referred to, who updates the data, and what has not been touched in the last several years. When forming the team, the project manager pulls together a team representing all stakeholders. The project manager is careful to:

- Ensure all internal and external groups are represented, and

- Select participating representatives based on their broad understanding of their function and current processes. Often these people are the busiest in any organization and in heavy demand. He chooses substitutes carefully and still involves the real experts on the current processes even if they can not make it to the first round.

The project manager's team would comprise the following six to ten people:

- Internal functional users of library data (one or two people),

- Internal owners or creators of data (one or two people),

- IT experts in digital, library, or document management technology (one or two persons),

- Customer-facing representatives from product support or customer service centers (one or two persons),

- Quality (as a function) representative (one person) unless the project manager assumes this authority, and

- CRM project leader (one person).

After several iterations and validations, the team prepares a typical flow chart of process activities (shown in Figure 4.5).

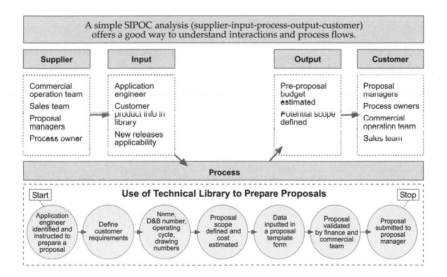

Figure 4.5: A Typical As-Is Process Map

Conduct a Gap Analysis

Conducting a gap analysis begins with measuring the current state of probable process candidates for outsourcing. If you don't know what the current internal costs are for accomplishing tasks you plan to outsource, how can you know how much you will save? Perform a gap analysis to define current state costs, business processes, quality metrics, and procedures. Understanding and articulating what you want to do and what you need from your potential outsourcing partner is a key step. Thinking about the feasibility of outsourcing a particular process is critical.

Analyzing data you gathered on your as-is status and comparing it with what others can do is the most exciting part of deciding what processes and functions to outsource and when. For example, if the product and technology gap between your company and your competitors is marginal, you may seriously evaluate implementing a game-changing plan before you are forced to exit the business from price wars.

Analyze each gap and decide what to outsource relative to the ROI, time line, and where it fits into your one-year, three-year, or five-year plan. An apples-to-apples gap analysis will point to several simple conclusions that will converge to form a sourcing plan applicable to a specific project but aligned with the overall business strategy. Some questions to ask during the gap analysis related to our hypothetical example follow:

- Does your company have the skills to complete this work? If not, would you prefer using your highly skilled staff to complete a low-end job like scanning paper documents?

- What skills and infrastructure does the project require?

- After this project is finished, what will the employees assigned to it do? Are their skills considered core to business growth? It may be more risky to add more heads as it may delay the project and exceed the allocated budget.

- Can 80% of the solution achieve the target goals at this point rather than shooting for the perfect solution?

- How do you manage the risk of the vendor losing your drawing if you send them overseas for scanning? Are there any safer locations that can do the scanning for you at a lower cost?

Benchmark

If the process baseline is not clear, the outsourced project will be doomed. Functions, processes, locations, third-party agreements, or projects that will be part of the outsourcing agreement are termed in scope; those that are not are called out of scope. Part of the scope definition includes establishing an appropriate baseline, which outlines the current service delivery costs, service levels, and benchmarks and serves as a guideline for the future or desired state. It's critical that you understand your current baselines so that you can define project scope more easily when you enter into contract negotiations.

Benchmark Product Gap

Before designing or deciding what portion of the process map can be outsourced, you need to benchmark the corresponding best-of-breed solutions. In our library example, this might entail searching the Internet, visiting good local libraries, studying companies with good customer response times, and identifying best practices from traditional libraries. Make sure that this exercise is given to someone on your team who can glean useful information from the volumes of data available on the Web. An evaluation of this kind should take a few days rather than a few weeks in our example case. A product benchmark matrix can be prepared.

A lack of adequate, validated data often serves as the Achilles heel of most strategic plans. Many companies depend upon research reports commonly published by independent marketing research firms. It is important to drill down the source, quality, and validity of that data. You should slice and dice thoroughly: global markets, regional play, product segmentation, product-specific consumer pockets, seasonal impacts, and so on. Validate these reports with your own field marketing, sales, and customer inputs.

Benchmark Technology Gap

Since our example is characterized as a digitization project, an IT leader would likely be in charge. The leader would have to resist the urge to jump to a technical solution at this stage. His aim (and your aim) is to identify technologies available in the market, in the company stack, and in use by the products just benchmarked. Once again, this evaluation should only take a few days.

A technology matrix can be assembled quickly. Every effort should be made not to select a technology solution and start changing your processes right away. We have seen hundreds of projects where "out-of-the-box" technology solutions are applied to problems only to end up customized to the point where the original "out-of-the-box" solution becomes unrecognizable.

Benchmark People Skills

It is important to know what activities people spend their time on when executing their work, such as organizing meetings, preparing for presentations, making travel arrangements, handling fire drills, or filling out forms. You might be surprised to know how your employees are spending their time when they say that they are managing a project.

Conduct activity surveys and reconcile the feedback with the jobs people have. This kind of feedback highlights areas that may be good candidates for outsourcing. What activities are back-end or front-end (customer-facing)? This exercise also helps you separate repeatable processes from specific skills that are needed for work.

Not all projects require this survey exercise, but it can be useful for annually calibrating the utilization of talent pools or when major company initiatives are launched. Use the information from these surveys to decide whether you have the skills to execute on any project the moment process, product, and technology maps are done.

The survey results will also tell you how much time expensive, skilled employees are spending on low-level tasks. If managers are devoting 20% of their time to organizing staff meetings or approving travel expenses, your company may want to institute some changes.

Applying this information to our digital library example, the company could find after surveying employees that 80% of query response time was consumed by the product support engineer collating information for that customer because it was not indexed properly. The company would likely make a note to fix this problem during the digitization project.

Benchmark Tools

The next task centers on identifying what tools are involved in your processes. What computers, telephones lines, network connectivity, communication lines, and other gadgets are present? Are they compatible and interoperable? Should you implement some standards to drive better operational efficiencies going forward? Taking inventory will help you select the same tools for your entire global outsourcing team and enable more efficient execution.

People and process improvements take priority, while tools come last. Tools are important, but they should not drive the project. This is precisely where many companies, especially small and midsize ones, go wrong. They adopt all the cool gadgets that come on the market, resulting in a cost structure that doesn't really increase productivity. Competitively speaking, high efficiencies can still be achieved with well-proven tools of today rather than tomorrow's. If in doubt, lean toward a fast follower strategy when investing in tools.

Good tools in the hands of skilled people using robust processes is the best combination any business leader can strive for.

Select the Business Process

Process selection represents an important step of the strategy process. The general rules of thumb when selecting processes for global outsourcing: pick commodity processes where scale matters or pick processes where talent matters or pick processes that are constantly the root cause of customer complaints.

Regardless of the process, the structure that delivers the best results is simple: keep the input-related work onshore, migrate the heavy-duty or mundane process-related work nearshore or offshore, and keep the output-related work onshore.

To illustrate this rule better consider the accounts payable process: The input-related tasks of capturing invoice information is done in the United States, the images are sent offshore for processing, and the data is sent back to the United States for output-related tasks such as check production. The more complex the process, the shorter distance you should send it.

Business Process Evaluation

Companies need to carefully evaluate their business processes to determine:

- What processes should be outsourced?

- When should the processes be outsourced?

- Where should they be outsourced to?

- How should they be outsourced?

Once you have decided that your business can benefit from outsourcing, it is time to evaluate the scope of the process selected and the ROI of global outsourcing. Before you invest time and money developing an RFP, choosing a vendor, and negotiating a contract, you need to be certain that the business case for outsourcing is airtight.

Begin with the end state in mind. Figure out the capabilities the company needs to align outsourcing operations with business strategy. Which divisions, functions, or processes of your organization should fall under your initial outsourcing scope? Outsourcing has its fair share of success stories, but it's important to realize that some functions or processes should never be sent offshore. For instance, pharmaceutical companies should not send their research offshore if they are worried about intellectual property (IP) issues.

To achieve the maximum benefits of outsourcing, companies must closely evaluate their processes and the sources of information that feed into them. After this self-examination, companies can delineate their core and noncore processes. This evaluation substantiates which processes should be outsourced and which processes should remain in-house. There is no point in outsourcing a poorly understood process.

Keeping your culture, customers, and employees in mind, determine what processes you want to outsource. Inbound calls or outbound calls? Telemarketing? Catalog sales? Technical assistance? Early-stage payment delinquency? Processes should be selected based on savings potential, labor attributes, interdependencies, and regulatory constraints.

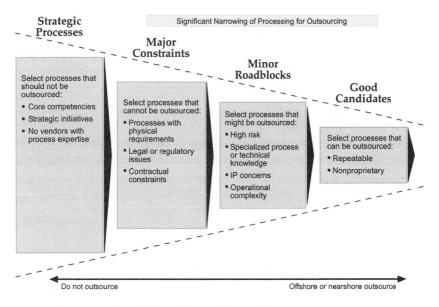

Figure 4.6: Process Selection

Some criteria to consider when selecting a process to outsource are:

- If the process has a large cost base.

- If the process is labor-intensive.

- If it has interlinkages that would be violated by relocation.

- If the skills to complete the process are available offshore.

- If a significant wage level differential can be created by outsourcing.

Factors in Process Selection

The following factors can be used to select process or application candidates for outsourcing.

- **Degree of customer interaction.** The level of face-to-face contact and communication with the customer or end users is one of the most critical factors for determining the suitability for outsourcing and the possible location. Projects that don't require much face-to-face, customer, or end-user interaction are typically more suitable for nearshore or offshore delivery.

- **Level of process integration.** Processes or applications being reviewed for outsourcing potential should not have a high level of integration with other processes or systems, unless the majority of the systems are part of an entire application targeted for outsourcing.

- **Criticality of business initiative.** Choosing a process or application that is not labeled a critical business initiative will limit the problems that arise in outsourcing. For instance, in IT, application maintenance is low risk. The application is relatively stable, which enables the vendor to focus on the process, methodology, and workflow rather than on time-critical error fixes and downtime.

- **Visibility.** Some companies initially select low-visibility projects so they can smooth out the outsourcing wrinkles without undue business risk. After a successful outsourcing initiative, they will choose a project with higher visibility. Another advantage is that there is less scheduling pressure with low-impact applications.

- **Documented process.** The amount of documented information available for a process or application is an important factor to consider during selection. Projects with more documentation on hand will likely be implemented faster and at a lower cost than those where there are limited process flows, system binders, or database details. Although all processes should be thoroughly documented in their current state before outsourcing occurs, having this information already on hand is a plus. It also limits vendor interactions with internal employees who may be resistant to outsourcing.

- **Employee backlash.** A backlash against offshore outsourcing exists in today's economy. People who have lost their jobs because companies have outsourced to companies overseas are resentful. There is no way to avoid this type of reaction. Companies need to be aware of the potential backlash that can occur.

- **Customer backlash.** Many companies are struggling with the negative backlash stemming from sending work to third-party vendors located in other countries. Your company will need to consider this issue when planning your outsourcing strategy. Some mortgage firms have innovatively approached the issue by giving customers a voice in the matter. E-Loan offers borrowers the choice of having their loans processed in the United States or India. According to the company, many of the borrowers select India once they realize their home equity loan will be processed two days faster than it would be in the United States.

- **Payback period.** The financial justification should ensure a payback period of 12–18 months. If outsourcing ITO, then the application should be scheduled to remain in use for at least two years. This will provide sufficient time to ensure that an adequate payback period is realized.

- **Hardware or software restrictions.** Make sure to look into the vendor's hardware or software applications if you are planning on outsourcing. Who will provide the hardware and software? Will licensing problems occur? Who will own the hardware or software? The answers to these questions could diminish the feasibility of outsourcing, particularly to a nearshore or offshore location.

Define the Financial Justification

Every global sourcing project needs careful financial justification as part of the business case. Because so much of the benefit of outsourcing projects lies in the future, it is hard to know when or if they are going to pay off, which stresses the resource and budget allocation process. Given finite resources, how can managers choose between onshore projects that have a near-term and quantifiable outcome and offshore projects with returns that are hard to estimate? Developing a well-researched financial model with assumptions clearly stated is a mandatory step.

Part of every financial model is a cost-benefit analysis. Outsourcing cost-benefit analysis takes each task of a business process and defines its value and the basis for measuring its benefits or effectiveness. Then the costs of performing each task are reviewed, taking into account labor, technology, and other cost variables. Care must be taken to evaluate alternatives on the same cost and benefit basis, a task with which many companies struggle. They do very little detailed analysis of their current state and costs. The tendency to wing it and not be data-driven leads to poor strategic choices.

Total Cost Analysis
There has been much written about the cost savings from outsourcing and offshoring in particular. On one side, you have vendors touting savings of 50% or more. On the other side, you have companies complaining about hidden costs and problems. No matter whose side you take, understanding the true cost of outsourcing is a complex issue and one that companies often do not thoroughly understand.

Even experienced multishore vendors seem to be having problems. Take Sykes Enterprises for example. The Florida-based BPO company announced in 2005 that it was relocating its India call center to the Philippines. The move out of India was based mostly on the inadequate rates of return at the Bangalore call center and the marginal competitive advantage of Bangalore operations. A Sykes official also mentioned that some of its clients had complained that their customers were having trouble understanding the accents of the Indian call center reps.[9]

This example highlights the challenges of offshore execution and the importance of total cost analysis that questions or supports assumptions.

Cost Factors
Vendors have been known to inflate cost savings that can be achieved from outsourcing ITO or BPO. Although offshore vendors have substantially lower labor rates, you must look at the costs for the project's entire lifecycle — from contract signing to project completion.

The rate for an entry-level offshore developer working in India ranges from $20–$40 per hour, compared with $100–$150 per hour or more for a U.S. developer. The offshore developer's rate also tends to come in lower than the fully loaded internal cost of an in-house U.S. developer.

However, the hourly rate for an offshore developer who works in the United States will typically range from $55–$90 and may be higher than the fully loaded internal rate. Thus, it is critical to quantify how much of the service provider's work will be done offshore and how much will be onsite. A useful guideline is that significant cost savings will not be achieved unless at least 70% of the total labor hours can be executed remotely at an offshore location.

Additional quantitative factors include:

- **Number of resources.** The level of personnel involved in the engagements directly determines the scale of the project and correlates to the savings realized.

- **Duration of assignment.** The savings achieved will vary significantly according to the duration of the engagement. For example, the savings from a multiyear offshore outsourcing arrangement would be very different from those of a three-month assignment.

- **Technology platforms.** The specific technology platforms involved in an outsourced project may affect the supply and demand of specific skills. For example, it may be difficult to find highly skilled resources for emerging technologies or for legacy technologies, so these resources may be priced at a premium.

- **Scope of engagement.** The statement of work that defines the project and the vendor's role in the overall effort will also drive the savings achieved through the effort. As the scope of the effort increases, the benefits will increase as long as the risks are managed.

V. Bharathwaj, vice president of global marketing for 24/7 Customer, says, "24/7 is utilizing an integrated seat model. For one existing client, we provide customer support work during their daytime. During their nighttime, we use the same set of seats for their back-office services. The client utilizes that seat better, so the cost per transaction decreases."[10]

As enterprises evaluate the suitability of projects for offshore delivery, they should apply a framework that is composed of quantitative and qualitative factors. This framework will assist them in minimizing the risks of early pilot offshore projects and will lay the foundation for future success.

Rank the Processes

Once you have gathered all the information on your current state processes, conducted your gap analysis and determined the financial justifications, you should rank which processes would be best suited to outsource. Rate them after you have completed the following analysis:

- Opportunity analysis: identifies the processes that can be outsourced and the prioritization.

- Site analysis: determines the appropriate location for the process (onsite, offsite, nearshore, or offshore).

- Cost analysis: reviews the financial justification and business case.

Classify them into three categories: probable, possible, and unlikely to be outsourced. The probable ones are your best bet.

Summary

Global outsourcing must be tied to your tactical, short-term, near-term and long-term growth goals. Global outsourcing affects processes, people, roles, structures, morale, and expectations. In the face of potential disruption, succeeding in outsourcing requires planning discipline.

Global outsourcing works well if it is done one business process at a time. Understanding, modeling, and redesigning the business process landscape makes execution easier. Investing resources upfront to measure the current state of your products, technologies, people skills, methods, and tools is essential. If you do not know what you are outsourcing, then you never know what you are going to get in return. Fix the process first and then outsource functions that make sense per your growth plans.

Map the detailed workflow of the process the way you would do it yourself. Parse out components that do not require your core competencies. Identify start and exit decisions for the project. Remember always that a key objective of planning is to mitigate the execution risk associated with global outsourcing.

Chapter Five

Determining the Right Business Model

What business model should you choose for your global sourcing strategy? Should you outsource (buy), set up our own (make), or create a hybrid? Guiding these decisions are the three C's of outsourcing strategies: customers, cost, and core. This chapter aims to help you decide which business model will help you achieve goals along these three dimensions. It analyzes the business models that are shaping the global outsourcing landscape, from staff augmentation and offshore development centers, to global delivery models and shared services centers.

Introduction

Today's market leaders understand the battle in which they are engaged: to constantly redefine value by reducing costs; to focus on core operations; to increase flexibility and capability; to maintain and raise service quality; and, finally, to build competitive advantage through operational excellence, not just innovation. They are well aware of the urgent need to create new capabilities that render their rivals' positions obsolete.

In the early 1990s, some first-mover companies aggressively adopted outsourcing as a core tenet of their operating strategies. Former General Electric (GE) Chief Executive Jack Welch is reported to have declared that "70-70-70" would be his company's rule for sending technology work offsite: 70% would be done by outside suppliers, 70% of that overseas, and 70% of that in India. Welch's vision was to recreate the company using offshore resources, especially Indian ones.

GE in India

GE was no stranger to operating in India. In fact, GE has been in India since 1902 when it installed the country's first hydropower plant. In 1930, the multinational set up IGE (International General Electric) to sell GE products and services that were not represented in the region.[1]

GE's growth in India began in earnest in 1992 when the company's medical systems, appliances, plastics, and lighting units all formed joint ventures with local companies. In 1993, GE Capital gained approval for a wholly owned, non-banking financial services company in India. Between 1992 and 1995, the company focused on growth and acquisitions. By the close of 1998, most of GE's major businesses — aircraft engines, broadcasting, capital services, lighting, medical systems, industrial systems, plastics, power systems, and transportation systems — had a presence in India.

The Indian operations grew steadily, based on positive results. GE was impressed by India's progress in terms of the BPO infrastructure, mature methodologies for migrating work there, strong work ethic among the BPO workers, desire to please the customer within the captive operations, supportive business climate, and tax breaks.

The Onshore-Offshore Relationship Between GE and Patni

To better understand the evolution of onshore-offshore relationships, let's look at GE and Patni Computer Systems.

Patni's relationship with the GE Group commenced in 1990. During the initial phase from 1990–94, Patni executed application support and development assignments, primarily on IBM mainframe systems. Most of the engagements were priced on a time and material basis.

In 1995, Patni marked the next phase of the relationship by founding a dedicated ODC for the GE Group in Mumbai. The amount of fixed-price work Patni completed also rose. In 1999, Patni became one of GE Group's strategic offshore outsourcing partners. Starting in 2001, Patni and the GE Group settled on a fixed-price, SLA-based engagement model for most projects.

Under the master services agreement, Patni has undertaken projects for GE's consumer finance, consumer products, insurance, aircraft engines, plastics, supply, and employers reinsurance divisions in the areas of application support, new program development, infrastructure management, business intelligence solutions, and software package implementation.

Every vendor needs to show continuous improvement to survive as a GE partner. To strengthen the customer relationship, Patni:

- Enhanced processes and methodologies using the Six Sigma framework;

- Completed a significant portion of the work from offshore centers to reduce costs;

- Delivered on service levels on a fixed-fee basis;

- Built centers of excellence that help deliver solutions in emerging technology areas; and

- Developed expertise in various industry domains such as insurance, financial services, and manufacturing.

In return, GE Capital became a shareholder of Patni in 2000 and benefited from the company's subsequent IPO. Patni, on the other hand, derived revenues of $80.9 million in 2001, $95.5 million in 2002, and almost $105 million in 2003.

GE's Low-Cost Outsourcing Strategy

In 2001, GE India's revenues and orders exceeded $1 billion for the first time.[2] In 2004, GE had 20,000-plus employees in India, 70% of whom supported GE globally. If the company's software supplier head count is factored in, the total number of GE related employees in India alone is estimated to be greater than 35,000.

GE's activities in India can be grouped into six categories: 1) local market sales and services, 2) sourced software in Global Development Centers and Global Engineering Centers, 3) GE-owned technology and software operations, 4) back-room services such as call centers and legal and accounting processes, 5) exports of components and products made by GE, and 6) sourcing of components from key suppliers for export to GE's global manufacturing locations.

Each of these six businesses helps drive GE's four corporate initiatives — globalization, services, Six Sigma quality, and e-business. For example, the company's globalization initiative centers on a high-quality labor pool, low-cost suppliers, and engineering and manufacturing plants in less expensive countries such as Mexico, China, India, and Russia. Through globalization, GE hopes to:

1. Generate cost efficiencies in its back-office business processes and free up money to invest in new initiatives,

2. Upgrade business processes and provide flexibility to respond to changing business needs, and

3. Create new capabilities and leverage them to achieve new strategic growth objectives.

The results of GE's low-cost outsourcing strategy have been remarkable. According to a 2002 Nasscom-McKinsey report, the multinational has achieved annual savings of $340 million from its Indian operations. More recently, GE forecasted savings of $1 billion by 2005.[3]

Selling General Electric Capital International Services

As offshore outsourcing matured in India, GE elected to sell a 60% stake in General Electric Capital International Services (Gecis), its global BPO operation, to two venture capital companies, General Atlantic Partners and Oak Hill Capital Partners, for $500 million.

In recent years, the division had grown so large that it had become unwieldy. Gecis numbered 17,000 employees located in four different countries, about 12,000 of whom were in India. Ultimately, the price tag and the labor involved in managing a captive center have led several companies to reject this model in favor of hiring a third-party provider.

In a November interview with the *Financial Express*, Pramod Bhasin, the president and CEO of Gecis, explained, "This is a dynamic business, and third-party contracts worldwide will grow. I believe that captive business in BPO operations will slow down." He added, "I also believe that captive businesses will not be as popular as in the past."

Despite the divestiture, GE remains a high-profile outsourcing success story. It has brought to back-office services the kind of cost deflation previously experienced in manufacturing. GE, however, is by no means the only poster child for global outsourcing. Similar stories are emerging in other industries as corporations integrate global outsourcing into their overall business strategy to achieve a low-cost advantage. In consulting circles, this is called a "total cost strategy."

As GE's behavior illustrates, global outsourcing — onshore, nearshore, or offshore — has surfaced as a strategic and tactical method of meeting cost and overhead management needs. However, the challenge of global outsourcing lies not in envisioning it but in executing it. How do you select the right delivery model for executing outsourcing among the options for external contractors, joint ventures, and insourced "do-it-yourself" shared services centers?

Each of these models has advantages and disadvantages. Managers need to know how to compare the different approaches to ITO and BPO so they understand what they are getting into with global outsourcing.

The Three Phases of Global Execution

As the pressure on companies to lower costs and maintain or improve quality continues unabated, outsourcing strategies are steadily moving away from the label of "something to consider" to "something that must be done." Once viewed as a cost-cutting option, outsourcing is fast becoming a new frontier in competitive strategy.

What happens if your competitor achieves a lower cost structure? How will your firm respond to this threat? The pressure to establish nearshore and offshore operations is most acute among the larger service firms (Accenture, EDS, ACS, or IBM) and the major BPO companies (Hewitt in HR, ADP in payroll, and Sykes in call centers).

To combat continued pricing pressure and to win deals, vendors are scaling up in nearshore and offshore locations. ACS opened a service center in China in early 2005 to provide HR and other business processing outsourcing services. ACS already provides Motorola with HR services from an existing facility in China. EDS announced in February 2005 that it will likely establish an HR outsourcing center in China. EDS already operates IT outsourcing centers in several cities throughout the country.

Their logic is clear. Let's assume that offshore rates on average are 30%–40% below onsite rates. If you assume that 65%–70% of the work is done offshore, this would imply that the overall pricing structure of a global service provider like Wipro or Infosys is roughly 20%–30% below their competitors that lack an offshore presence.

The economics have led companies to rapidly make their way offshore. However, there is a right way and a wrong way to migrate offshore. What is the right way to migrate operations offshore? After examining the approaches of multiple companies with nearshore and offshore operations, we found that a successful strategy typically moves through three broad phases: entry, development, and integration.

Nearshore or Offshore Entry Phase

The primary goals of the entry phase are to establish a presence and gain experience with the nearshore or offshore model. That is, take what your organization does today and do it for less money. The choices for establishing a nearshore or offshore presence have largely been limited to do-it-yourself, in-house initiatives and outsourcing arrangements. In-house initiatives require substantial management resources. Mistakes can easily nullify the cost savings in the early years.

In selecting an entry model, operational risk must be weighed against potential cost savings. Operational risks inherent to establishing and conducting operations in international markets include:

- Cost structures and cultural and language factors associated with managing and coordinating global operations;

- Compliance with a wide range of foreign laws, including immigration, labor, and tax laws;

- Restrictions on repatriation of profits and capital;

- Potential difficulties protecting intellectual property rights in some countries; and

- Exchange rate volatility.

If the nearshore or offshore operations are not managed well, the operating performance can be adversely affected by these factors.

Nearshore or Offshore Development Phase

During the second phase of development the main objectives are increasing your presence and integrating core or mission-critical business initiatives with your nearshore or offshore operations. You can accomplish these tasks by transferring more management authority and value-added production to the nearshore or offshore affiliates.

However, the process of integrating a nearshore or offshore delivery model is more difficult than hiring several hundred foreign employees. It requires a more fundamental organizational restructuring, realignment, and integration to rebalance the processes in the firm.

Nearshore or Offshore Integration Phase

In the third phase of integration your mission is to integrate the nearshore or offshore activities with regional and global efforts. The operational risk is deemed minimal, and your firm moves from noncore, cost-focused activities to core, value-enabling activities. Sending work out of the country becomes a normal way of doing business.

Table 5.1 illustrates the key goals, the roles of the offshore and corporate offices, and the ideal manager profile for each of these phases. Because most firms find themselves at the entry phase of offshore outsourcing, the discussion that follows focuses on issues salient to that phase such as ownership and location decisions.

	Offshore Entry	Offshore Development	Offshore Integration
Key Goals	▪ Determine the business model ▪ Select the location ▪ Define expected results ▪ Establish a presence	▪ Expand operation to several initiatives ▪ Migrate from a cost center to a profit center mind-set ▪ Seek positive P&L results	▪ Expand scope and capabilities
Role of the Corporate Office	▪ Get the right people on the team and set clear objectives ▪ Hire experts in key offshore countries ▪ Identify cultural differences ▪ Understand the legal framework	▪ Develop a phased approach for building an onshore presence ▪ Improve processes by setting aggressive goals ▪ Remain ready for a disaster with contingency plans	▪ Fully integrate offshore centers into regional and global operations
Ideal Offshore Manager Profile	▪ Entrepreneurial managers who are creative and flexible ▪ Managers experienced in starting operations in developing countries with numerous hurdles	▪ Senior manager with strong ties to leadership at corporate headquarters ▪ Managers skilled at communicating across a complex corporate matrix	▪ Senior manager able to work with several business divisions
Role of the Local Managers	▪ Establish local brand to attract talent ▪ Provide services to business units to migrate operations	▪ Manage awareness at corporate headquarters ▪ Coordinate activities of the business units	▪ Further integrate offshore operations into regional and global strategy

Table 5.1: The Three Phases of a Migration Strategy

The Two Dimensions of Every Business Model

To better understand your business model options, it is important to familiarize yourself with the two facets of every model:

1. Ownership or relationship structure (subsidiary, joint venture, or external vendor), and

2. Geographic location of the work (onsite, offsite, nearshore, or offshore).

In the next section, we explore the business models that emerge from the different combinations of relationship structure and geographic location.

Ownership Structure: External Vendor, JV, or Subsidiary?

A crucial issue in ensuring future offshoring success involves selecting the most appropriate ownership model. There are three different general relationship structures for outsourcing engagements:

1. Pure contract offshore outsourcing (buy or hire a third party),

2. Joint ventures (partnership agreement), or

3. Fully owned captive subsidiary (build it or insource).

Clearly, there is a varied, complex spectrum of ownership structures available with particular advantages and disadvantages for each. Let's look at them in more detail.

Pure Contract Nearshore or Offshore Outsourcing

Pure contract nearshore or offshore outsourcing is the phrase used to describe a company that relinquishes control of a noncore function to a service provider in a foreign country.[4] The external service provider takes over the function and completes much of the work offshore using low-cost labor. Contract outsourcing can lead to three different models:

1. Selective outsourcing in which firms send out a small subset of their business process activities.

2. Transitional outsourcing in which firms temporarily hand over a function to a third-party vendor and bring it back in-house later.

3. Total outsourcing in which external vendors take over the business process and do whatever the organization was doing for 20%–30% less cost.

Contract outsourcing is a "buy instead of make" decision. Its chief advantages are limited operational risk for commodity tasks such as help desks, payables, or reconciliation, the potential for cost savings, and the rapid speed at which it can be executed. Typically, it is faster to implement an outsourced project than a joint venture or captive center.

Joint Venture

A joint venture (JV) is the product of two or more companies pooling their combined resources to create a new entity to perform a business project together for a set period. JVs attempt to create common goals through joint equity ownership.

Unisys, a global IT services and solutions company, formed a joint venture called Unisys West with Australian financial service provider BankWest to take advantage of the significant opportunity in the western Australian market for BPO and ITO. Unisys West offers e-business solutions spanning hardware, software, and e-business. So far the JV has enjoyed success, reporting that profits grew by more than 60% and revenues expanded by more than 30% in 2004.

What is unique about JVs is their independence. They have their own management and the organizational freedom to develop a culture and practices different from either parent. From a benefit perspective, JVs are attractive since they can save both parents money because expenses, resources, and workload are shared.

Airline Financial Support Services Private Limited, or AFS, offers one of the earliest examples of an offshore JV. AFS was incorporated as a JV between Swissair and TCS in 1992 for providing offshore IT-enabled services to Swissair. AFS supplies a variety of services, ranging from airline revenue accounting, logistics management, and passenger interline billing, to frequent flyer program administration, navigation support, and customer care and analytics. AFS's client list has increased to include Austrian Airlines, Malmo Aviation, Loyalty Gate, Singapore Airlines, SN Brussels, and Unitpool. Swissair sold its stake in AFS to TCS on January 16, 2004.

In May 2004, Hildebrandt International, a management consulting firm, and OfficeTiger, a provider of support services with a major presence in Chennai, paired up to form OTH Services. The JV plans to compete for the business of Western law firms that are beginning to outsource legal services such as processing documents and preparing case briefs.

Captive Nearshore or Offshore Subsidiary

In the past, companies pursued the international outsourcing path via joint ventures. As business evolved and more core processes were deemed acceptable for offshoring, companies discovered that it was sometimes better to build their own subsidiaries ("make instead of buy"). Firms began to establish captive nearshore or offshore subsidiaries or foreign subsidiaries that completed all the ITO or BPO work internally.

Companies that select this ownership model tend to cite reasons of greater control and flexibility and lower long-term prices. In some instances, firms may wish to maintain control of the output by using a model that is more aligned with their internal culture. The captive model is especially justified in cases that involve sensitive intellectual property or a high degree of transaction or customer privacy risk.

Some of the companies that have built captive subsidiaries in India include HSBC (Hyderabad), American Express (New Delhi), British Airways (Mumbai), Citibank (Chennai), and Dell (Bangalore). Aside from India, companies have established captive subsidiaries in locations such as Ghana (ACS), Chile (Nestlé, Sodexho), China (Dell, IBM, Infosys), Ireland (Colgate, Hertz, Pfizer), and the Czech Republic (Sun and Symbol Technologies).

Interestingly, even companies with captive centers are broadening their outsourcing strategies, seeking to reduce their dependence on one country and outsource work to other offshore destinations.

Location: Onsite, Offsite, Nearshore, or Offshore?

Geographic location plays a key role in structuring outsourcing business models. Outsourcing can either be done onsite (on the premises), offsite (outside the premises but in the same country), nearshore (outside the premises in a country that is relatively close by), or offshore (outside the premises in a country that is a long flight away).

Global companies such as Electronic Data Systems (EDS) tend to blend all four location models. In March 2003, EDS fired its CEO, Richard H. Brown, after disastrous third-quarter results. Upon his arrival, the new

CEO, Michael Jordan, immediately began to take steps to make EDS more competitive against the low-cost outsourcing competition.

EDS, which makes the bulk of its revenues by running the back-office operations of big corporations, was losing ground to lower-cost outsourcing firms such as Wipro and Infosys. In July 2003, Jordan told employees, "The concepts of low cost and high value must be present in every action we take, in every service we provide, in every piece of new business we pursue."[5]

To improve its competitiveness, EDS moved quickly to lower its cost structure. It increased its head count in India, Argentina, Malaysia, Hungary, and Mexico, the countries in which it expected to have more than 10% of its workforce of 137,000 employees by year-end 2004.

EDS also created a global delivery model that increases customer choice. EDS's Best Shore initiative blends the onshore, nearshore, and offshore models, matching clients to different development or solution centers according to their particular requirements (industry, technology, or location). EDS predicts it will employ 7,200 individuals in its 16 global Best Shore solution centers.

Onsite Outsourcing

This location model mandates that all processes, starting with information gathering and ending with implementation, be carried out at the client's premises. The third-party provider utilizes its own workforce to service clients on their premises. This model ensures clients greater project control. It is also suitable for those projects that are mission-critical, location sensitive, and requiring of constant attention.

Fidelity Information Services, a division of Fidelity National Financial, offers onsite outsourcing services primarily for resource and software management. According to the company, clients don't have to contribute anything (except payment for services). The IT processing occurs at the client's site with Fidelity's equipment, software, and staff who operate and maintain the systems.

Offsite Outsourcing

This location model hinges on the service provider having an office onshore. The project or work may be done offsite, but it's still in the same country as the client. Not only is the offsite center close to the client, it may be used to provide support to an onsite team. Thus, the experts at the offsite center work in tandem with the corresponding onsite team to ensure timely, quality service.

Nearshore or Offshore Outsourcing

This location model dictates that the project-related activity is done at the vendor's premises nearshore or offshore. For U.S.-based companies, nearshore refers to countries such as Canada, Mexico, or Costa Rica, while offshore indicates countries such as India, China, or the Philippines.

Companies that are uncomfortable with the offshore distance are looking nearshore for application development as a risk mitigation strategy. Tufts Health Plan, a health maintenance organization (HMO) with 747,000 enrolled members and a network of 85 hospitals, decided to give nearshore outsourcing a try when the task of maintaining its managed care administrative system internally proved to be expensive. The HMO hired Keane to deliver, maintain, and support the administrative system at the vendor's nearshore development center in Halifax, Nova Scotia, Canada. By reducing resources dedicated to maintenance, Tufts has been concentrating on more strategic e-business initiatives.

The offshore model works best in instances when the project plan is well defined and the client requirements are clearly understood. The high level of risk associated with this model becomes an issue for some clients. Communication gaps between the vendor and client can result in the client's requirements not being captured accurately. Some analysts think that a 100% offshore model is not workable.

Tata Consultancy Services, or TCS, offers clients offshore or onsite delivery models. During fiscal 2003, offshore business contributed 34.1% of annual revenues, while onsite business accounted for 65.9%. During fiscal 2004, the offshore component rose to 38%, while onsite declined to 62%.

The bottom line: Numerous ownership and location options are available. Executives can use supplemental staff, temporary workforces, consultants, or contractors. They can outsource — hire external contractors to do some or all of the work. They can pool resources through strategic alliances and share in the results. Or they can meet their needs by creating entirely new entities through joint ventures with one or more partners.

To understand which business model (combination of ownership and location models) is right for you, it is useful to understand the nuances of what's being implemented by various companies.

The First-Generation Outsourcing Business Models

The many combinations of location and ownership structures give rise to several distinct business models (see Figure 5.1). In each model, the relationship between the client and provider is structured uniquely.

As you look at Figure 5.1, you will notice that some of the cells represent business models while others are more like delivery models. A business model typically illustrates how a firm makes money. This is relevant and pertinent for third-party vendors. However, for companies that are building captive centers, offshore is part of their overall strategy, more of a delivery mechanism than a new business model. Different models are appropriate at different levels of organizational maturity and complexity.

Internal Delivery (Department-Based Model)

This is a delivery model with which every manager is familiar. In this model, an internal department provides services — finance and accounting, human resources, or information technology support — to other business units and implements new services through internal projects. The internal department and business unit involved manage the relationship directly. Internal delivery is the most flexible model because the unit manager may change the rules and the processes as much and as often as needed. Nevertheless, it is also the most limited outsourcing model with regard to scale (dimension of operations) and knowledge (experience, innovation, and available additional resources).

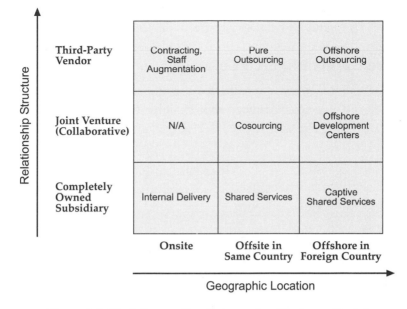

Figure 5.1: First-Generation Outsourcing Business Models

Offsite Onshore Shared Services

The shared services approach eliminates the duplicate processes, activities, and staff that individual business units have and brings them together to achieve critical mass. Paying for each business unit to manage its own finance and accounting, human resources, or information technology support is costly. These "cost center" functions, while necessary, are not strategic. It makes more sense to consolidate these nonstrategic processes and generate economies of scale.

Companies execute the shared services model by bundling selected supporting processes and activities into a separate division or organization. This entity treats these processes as its core business and is measured by its own unique profit and loss (P&L). Bundling services into an independent organization means that some or all of the employees who support them also have to move to the new entity.

A 2001 study conducted by PriceWaterhouseCoopers monitored companies that moved financial processes to shared services centers. Those that moved their customer invoicing and accounts payable processes saved the least relatively (40%), while those that transferred accounts receivable and general finance functions realized the highest savings of 50% and 75%, respectively.

Offshore Captive Shared Services

Taking the shared services and housing them offshore leads us to the captive shared services delivery model. The product of this "do-it-yourself" offshore model is a center set in a foreign country that is dedicated to serving the different business units or sales, general, and administrative (SG&A) functions of a large company. This model is very common in multinational firms that wish to control their BPO operations, quality, and intellectual property.

American Express was among the first to establish a back-office, captive shared services center in India in 1993. Other companies that have followed suit include British Airways in 1996 and Gecis in 1998. Since 2000, a growing number of Global Fortune 500 firms including AOL, Citigroup, Dell, Hewlett-Packard, HSBC, and JPMorgan Chase have established captive operations.

Oracle numbers among the many corporations developing captive centers in India in a bid to retain a cost advantage over competitors. Oracle India employs over 6,500 people and is shifting a large portion of its developmental work from its centers in California, Sydney, and Dublin to India.

Oracle's competitor SAP AG has adopted a similar strategy. In 1998, SAP created a strategic development center called SAP Labs India. Since then, it has become one of the fastest-growing SAP subsidiaries. In 2003, SAP's Bangalore, India, development center had around 1,000 employees. In 2004, CEO Henning Kagermann announced that SAP was planning to increase the number of staff to 3,000 by 2005. It will become SAP's largest development hub outside Germany.

Captive IT development centers, however, are not for every company. Some firms that have started on this path have sold their Indian operations to vendors. For instance, Wipro bought Ericsson's research and development units in India, and HCL Technologies, one of India's largest IT services firms, bought a 51% stake in the holding company of Deutsche Software (Deutsche Bank's IT services subsidiary).

Cosourcing

The term cosourcing describes companies that execute a shared services center with an external vendor. Cosourcing, a fancier term for joint venture, is more of a strategic alliance based on shared objectives that reflect the appropriate balance between control and flexibility. Cosourcing is a viable model for organizations uncomfortable with outsourcing a complete business process; outsourcing some parts to a joint venture with a vendor may offer a temporary or final solution.

Cosourcing can also serve as an intermediate step to full global outsourcing. In October 2001, HCL Technologies entered into a strategic alliance with British Telecom by acquiring a 90% stake in BT's Apollo Contact Center located in Belfast, Northern Ireland. Now operating as HCL Technologies BPO Services, the Belfast facility is a central part of BT's next-generation contact center strategy. BT has steadily leveraged HCL's BPO unit to develop a global outsourcing model.

Stating that outsourcing doesn't have to be an all-or-nothing proposition, Deloitte offers a tax cosourcing service. Customers keep their strategic tax functions in-house and outsource those that monopolize resources and aren't value-added. Deloitte customers choose what to outsource, when, and for how long.

Cosourcing Example: AT&T and Accenture

The cosourcing model aims to combine the strengths of the vendor and the client. That was the intent of AT&T and Accenture, which announced a five-year, $500 million, cosourcing arrangement designed to transform AT&T's residential credit and accounts receivable management functions and provide new capabilities and efficiencies. In particular, the agreement is intended to help AT&T expand its service portfolio, increase marketing flexibility, improve uncollected receivables, enhance operational efficiency, and reduce costs.

Accenture will manage the integration of planning, initiative execution, and collections processes across multiple organizations within AT&T Consumer. Approximately 45 AT&T employees whose work is within the scope of the agreement will transition to Accenture. In addition, approximately 250 other AT&T employees will be part of the cosourced operation and remain on the AT&T payroll.

The cosourcing agreement has been structured so that AT&T will retain control of business planning, credit policy, and customer interaction. Accenture will lead the transformation program and be responsible for the credit risk management and collections functions. In addition, Accenture will build and deploy capabilities to enable AT&T to support its growth objectives while mitigating risk and reducing uncollectibles.

Cosourcing is an option when firms don't have the skills or the money to set up a shared services center on their own or simply don't have the management bandwidth given the magnitude of the other tasks on their plates. The advantage for companies that cosource is that they don't have to pay for everything upfront. The advantage for vendors is that they gain a guaranteed revenue stream.

Offshore Development Centers

In the software industry, joint ventures with offshore vendors are common, so common that the industry developed a term for them: offshore development centers (ODCs). An ODC is a dedicated, customized, and secure development center established by a vendor for a customer who needs to outsource substantial software development, maintenance, or engineering work. This model gives the customer more control but requires much more management attention.

In the mid-1990s, GE began a businesswide initiative to establish dedicated software and engineering development centers with several Indian vendors such as Tata Consultancy Services, Satyam, and Patni. Each vendor established facilities dedicated to GE with separate entrances, security, and firewalls in cities such as Mumbai, Bangalore, Hyderabad, Delhi, and Chennai.

These software and engineering development centers act as extensions of GE's individual business IT or engineering teams and ultimately report to the global business chief information officer (CIO) or engineering leader. The CIO reviews current suppliers, selects new ones, and negotiates contracts. These centers have proved highly successful, growing from just over 600 software designers in 1995 to 6,500 in 2005. In 2001, GE's savings from the project exceeded $250 million and were projected to grow to $600 million in 2003.[6]

In 2002, GE established two wholly owned software development centers (as opposed to the jointly owned centers we just described) to develop key in house expertise for more highly valued and proprietary software. Increasingly, many U.S. technology companies are considering starting 100%-owned subsidiaries in countries like India instead of working with an offshore IT services vendor. The main reasons being: 1) the cost savings associated with an offshore subsidiary can be as high as 40% when compared to a vendor partnership; 2) direct control on hiring and retention of offshore resources; and 3) the ability to retain intellectual property within the company.

ODCs typically are dedicated to a particular client's business and are equipped with hardware, networking, and software applications that replicate the client's facilities. A typical ODC provides the services outlined in Table 5.2.[7]

Facilities Management	Operations Support	Staffing, HR, and Training
▪ Office infrastructure ▪ Physical security ▪ Communications infrastructure ▪ Technology equipment ▪ Standard office software	▪ Data security and backup ▪ Computer maintenance ▪ Systems administration ▪ Accounting services ▪ Office administrative support ▪ Visa and travel support ▪ Government liaison	▪ Recruiting and hiring ▪ Orientation and training ▪ Retention program ▪ Taxation and HR compliance ▪ Employee benefits ▪ Outplacement

Table 5.2: Services Provided by Offshore Development Centers

Target Corporation, a $26 billion retailer, set up a dedicated ODC in Chennai, India, with TCS. Using the hybrid onsite-offshore model of delivery, TCS provides application development, maintenance, and production support to all of Target's divisions in e-commerce, stock control, warehouse, supply chain, credit, and corporate services.

MasterCard International, one of the most recognized brands in the world, also built an ODC. MasterCard recognized that offshore outsourcing could not only save money but also generate it. In June 2001, MasterCard launched an ODC with Mascon Global. Mascon-MasterCard

Global Technology Services develops and maintains software for MasterCard's core processing functions — authorization, clearing, and settlement. The business model behind this is a joint venture, with Mascon owning 51%.[8]

How Does the ODC Model Work?

To understand the role of an offshore development center, it is useful to look at the lifecycle of a typical third-party vendor software development or maintenance project. At the beginning of the project, the ODC assigns a small team of two to five people with varying skill sets — business analysts, project managers, and IT professionals — to visit a customer site and determine the scope and requirements of the project.

Once the initial specifications of the engagement are documented, the project managers return to the offshore location to supervise a much larger team of ten to 50 IT professionals dedicated to application development. A small team remains at the client's site to track changes in scope and address new requirements as the project progresses.

Once the development stage of the assignment is completed and tested, a team returns to the client's site to install the newly developed system and ensure its functionality. At this phase of the engagement, the vendor will often enter into an ongoing agreement with the client to provide comprehensive maintenance services from one of its offshore software development facilities.

In contrast to development projects, a typical maintenance assignment requires a larger team of ten to 20 IT professionals to travel to the client's site to gain a thorough understanding of every aspect of the client's system. The majority of the maintenance team subsequently returns to the offshore software development facility where it assumes full responsibility for day-to-day maintenance of the client's system, while coordinating with a few professionals who remain stationed at the client's site. By pursuing this model, the company completes a significant portion of its project work at its offshore software development facilities.

Sophisticated project management techniques, risk management processes, and quality control measures such as ISO 9001 and the Capability Maturity Model are necessary to complete projects seamlessly across multiple locations. These processes govern the entire software product lifecycle, from requirements to testing and maintenance.

The software product engineering and IT industry has grown rapidly over the last decade through the provision of outsourced programming and IT services. In an era where innovation centers on software, we expect the ODC model to be widely adopted.

Staff Augmentation, Contracting, or Temporary Services

The oldest onsite outsourcing model is staff augmentation, contracting, or temporary services. In this model, corporations leverage supplemental staff to contain costs and handle overflow work. Staff augmentation reduces the costs associated with hiring, benefits, and termination, as well as the expense of recruiting, training, and retaining personnel. In-house resources can be redeployed on revenue-generating and strategic activities.

The staff augmentation model can also utilize offshore resources. Actually, many offshore vendors first started as "body shops" that provided staff augmentation. These vendors thrived in the late 1990s when it was extremely difficult to find qualified employees.

Pure IT or Business Process Outsourcing

Pure outsourcing is the most classic of the first-generation nearshore and offshore outsourcing business models. In this model, companies delegate one or more business processes to an external provider that owns, administers, and manages the processes based on predefined and measurable service level metrics.

Pure outsourcing is based on a multiyear (five- to ten-year) contract with a single vendor for all the in-scope services. It comes in two forms: information technology outsourcing (ITO) and business process outsourcing (BPO). In this model, vendors usually handle a large part of the customer's IT or process needs. Companies commonly cite 1) a lack of staff with appropriate skills and 2) not enough time to do the job right when explaining why they chose this model.

The ITO model really began in 1988 when Eastman Kodak outsourced its corporate IT infrastructure (17 data centers and all its networks and desktop systems) to IBM. The ten-year deal was estimated at $250 million. Since then, several companies, such as DuPont, GM, United Technologies, and Xerox, have outsourced most of their IT infrastructure.

The advantages of this model are a lower cost of procurement, reduced management overhead, and service provider familiarity with client needs. The disadvantages are the captive or even exclusive relationship and the tendency of service provider investments to set the pace for innovation.

First-Generation Nearshore or Offshore Outsourcing

In this model, foreign companies come to North America or Europe to sell projects. These projects are then executed completely nearshore or offshore with local, lower-cost labor. This model was first seen in contract manufacturing and then spread to IT for projects involving Y2K remediation, euro conversion, software development, and application maintenance.

The first generation of nearshore and offshore outsourcing was attractive for CIOs in the financial services, high-tech, and retail industries who did not want to hire in-house staff or expensive consultants for simple tasks. In addition, the U.S. unemployment rate during the 1990s was very low, which made it hard to recruit employees. As a result, many organizations turned to nearshore and offshore vendors to take care of their staffing problems. Their actions facilitated better utilization of in-house personnel and helped them to rapidly turn projects "on" or "off" based on business demand.

The first generation of nearshore and offshore outsourcing did suffer from some limitations. The modus operandi was to throw low-cost talent at a variety of problems, which works well for defined commodity tasks that do not require much communication; however, in a business process environment (customer care or transaction processing) that calls for ongoing interaction, the classic hand-off model is not a good match. Much more integration between the firm and the offshore vendor is necessary for larger, more complex engagements.

The Second-Generation Outsourcing Business Models

As customer needs evolve, second-generation business models are emerging. They tend to be more sophisticated and to span multiple models of the first generation (see Figure 5.2). These combination models include:

- Global delivery or blended outsourcing models (practiced by large global vendors),

- Hybrid delivery model (practiced by midsize and large offshore vendors),

- Global shared services center (practiced by large multinationals),

- Build-operate-transfer (BOT) model (practiced by risk-averse corporations), and

- Nearshore or offshore multisourcing model (practiced by experienced conglomerates).

Global Delivery Model

A blended outsourcing or global delivery model (GDM) is one in which a company outsources to a multinational service provider such as Accenture, Unisys, EDS, TCS, Infosys, or IBM that offers a mix of onsite, offsite onshore, and offshore resources.

Accenture, for example, is transitioning its service offering mix to a GDM in an effort to improve its cost structure and margins. In response to rate pressure from offshore firms, Accenture has been establishing its nearshore and offshore presence with more than 40 low-cost delivery centers worldwide. Accenture has hired more than 8,000 employees in locations such as India, China, the Philippines, and Spain, up from 4,000 in 2002 and expected to increase to 12,000 by year-end 2004.[9]

Accenture is facing tough competition from the Big 5 Indian vendors — TCS, Infosys, Wipro, Satyam, and Patni. TCS, for instance, has built an integrated GDM that allows it to fulfill client requirements for onsite and offshore delivery of IT services. Onsite delivery is performed through a combination of employees based at client premises and situated in over 100 international offices and global development centers in 17 cities in nine countries outside India. The offshore delivery is performed through development centers located in 14 cities in India, which include a number of dedicated ODCs.

GDM Example: Motorola and ACS

The Motorola and Affiliated Computer Services (ACS) relationship typifies the global delivery model. Motorola took a bold step in converting its HR functions from a cost-center model to a profit-center model when it outsourced them to ACS. In December 2002, Motorola signed a ten-year HR outsourcing contract with ACS valued at $650 million. According to the contract, Motorola transferred 600 employees and a substantial part of its HR systems, software, and process capabilities to ACS.

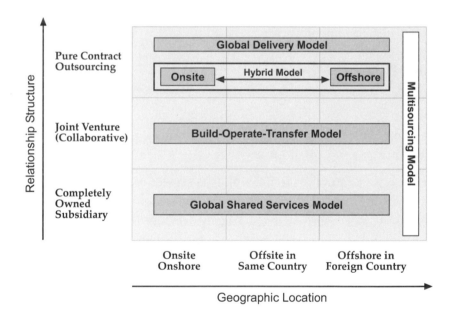

Figure 5.2: Second-Generation Global Outsourcing Business Models

ACS combined the capabilities of Motorola with its BPO abilities to create a new, wholly owned ACS business that 1) supports Motorola and 2) provides HR BPO solutions to other customers worldwide. Established in 2004, Motorola has the potential to share in the financial performance of the new business unit, that is, receive commissions based on predetermined revenue target growth by ACS Global HR Solutions.[10]

ACS operates global facilities in Mexico, Guatemala, Jamaica, the Dominican Republic, Ghana, Spain, Fiji, and India. ACS Global HR uses these offshore centers to provide HR information systems, benefits administration, global relocation, employee assistance, HR selection and assessment, learning services, employee call centers, as well as compensation, staffing, and performance management systems and processes. As the HR needs of companies expand, ACS Global HR Solutions is positioned to expand the breadth and depth of its offerings.

GDM Dynamics

The GDM allows vendors to innovatively distribute and manage engagements across multiple global locations. The advantage of this model is that the company initiating the outsourcing receives a lower rate without the risk. If faster time to market is a primary delivery objective, the GDM can accommodate this requirement by divvying up work efforts across onshore, nearshore, and offshore development facilities.

Large corporations that hire global outsourcers such as Sykes, SITEL, Convergys, Wipro, or Infosys often prefer this distributed approach. The distribution varies according to the demands of the project.

Vendors have given the GDM a variety of marketing names: best shore, any shore, right shore, and multishore. Whatever it is called, its objective is the same: to distribute and manage engagements and resources across multiple global locations, thereby allowing the service provider to better respond to client requirements from around the globe. If disaster strikes any of the vendor's locations, it can immediately shift work to other locations so that there is no interruption in business processes.

The biggest advantage of the GDM is that it saves the client from investing in a huge team of employees for multilocation projects. It adapts to the client's changing requirements and, if there is a sudden need for more resources, the service provider can supply them at once to the client and later relocate them to other, more convenient locations.

Hybrid Delivery Model (Onsite and Offshore)

Hybrid outsourcing combines onsite and offshore services to deliver results at reduced cost. The hybrid outsourcing model, also known as the dual-shore model, is favored by midsize service providers headquartered offshore in countries such as India.

How does it work? Consider the case of a software development project: The local onsite team manages the project's program management office (PMO) and supervises the client-facing components of the project, such as requirements gathering and user-interface development. The onsite operation may control a defined portion of the project that requires interaction with the subject matter experts and software architects onsite. The offshore facilities take care of the coding, testing, and bug fixing so work can be performed around the clock.

In a dual-shore model, requirements gathering and the development of detailed specifications is done onsite, while programming or process work is done offshore. This model maximizes efficiency in resources and costs. Ideally, 20%–30% of work is done onsite, whereas 70%–80% is sent offshore, depending upon the criticality of the project.

The hybrid model is one of the most popular to have emerged so far. Its proven benefits include continuous, near 24-hour work cycles; lower-cost resources; the ability to structure and assemble teams with diverse, multiple skill sets; and the flexibility to quickly scale (up or down). Some of its attractiveness stems from the fact that it enables clients to directly interact with the service provider through the onsite team, while enjoying the benefits of offshore outsourcing.

The model's challenges include project management and administration costs, optimization of cross-cultural communication, and the supervision of onsite teams.

Global Shared Services Model

Global shared services centers, also known as captive centers or offshore insourcing, are a combination of onshore shared services and offshore captive centers. They are the product of multinationals' efforts to consolidate their scattered, autonomously run internal services operations into mega-service centers.

These centers strive to create a customer-focused mind-set, which enables high-quality, cost-effective, and timely service. The global center is run as an independent business, with its own budget and bottom-line accountability. GE, HSBC, and American Express are considered the most sophisticated in deploying this model.

How does the global shared service model work? A look at the best-practice example of GE Capital International Services (Gecis) offers some insight. Gecis provides back-room services to GE Capital and GE industrial businesses at significantly lower costs and higher quality levels.[11]

Gecis began with simple data processing and has moved up the value chain to support more complex processes from diverse businesses across GE. Gecis has nine centers of excellence (CoEs) in the following areas: finance and accounting, insurance, collections, customer fulfillment, industrial and equipment, analytics, learning and remote marketing, IT services, and software.

Table 5.3 lists some of the situations and processes that three of these CoEs handle.

Gecis Contact CoE	Gecis Finance CoE	Gecis Transaction CoE
■ A store representative calling for approval of a credit card purchase ■ A credit card holder with a question or reporting a lost card ■ An automobile owner calling to report an accident ■ A medical systems field engineer ordering a spare part ■ Collection calls to credit card holders requesting past due payment	■ Over 60% of GE's accounts payable — 6 million invoices annually ■ Daily cash settlement to private label credit card services ■ Account reconciliation for 28 GE businesses ■ Financial planning and analysis ■ Financial closing for six businesses ■ Balance sheet reporting for 11 businesses	■ Application claims ■ Claims processing ■ Billing ■ Collections ■ Underwriting ■ Loan approvals ■ Order processing

Table 5.3: Services and Processes at the Gecis Centers of Excellence

Gecis also supports other back-office functions. The IT-enabled services center provides help desk and network management. The analytics center conducts data mining and analysis for GE and its customers. E-learning assists with employee training and assessment. Gecis even employs doctors to evaluate and classify medical claims. Currently, Gecis is the largest captive shared services employer in India with more than 17,000 employees.

Captive shared services centers possess significant advantages. First, they have guaranteed markets for their services and an established management hierarchy. They also alleviate some of the organizational issues such as control and politics that crop up when firms relocate back-office activities offshore to external vendors. Multinationals are leading the way in establishing global shared services centers.

Build-Operate-Transfer Model

For many of the companies that have started their own foreign subsidiaries, the process has not been as smooth as they expected. They faced obstacles — legal, taxes, hiring, and management — from start to finish. While some companies have taken a long time to attain a steady state, some are still struggling, and a few even closed their operations.

The rise of captive subsidiary failures led to the evolution of a new business model in the outsourcing industry called a build-operate-transfer (BOT). In this model, a firm contracts with a service provider to build a shared services facility or offshore development center and operate it for a fixed interim period.

The logic behind the BOT model: Companies can initiate operations and reach operating stability much faster with the help of a service provider than they can with an in-house effort.

A typical BOT is built and managed in three phases:

1. **Build.** The vendor provides a complete solution for building a presence in a particular country. The clients receive their own office space and establish their own brand identity at a lower price than comparable outsourcing arrangements. The vendor's staff takes care of all administrative and legal issues, from real estate, utilities, and permits, to computers, communications, and office supplies. The vendor also provides the professional support staff and operating licenses to run functions such as call centers.

2. **Operate.** The supplier delivers a comprehensive set of operational management services, from HR and staffing, to accent training, accounting, payroll, legal, facilities, and security. The clients are able to focus their management time on their core business rather than on operational issues.

3. **Option to Transfer.** The offshore partner cannot lock in clients. The clients have the option to bring the operation in-house at any time. The outsourcing contract should detail a well-defined process to ensure a smooth transition. Typically, the contract includes a clause that says the client has the option to buy the entire operation after a fixed period. A BOT gives the client the ability to quickly realize the benefits of outsourcing with limited execution risk while minimizing upfront costs and long-term financial risks.

The BOT model is ideal for a risk-averse company. Building your own subsidiary in a foreign country requires much knowledge and information about the country and culture, as well as the right personnel. If you aren't up to the task of gathering this information, then a BOT solution may be the right answer for your company. The BOT model is usually found in the civil and construction engineering business, especially in the maintenance of highways and airports. Now the BOT model is becoming popular in the offshore outsourcing world.

Ernst and Young surveyed Indian BPO companies and found that almost 13% of those vendors have entered into BOT contracts. Aviva Plc, the U.K. insurer, signed three different BOT contracts for business process outsourcing services with Mumbai-based WNS Global Services, Delhi-based EXL Services, and Bangalore-based 24/7 Customer.

BOT models tend to build on first-generation ODC models. With the ODC model, the basic framework is in place for the "build" and "operate" parts. With the BOT model, there is an additional option to "transfer" the operations after a certain period. This arrangement affords customers bottom-line enhancements and fully offloaded costs, risks, and ownership of the new venture. It minimizes the risk of execution and allows companies to spend more money on core functions.

Multisourcing: The Hub-and-Spoke Model

Similar to the Chinese proverb that states a clever rabbit will have three openings to its den, many companies will work with multiple offshore or nearshore vendors to mitigate risk. For instance, a company might establish a shared services center for its finance and accounting operation; it might rely on a third-party vendor for its call center operations; and it might have a joint venture with another vendor for its R&D.

Multisourcing is the practice of executing multiple nearshore or offshore business models simultaneously. This portfolio approach has three strategic objectives:

- Diversify risk by leveraging multiple service providers and encouraging competition to ensure continuous improvement;

- Control risk by leveraging multiple geographic locations; and

- Employ a variety of business models to minimize risk and maximize control.

Multisourcing helps companies achieve the advantages of a best-of-breed strategy and builds in more flexibility. Citibank and American Express have both taken a multisourcing approach that resembles a classic hub-and-spoke model. They have offshore operations of their own, as well as three or four partners with whom they collaborate. This is an interesting model as the businesses get some of their partners to actually work with them in their own hub centers, train them, and then send them back to the spoke center.

A narrower view of multisourcing is simply doing business with multiple vendors to mitigate risk. New York–based Guardian Life Insurance Company embraces a multisourcing approach. The insurer contracts with Patni Computer Systems (Mumbai), NIIT Technologies (New Delhi), and Covansys (Michigan). Instead of awarding one major, long-term contract to a single supplier, Guardian is mitigating risk by working with a consortium of vendors to create a multilocation, distributed delivery model.

The rise of multisource deals could be a sign that companies are taking a more cautious, risk-averse approach to outsourcing. In the case of

Guardian and others, multisourcing works because the organization has the internal ability to manage and integrate multiple providers (products, projects, and services) to derive a single solution.

When should organizations choose full-service outsourcing (using one provider) over multisourcing portfolio approach? It depends on the maturity of the organization. Companies that are new to outsourcing tend to multisource until they get comfortable with the whole process. When they renegotiate contracts later, they give more thought to using one provider. Often, to reduce complexity, very large businesses look for one dominant provider that will work with a big network of companies.

Understanding the Outsourcing Revenue Models

No business model discussion is complete without some mention of the underlying revenue models. In order to help you understand the revenue models, we should note that outsourcing comes in two flavors:

1. Task-oriented (piecemeal): take my tasks and complete them for less money.

2. Process-oriented (comprehensive): take over my business processes and provide them back to me as a service.

The task oriented and process-oriented revenue models are quite varied in outsourcing. The task-oriented BPO contracts gravitate towards time and material and fixed-price models. The process-oriented BPO contracts range from cost-plus models to fuzzier risk-reward ones. Let's look at each revenue model in more detail.

Time and Material Revenue Model

The simplest pricing model is time and materials (T&M) billing. The T&M model is an attractive option when scope, specification, and implementation plans of a project are not easy to define at the outset.

The challenge in the T&M model is adhering to very strict project management and reporting practices whereby task sheets are generated on a daily or weekly basis for each employee on the project. If there is lax oversight of the work, then T&M can become very expensive.

Fixed-Price Revenue Model

Outsourcing vendors use the fixed-price or fixed-time model to effectively sell their services to clients. Customers are attracted to this model because of the upfront commitment on timing and the concept of risk sharing on potential cost or time overruns.

Under this option, the customer pays a prenegotiated, fixed price for the complete project, which is linked to well-defined deliverables. It is suitable for customers with clear requirements and project schedules. Changes in scope are subject to a predefined, fixed hourly rate and must follow a standard, already established change request procedure.

When bidding for fixed-price, fixed-time engagements, vendors must accurately estimate the costs and timing of completing the projects based on the processes they plan to use, the professionals they plan to staff on the engagement, and past project experiences. Vendors bear the risk of cost and time overruns as a result of any unforeseen costs or delays associated with the performance of these engagements, including delays caused by factors outside their control.

Cost-Plus Revenue Model

This model is typically used in tandem with the BOT model or for complex multiyear, multi-element arrangements. It is also the model behind the dedicated development center (an extension of a company's software engineering facility).

This revenue model is popular among large companies that seek long-term gains from global outsourcing. These contracts are principally structured on a fee-for-service basis and stipulate that the vendor receives a fee that is no greater than the client's historical cost of operating the functions assumed by the vendor. For some components of the outsourcing fees, vendors provide negotiated discounts from the client's historical costs. After vendors have recovered their costs or achieved a negotiated minimum cost reduction, they may be required to share further savings with the clients in a negotiated gain sharing arrangement.

Risk-Reward Revenue Model

Vendors that enter multiyear partnerships with clients favor risk-reward or gain sharing models for outsourcing contracts. Since the goal of outsourcing is to help clients become more effective in their business operations, vendors are open to linking their revenues with the actual benefits their clients realize.

This type of contract is also known as value pricing, or "pay as you save," whereby the outsourcer builds first and is paid as savings materialize. These are performance-based contracts, tying payments to business performance.

The drawback of this model is that revenue recognition on the vendor side becomes an important accounting issue. Vendors typically can recognize revenues and profits as work progresses based upon the proportion of costs incurred to the total expected costs. Vendors maintain for each of their contracts estimates of total revenues and costs over the respective contract term. For purposes of periodic financial reporting, vendors accumulate total actual costs incurred to date under the contract.

Summary

A crucial issue in ensuring outsourcing — onshore, nearshore, or offshore — success is selecting the appropriate business model.

Global outsourcing can be implemented using a variety of structures ranging from captive centers to third-party outsourcing vendors. The distribution of activities across the various delivery models may vary from one project to another, depending on the effort involved, speed of execution, level of interaction, and cultural and time zone differences.

Managers should understand the underlying revenue and pricing models. Current revenue models for outsourcing vendors are similar to those of traditional service firms or professional service organizations, such as accounting or law firms. In general, the number of billable consultants, their utilization, and average hourly bill rates determine revenues. We envision more progressive revenue models developing over time.

In summary, the more time you invest in choosing the right business model, the higher your probability of success.

We have reached the end of the second section of this book, planning. To recap, Chapter 4 focused on setting the corporate strategy and examined how to select business process candidates for outsourcing. Chapter 5 presented the different ways business models can be structured, or the "how" of outsourcing.

Our objective in the next section of the book — Chapters 6 through 9 — is to help readers understand the vendor, location, and contract decisions that will need to be made.

Chapter Six

Finding Vendors — Creating Effective RFIs and RFPs

Once the strategy is firm and the business requirements are clear, it's time to initiate the request for information (RFI) and the request for proposal (RFP). This chapter guides you through both processes. By the chapter's end, you should be able to explain how an RFI differs from an RFP, what the elements of a good RFP are, what some common pitfalls to avoid are, and how the RFP process works in the real world.

Introduction

The RFI and the RFP are essential elements of any outsourcing engagement. The RFI gathers intelligence about the feasibility of a project. At the conclusion of the RFI process, companies decide whether to proceed with an RFP. If they elect to proceed, they also have to determine the scope of services to be outsourced.

An RFP describes much more than specific project requirements. Its contents are a good indicator of companies' business strategy and immediate needs, as well as a reflection of the health of internal processes, technology, work culture, and tools. It is a barometer for gauging companies' process rigor, methodologies, and planning maturity.

A poorly written RFP wastes everyone's time and money and fails to achieve a project's stated goals. Such an RFP leaves much room for misunderstood expectations and leads to protracted negotiations and damage control meetings. The cause of a failing project can often be tracked to a badly written RFP.

Request for Information (RFI): A document requesting information from potential outsourcing vendors demonstrating their capabilities, resources, experiences, and overall approach to providing services. Often, response to the RFI is required for participating in the subsequent RFP process.

Request for Proposal (RFP): A document detailing a customer's outsourcing requirements and the evaluation criteria that will be used for selecting the ultimate provider. RFPs are typically sent to a limited number of potential providers, around three to five, that have been previously qualified as capable of delivering the needed services.

Request for Quote (RFQ): Consultants and experienced users sometimes issue an RFQ rather than either an RFI or RFP. The RFQ is more money-oriented (How much will it cost to do this?) rather than gathering information on what's possible.

Table 6.1: Defining RFIs, RFPs, and RFQs

The End-to-End RFP Process

Outsourcing initiatives fall into two categories: sole-source negotiations with a single vendor or an RFI/RFP process aimed at finding a small subset of vendors that fit the organization's needs.

Companies select the sole-source option if they know the vendor that they want to outsource to and if they are not willing to open up the bidding process. Companies that want to learn more about new methods, vendor capabilities, and options lean toward the more time-consuming RFI/RFP route. We call this "competitive intelligence gathering," or receiving a free, vendor-sponsored education.

The RFP is a subset of the broader vendor selection process (see Figure 6.1). The end-to-end process, from creation and release to contract award, is a lengthy one. At a minimum, it takes two to three months to complete, but can take as long as nine to 12 months from start to finish, depending on the complexity of the contract. Often companies hire sourcing consulting firms to help manage the RFP process and define the important business and process requirements and information needed.

Companies often lose negotiating leverage by exposing their most powerful piece, the RFP, prematurely. Instead of directly engaging in an RFP process, the smarter firms are choosing to issue an RFI first. If done right, the RFI is sometimes the more effective opening move of a strategic outsourcing project.

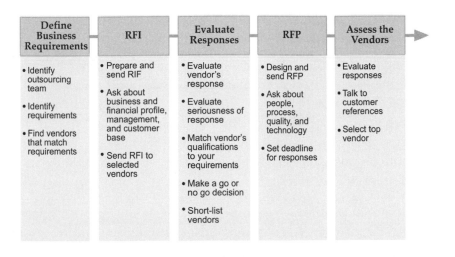

Figure 6.1: The RFI and RFP Process

Request for Information

The RFI provides material for the first few rounds of vendor evaluations. Organizations sometimes use it as a "tire-kicking" effort to validate vendor interest and to evaluate what is going on in the outside world.

A good RFI encourages vendors to respond freely in the absence of the constraints of a highly formal RFP. The RFI process is the vendor's chance to sell the company's strengths and features. It offers businesses, usually under nondisclosure agreements, the opportunity to learn not only what vendors can do now, but what they plan to do.

An effective RFI defines as specifically as possible the business requirements that are important to a company. In order to receive comparable information from multiple vendors, companies should prepare a questionnaire to send to vendors that are invited to participate; otherwise, it will be difficult to compare and evaluate responses objectively (apples to apples).

Structuring the RFI

The RFI questionnaire should explain your company's business goals, objectives, and the reason why you are looking for a vendor. Potential questions could relate to vendor size, stability, location, infrastructure, quality processes, and skill sets. A sample questionnaire could include some of these categories:

- **Business profile.** This section would ask for a general overview of the vendor, its history, capabilities, and markets served. Specific questions could include the following: How long has the vendor been in business? What is its business model? How large is it? How many locations does it have and in which countries? What are the vendor's onshore, nearshore, and offshore capabilities? What are its areas of expertise?

- **Financial profile.** How financially stable is the vendor? Request a copy of the most recent annual financial statement and at least two bank references.

- **Customer base and references.** Can the vendor provide long-term client references? Ask the vendor to provide the last three contracts it signed as references.

- **Management.** This part of the questionnaire would seek an overview of the vendor's organization, with key executive personnel identified. Sample questions could include the following: What experience does the management team have? How will senior management participate in the planning process?

- **Employees.** What educational requirements does the vendor have? What employee retention initiatives does it have in place? What training programs are established? Will the vendor use subcontractors? Can the vendor scale up quickly?

- **Process.** What quality certifications has the vendor achieved? Does the vendor have relevant experience in the area or industry applicable to your company? Does it have a defined project management methodology? Does it have quality control measurements in place?

- **Infrastructure.** Does the vendor have the facilities to deliver what you need? Are its telecom and IT infrastructures state of the art? Has it instituted contingency or redundancy plans?

- **IP protection and data security.** What security measures will the vendor take to protect your intellectual property? What procedures has the vendor set up to protect your data?

- **Delivery.** This section would request the vendor to state the performance commitments and guarantees that it would offer. Suggested questions could cover the following: What are the vendor's reporting guidelines? What are the escalation procedures? What personnel will the vendor assign to coordinate and communicate reports and review performance?

Too many questions can cause data overload. With an RFI, you could get reams of data from vendors. You have to be ready and able to analyze it. If you're not, an alternative is to ask vendors to come in and give detailed presentations, offering your company a taste of what is available in the marketplace and affording vendors the opportunity to ask a few questions of their own.

Sending the RFI to the Right Vendors

To choose a service provider, you must first get the right vendors to respond to your RFI. In general, four types of vendors exist.

- Niche vendors offer specialized skills or location expertise but have a limited ability to scale. A competent IT services company that is based primarily in India or China with a token onshore presence is a good example of a niche vendor. GE often does business with this type of company.

- Transaction providers handle a limited set of outsourced processes, such as data entry or payroll. They perform the task efficiently but do not usually transform or re-engineer the process. Transaction outsourcing is the quickest and easiest, but it is so narrowly defined that it fragments processes since third-party vendors handle certain activities and others remain in-house. The typical transaction contract value is $1–$5 million, and the average contract length is one to two years. SLA metrics are usually based on the number of transactions. Examples include payroll (ADP), call center (Sykes), and customer billing (Convergys).

- Process providers focus on multiple, related processes, such as call center or tax accounting, and take responsibility for the processes they manage. SLA metrics are usually based on process outcomes. The typical full-service provider contract value is $5–$10 million per year, and the average duration is three to five years. Examples include contact center (eTelecare), accounts payable (Core3), and application development (Keane).

- Full-service providers handle several business processes, such as human resources (HR) or IT. Comprehensive providers take full responsibility for the complete processes they manage and typically offer to re-engineer the process to make it more efficient. They often take over existing operations and hire hundreds to thousands of the client's employees. The typical contract value per year is $50–$100 million, and the average length is seven to ten years. Examples include HR (Hewitt, Accenture) and finance and accounting (Affiliated Computer Services, EDS).

Usually the RFI is sent to vendors based on the project's scope and objectives. Will you be outsourcing one well-defined task, several processes, or a total end-to-end process? If you are looking to improve a process, you need to find a vendor that has expertise in that area and is willing to re-engineer the process. Understanding what you want to accomplish will help you define the type of vendor you should target.

Analyze and Evaluate Information

Once vendors have completed and returned the questionnaires, match their responses to your requirements and weight the criteria based on importance. Eliminate vendors that do not meet your needs or have not responded to the specific questions.

The best way to choose the most legitimate and effective vendor is by conducting an extensive evaluation to determine suitability or compatibility concerning procedures, quality assurance controls, infrastructure, and security. It is important to find a vendor consistent with your company's business objectives.

Throughout the entire process, it pays to think out of the box as you analyze responses. In other words, look for potential problem-causing scenarios. One important response to consider is whether the vendor relies on external subcontractors to deliver services. If the answer is yes, you will need to dig deeper and evaluate the subcontractors. Why is this important? Consider the following real-world example: The University of California, San Francisco (UCSF), Medical Center used three subcontractors for patient record transcription. The first contractor was a Bay Area transcription service, which UCSF had worked with for many years. This firm regularly used about 15 U.S. subcontractors. One subcontractor, a woman from Florida, also used subcontractors. One of the Florida woman's transcribers, a Texan, sent his work overseas to Pakistan. The Pakistani transcriber threatened to post UCSF's patient files on the Internet unless it assisted her in resolving a financial dispute with the Texas man who had hired her. She attached actual UCSF patient records to her e-mail threat. After receiving payment from the subcontractor, the transcriber withdrew her threat.[1]

So be thorough in your RFI questionnaire and your analysis of the responses will yield useful insights. The goal is to avoid potential problems downstream by identifying and resolving them early.

An RFI questionnaire is a very useful data collection tool. Vendors realize that if they respond to an RFI intelligently and promptly, the likelihood of their getting a copy of the RFP increases.

The Go or No Go Decision

The information obtained from the RFI process can help vendors make the "go or no go" decision. The data provided should identify the availability and viability of outsourcing, cost estimate ranges, and risks. While there are many other considerations relevant to the decision to go forward with a project, the RFI can be a valuable tool for collecting some of the required information.

In addition, the RFI can serve to validate the decision to proceed with a project and provide another level of detail for developing project requirements. The RFI will supply an overall sense of what solutions are available in the marketplace to solve the particular business problem.

Short-List Vendors

Once companies have assessed the RFI information and chosen to proceed, it is time to short-list the vendors for the RFP process. The vendor short-list normally consists of three to five respondents. It presents an opportunity to start developing a relationship with the potential service providers through increased communication of your business needs and requirements.

Expanded communication also allows prospective vendors to articulate their methodologies for enhancing or modifying the outsourced process to achieve greater efficiency. The time spent working with the short-list candidates to refine the requirements and critical success factors is valuable. It foreshadows the future client-vendor relationship. Now you are ready to circulate the RFP that clearly communicates to service providers what your company seeks.

Request for Proposal

The goal of this step is to distribute the RFP to at least three suppliers in the short-list, assist service providers with their proposal development, evaluate the proposals, and select the best ones.

The relationship between the RFI and RFP is complementary. Once the "go" decision is made, information developed by the RFI can be used to seed the solution requirements section of the related RFP. A better understanding of project scope and requirements, as well as a list of qualified suppliers should now exist. Leveraging the information-gathering focus of the RFI will lead to an unambiguous, concise RFP that articulates the business need.

To understand the entire end-to-end process, consider Delta Air Lines' quest to cut costs by outsourcing reservation centers. Figure 6.2 illustrates the process that Delta undertook when it outsourced some aspects of its reservations centers.[2]

Elements of a Good RFP

An RFP spells out requirements in detail — relevant skill sets, language skills, IP protection, infrastructure, and quality certifications — and gives prospective vendors the information they need to prepare a bid.

The responsibility of developing the RFP rests with your sourcing leader, but different aspects of it require input from other domain experts. It is not the length of the RFP that matters, but the coverage of different issues involved in global project execution.

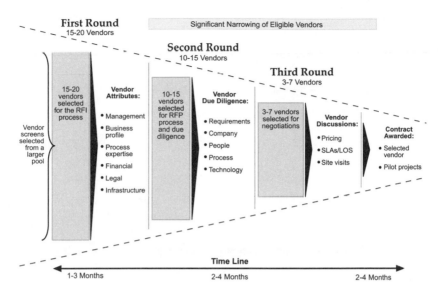

Figure 6.2: The RFP Process in Action

A good RFP includes sections on five elements:

1. Business requirements,

2. Vendor's company information,

3. Vendor's people information,

4. Vendor's process and methodologies, and

5. Vendor' technology skills and expertise.

Let's look at the information each section should cover.

Business Requirements

The RFP process should serve as a mutual learning process for your company and the potential vendors. The requirements section details your company's needs. At the very minimum, a requirements section should detail the project's scope, deliverables, performance and fulfillment requirements, and liquidity damages.

Project Scope

Be specific to the project. Identify the project's overall objective and how to define its success. Describe the project in terms of its skill, size, content, volume, and time line. A short paragraph normally suffices. Highlight key relevant or related business process interdependencies and the importance of quality as appropriate. A word about the interdisciplinary nature of the project and its regional, global, or local reach may be relevant in some cases.

Deliverables

To document deliverables, you should refer to your process map and identify touch points and hand-offs between the vendor and your company. Itemize deliverables, explaining what will be delivered when and outlining the role of the vendor and the company at each point.

Performance and Fulfillment Requirements

Here, the RFP must explain the quality and time frame guidelines for the deliverables. Depending upon the project, they could be written in very simple language, or they may have to be tabulated in detail to make the project execution resilient. Is the delay for a particular task acceptable if the deliverable is delayed by 4 hours, one day, or one week?

The upper and lower bounds for delivery of each milestone and the project item must be quantifiably defined. Early delivery may not necessarily always mean a better solution. For instance, you may not have storage space ready for shipments that arrive ahead of schedule.

Fulfillment terms must define when a task is considered complete. The requirements mentioned in this part of the RFP will roll into the individual project performance scorecard. Chapter 12 contains more information on performance measurement.

Liquidity Damages

The conditions and amount of liquidity damages for the failure to perform and fulfill must be spelled out concretely, consistent with the same definitions used for deliverables and the project plan. Make sure the number is measurable, but remember that unreasonably heavy-duty penalty clauses drive vendors to resort to defensive tactics — trying to prove timely delivery through frivolous compilation of records — rather than effective and productive execution.

Assessing the Vendor

External service providers differ significantly in terms of performance, style, and experience. The company section of the RFP details the vendor's stability, services, and reputation.

Topic	Discussion Points
Company stability	Financial stability, experience, year of establishment, size, company growth, and funding position.
Company vision	Vision and values.
Management	Experience of management team.
Services	Areas of expertise, customers.
Culture	Openness, flexibility, learning, and communication.
Reputation	Project management, infrastructure reliability, and customer relationships.
Pricing	Cost of the agreement, any exception cost based on performance metrics, price stability, and hidden costs.
Location	Country, language, and time zones.
Legal	Contract agreement, indemnities, the transfer of people, and how the contract might be terminated.
Flexible contract	Schedules and deliverables, SLAs, guarantees, payment, conflict resolution, term, expiration, and renewal options.
Facilities	Security procedures such as access cards. Expansion capabilities in the current or new facility or city.

Table 6.2: Topics to Cover in the RFP's Company Assessment

Simply offering onshore, nearshore, or offshore resources does not guarantee that a company has the skills, processes, or management capabilities to support a truly global sourcing model. Carefully evaluate the vendor's reputation, references, culture, and management style.

The vendor you are considering may be riding the newest outsourcing wave and may not have developed adequate processes and relationships to stay in business for the long haul. Hence, it becomes crucial to try to gauge the stability of the offshore vendor.

Assessing the Vendor's Employees

The people section of the RFP details the resources assigned at each level: project management, middle management, team leader, and task.

Topic	Discussion Points
People quality	Quality of resources, hiring policy, experience, education, skill set availability, and frequency of employee background checks and formalized performance reviews.
Training	Training programs for new employees, accent neutralization training, documentation, and ongoing skills training.
Language	Languages used for oral and written communication.
Compensation	Compensation levels, industry compensation averages, and benefits.
Scalability	Manpower abundance, as well as depth and knowledge of employee resources.
Retention	Retention rate, policies for keeping employees, average employee tenure, country's average turnover rate, and frequency of employee satisfaction surveys.
Other resources	Tendency of the vendor to use other companies for resources (also obtain information on that company).

Table 6.3: Topics to Cover in the RFP's People Assessment

People Quality

As people-intensive businesses, outsourcing companies find attracting, training, and retaining skilled professionals challenging in the fast-growth offshore markets; therefore, it is important to study skill levels, hiring profiles, training programs, and retention capabilities.

For instance, customer service reps (CSRs) play a significant role in the success of offshore call center projects. With high CSR attrition rates prevalent, the vendor should have defined programs to ensure new CSRs are adequately trained and certified.

Skill Sets

The RFP must list the required skills for workers expected to be involved in the outsourced project. Including such a list will help vendors match the right employees with the right jobs, as well as accurately estimate cost of labor per industry standard rates for a particular skill set.

Typically companies will include an appendix in the RFP that describes the requisite employee skills, titles, education, work and project experience, certifications, and domain knowledge.

Assessing the Vendor's Process Capabilities

The process section of the RFP details project management, quality, and security.

Topic	Discussion Points
Project management	Project planning, risk management, communication, reports, supervisor-to-employee ratio, and presence of documented escalation procedures for problems.
Project quality	Standards, reviews, testing, certifications, and satisfaction measurements. The most widely known standards are ISO 9001 and the Capability Maturity Model (CMM).
Regulatory compliance	Compliance with regulations such as the USA Patriot Act, Sarbanes-Oxley Act, and the Health Insurance Portability and Accountability Act.
Intellectual property (IP) security	Vendor's policies on duplicating project information, IP rights, noncompetition and nondisclosure terms, and history of piracy.

Table 6.4: Topics to Cover in the RFP's Process Assessment

Project Management Requirements

A well-executed outsourcing project depends on the managers behind it. The RFP's project plan should name the people from your company who will be involved, as well as their roles and responsibilities, qualifications, and contact details. The potential vendors should supply the same information. With this information in hand, companies can begin building a proper transition team without having to start the discussions all over again. For more information on transition, refer to Chapter 10.

Project management requirements are much more effective if they include details such as the estimated size of the team, in addition to the location, qualifications, and availability of backup personnel.

Communications Requirements

The need to regularly communicate project progress at all levels should be listed in the RFP. Communication may vary from project to project, but the guiding principle should be that you have at least the same intensity of communication (frequency, means, and duration) as you have within your own organization. You should select a reasonable format and go with it, with an option to revisit as needed. Perhaps a daily report would be the best fit? Or a weekly report? Or a monthly report? Maybe a hand-over meeting would work best when a deliverable is shipped out? It all depends on the project scope.

If necessary, this is a good place in the RFP to include a time overlap clause for vendors located in different time zones, so that they are available to talk when you call. Effective communication is an important aspect of global project management and is discussed at great length in Chapter 10 from an execution standpoint.

Assessing the Vendor's Technology Infrastructure

The technology section of the RFP details the infrastructure stability and disaster recovery abilities of the vendor.

Topic	Discussion Points
Technology	Domain, applications, and infrastructure expertise.
Software infrastructure	Availability of all your software environments, such as your operating system, databases, and application servers.
Hardware infrastructure	Equipment quality and condition, cabling plan, and disaster recovery plan. Network infrastructure security, safety, and reliability for remote access.
Power backup	Availability of additional resources for power outages.
Internet and communication	Multiple levels of Internet connectivity, such as a leased line, broadband DSL, or ISDN.
IT support staff	Number and skills of IT staff supporting technology. Training requirements for IT staff.

Table 6.5: Topics to Cover in the RFP's Technology Assessment

If your company ranked technical skills as the most important criteria for success, look at the technical expertise of the proposals before you look at the costs. You want to be sure the vendor will be able to deliver what is important to you, as opposed to just focusing on price.

Industry-Specific Requirements

Knowledge, skills, and process compliance should be industry-specific and mentioned in the RFP. What standards do you expect the vendor to follow? If this is an IT project, you may be looking for Microsoft, SAP, or Oracle certified professionals. If this is a healthcare-related project, you may be looking for a HIPAA compliant process for data security.

Vendor Supplied Materials and Information

It is important to clarify the use of vendor-supplied equipment in the RFP whether for purposes of resource management, data security, or IP protection. Who will supply the laptops, servers, printers, development environment, test benches, and other material for the work to be done at the company or at the vendor location? How will the firewalls be set up? What will happen to the records and information?

Companies should also account for any collateral support they may provide at the outset, such as initial training, access to different databases, technical support, or any other material support.

RFP Process in Action: Lehman Brothers

Of all the industries, the financial services industry leads the business world in IT offshoring. A case in point is the investment bank Lehman Brothers. In 2001, Lehman saw that its revenues were diminishing and its IT costs were ballooning, so it initiated an offshore strategy to reduce its IT costs by 2003. A sizable part of the $700 million in IT costs was tied up in salaries for Lehman's total IT staff of 2,000.[3]

After a detailed analysis that included attending conferences, analyzing public documents, interviewing competitors, and talking with several outsourcing vendors, Lehman determined that it could optimize IT expenses. To gain experience and executive buy-in to the offshore model, the investment bank kick-started the process by initiating 80 pilot projects in the application development and maintenance area.

Lehman reviewed 15 vendors and picked three — Wipro, TCS, and Infosys. The investment bank conducted fixed-duration, limited scope projects with these vendors. One of the goals of the pilots was to let project managers become familiar with managing offshore vendors and fixed-price contracts, as well as providing vendors with business requirements. Lehman is estimated to have spent $8 million on 80 pilot projects over six months.[4]

Based on its experience and ROI data from the pilots, Lehman set up two dedicated offshore development centers (ODCs) with Wipro and TCS. It expects to obtain a 40% costs savings on development and cut costs by $50–$70 million in a three-year period.[5] The company is expanding the scope of its IT offshoring by creating its own captive center staffed by Lehman employees to do mission-critical software development, infrastructure maintenance, and research analysis.

Lehman is not alone in shifting work to lower-cost software development locations. Its competitors — Goldman Sachs, Merrill Lynch, Bank of America, and Deutsche Bank — have also adopted offshore strategies in an attempt to gain a cost advantage.

RFP Process in Action: Selecting Two Vendors

Many companies use the RFP process as a way to assess vendors, utilizing smaller pilot projects as a test. A midsize U.S. credit card company did exactly this. Trying offshore outsourcing for the first time, the company's senior managers decided to go on a tour to interview and evaluate numerous Indian vendors. They hired a consultant to help them identify which vendors to include on the initial long list. One of the decision makers was aware of alternative vendors in China, so they also visited a few companies in China.

At the close of the RFP process, the credit card company ended up selecting two companies to complete the same pilot project, one from India and one from China. This strategy worked out extremely well for the Chinese vendor as the larger Indian outsourcing company did not complete the project well.

Bleum, the IT outsourcing vendor based in China, was given several additional projects. The midsize companies now entering the offshore space for the first time are realizing that many of the larger U.S. or Indian vendors are not interested in the smaller contracts. After the contract is signed, it is difficult for these smaller companies to maintain the focus and commitment of the larger vendors. David Burke, vice president of sales and marketing at Bleum, says, "If you are a medium-size company, it can be difficult to get access to the mindshare and the resources of your large Indian supplier."[6]

RFP Pitfalls to Avoid

We often hear stories about the RFP process failing. Perhaps surprisingly, the source of the failure often resides with the company creating the RFP. Several factors can cause the RFP process to be suboptimal.

Lack of a clear sourcing plan. While most companies are aware of the need for a sourcing plan (that guides the RFI and RFP process) aligned with the strategic direction of the company, few have such plans. Faced with marching orders to outsource a project and time pressure to execute the assignment, managers don't feel that they are in a position to question the business motivation for outsourcing. The absence of a sourcing plan invariably leads to problems as people in charge of sourcing do not have clarity on the end goals.

Too procurement driven. Outsourcing success demands a different, specialized approach than procuring commodities from say China. Often, the process is given to the procurement department to manage. The problem with this decision is that sourcing managers know how to guarantee that the process is followed to the letter, but they might not have the background knowledge to be able to communicate effectively with the vendors. This delays the decision-making process.

No executive involvement. Unfortunately, executives usually do not get involved in the RFP process until the very end. They then do not have all of the information they need to make an informed decision. Companies can save themselves money and energy if they spend more time on the front end creating the right selection committee, developing an effective RFI or RFP, and bringing in the right vendors.

Lack of structure. Some large companies have dozens of outsourcing projects going on simultaneously across the organization. Most of these projects execute similar RFP processes with very little coordination, which leads to extra costs and overhead. To correct this, best-practice firms are creating vendor management offices (VMOs) to coordinate the RFI and RFP issues. The VMO typically becomes involved at the start of negotiations and helps managers figure out which vendor can offer the best price and service for the business process requested.

Skipping steps. RFIs and RFPs are not equivalent. The danger lies in the assumption that, with the information obtained from the RFI, one can proceed directly to negotiation and supplier selection. The RFI merely identifies options for proceeding and qualifies some potential suppliers. To be effective, the RFI must be used as a tool that helps the procurement team gain knowledge, formulate ideas, and develop a cohesive set of project requirements.

Summary

No matter the industry, every company has noncore functions that take resources and focus away from core strategic goals. The RFP process attempts to set of a chain of events in motion that transfers some or all of the responsibility for a particular service to an external vendor. In order to pick the most suitable vendor, you have to engage in the RFP process. A good RFP sets the right expectations and requirements. In this chapter, we have described the basic framework for creating an effective RFP, a process that can sometimes force companies to understand their internal issues.

It is important for your company to have some key people experienced in the RFI/RFP process or to hire a consultant if this is your company's first sourcing experience. A hasty sourcing plan that lacks proper understanding of the underlying processes and methodology is almost doomed to fail. Lastly, a good RFP will help your company negotiate your contract better.

1.	Company and financial stability
2.	Customer references and reputation
3.	Management
4.	Employee skills and expertise
5.	Infrastructure reliability
6.	Process expertise and methodology
7.	Cultural fit
8.	Scalability
9.	Flexibility
10.	Cost

Table 6.6: Summarizing the Top Ten Vendor Criteria

Chapter Seven

The Vendor Selection Process

Select the right vendor and outsourcing can be a powerful tool for achieving business objectives. Select the wrong vendor and outsourcing can be a quagmire of subpar business performance. Given its importance, vendor selection requires a multifaceted, multistage process to evaluate not only what service providers can do, but also how they do it. This chapter guides you through the steps of picking a vendor. It arms you with comprehensive information on how to choose a vendor that will deliver long-term, meaningful results and provides tips on vendor site visits and common pitfalls to avoid.

Introduction

Once companies decide that outsourcing is a beneficial strategy for them, evaluating vendors that will support long-term growth or cost management objectives is the next step. Some organizations want vendors that can provide most or all of the support for all of their outsourced processes. Others take a best-of-breed approach and obtain different vendors for each outsourced process. There is no right or wrong method for executing an outsourcing strategy.

If you decide to outsource to a third-party vendor, one of the most important tasks you will face is vendor selection. Many partnerships are long-term, with benefits and ROI accruing the more time is invested. With all the upfront work that outsourcing to a vendor entails, from contract negotiations to employee reassignment, it behooves companies to make sure the vendor they select aligns with their goals and corporate culture.

How you pick your vendor will have a significant impact on your success, so taking the time for due diligence is well worth it. How do you decide? How do you begin the painstaking fact gathering and analysis process? How do you determine how much industry knowledge vendors have?

How can you gain a sense of their processes and methodologies? Will cultural diversity inhibit effective communication? You will need to answer a host of questions.

The search for good vendors can be tedious. Many vendors that meet defined criteria will be unsuitable for a variety of reasons. Months of studying potential prospects, visiting companies, and negotiating costs may result in frustration and a temptation to quickly close a contract that could end in dissatisfaction.

The key to success, hard as it may seem, is maintaining discipline throughout the process. You should be aware that the offshore vendor selection process is different from outsourcing to a company within your own country. The difference in performance between the best and the worst offshore vendor is arguably larger than the differences among the performances of U.S. outsourcing companies.

This chapter highlights a vendor sourcing methodology that can help your company find the right vendor. The first step is identifying what type of vendor fits your needs.

Selecting the Right Vendor

Selecting the right vendor for a long-term relationship is a critical task. Vellayan Subbiah, vice president of sales and marketing at 24/7 Customer, agrees, "The offshore industry is in its infancy — it's only about three-and-a-half years old — so there are a plethora of vendors just like in the dot-com boom. Out of these firms, 50 will survive, and five will become great institutions. That's the way this space is going to shake out. So there is always a danger in the whole vendor selection process to go and pick somebody that may or may not be a survivor."[1]

A well-organized vendor selection process can take anywhere from six months to a year. When companies start the selection process, one aspect they tend to forget is the expense, which can range upward of 2% in addition to the annual cost of the deal.

For example, if your contract is estimated at $10 million, selecting a vendor could add expenses of $200,000. Associated costs include analysis and documentation of requirements, creation and dissemination of RFPs, evaluation of the RFP responses, contract negotiations, and the development of service level agreements. In addition, project leaders, staff, outside consultants, and legal fees must be paid.

According to Ron Kifer, vice president of program solutions and management, DHL Worldwide Express, "There's a lot of money wrapped up in a contract this size, so it's not something you take lightly or hurry with. There has to be a high degree of due diligence making sure that the company can respond to your needs." Kifer devoted several months to vendor selection before engaging Infosys to handle a startling 90% of development and maintenance work for DHL.[2]

As with any decision, the process of choosing a vendor should follow a well-established methodology that spells out the criteria and steps along the way (see Figure 7.1). At the end of this process, the goal is to select the best service provider for contract negotiation.

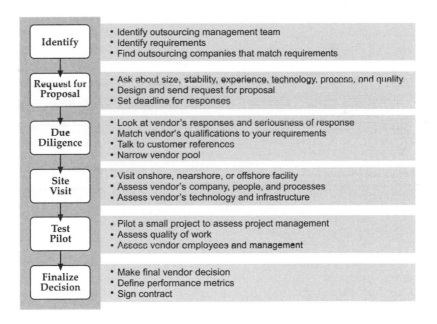

Figure 7.1: Vendor Selection Methodology

Identify: Assemble Your Core Team

As a first step, it is critical to form a core team that will participate in the evaluation of vendor responses and in the negotiations. The team should consist of individuals pulled from various groups throughout the company, such as subject matter experts (SMEs) from the business units affected, legal staff, and human resources personnel. For example, if you plan to outsource a customer care process, the team should have a substantial faction of people with significant collective experience in customer care.

The composition of the team will depend on the type of outsourcing being contemplated:

- Selective outsourcing occurs when companies outsource a portion of a business function, ranging from a single task (e-mail customer support) to an entire process (payroll processing).

- Total outsourcing happens when businesses outsource an entire business function such as human resources. It is also called transformation outsourcing since the decision is usually driven by the desire to transform the company.

- Transitional outsourcing describes when companies temporarily outsource a business process or function during a period of transition. Outsourcing a legacy payroll system while a new SAP module is being implemented exemplifies this type of outsourcing.

Depending on what is being outsourced, each team member should be assigned defined roles and responsibilities. Forming your core team at the onset of the process assures that everyone involved is fully informed and can make the best decisions moving forward.

The team's first task is to learn from the experiences of other corporations. Investing time and effort to learn best practices from peers and from organizations that have outsourced similar functions will maximize the effectiveness of outsourcing. The next step is external benchmarking to compare your current process to others in your industry. After this step you are ready to evaluate the RFP responses.

Evaluate the RFP Responses

Chapter 6 outlined the steps for creating an RFI and RFP. After you receive the responses back from the short-list of vendors, it's time for your core team to evaluate them. Vendors may propose different strategies when they respond to an RFP:

- Sole provider strategy in which one vendor delivers the entire service to the client.

- Cosourcing strategy in which two vendors work together to deliver the service to the client.

- Multisourcing strategy in which several vendors provide the services specified in the RFP. The customer takes on the responsibility of managing and integrating the services of the different providers.

- Alliance strategy in which several vendors collaborate to provide the services specified. Often one vendor assumes the primary role of interfacing with the customer on behalf of the alliance.

- Joint venture strategy in which a new business entity is formed by the vendors in providing the service to the customer.

Regardless of the structure, successful outsourcing relationships are a mutual commitment to improve the customer's business. If the stated requirements are met, then each individual or collective response that meets the RFP's requirements must go through a due diligence review.

Vendor Operational Due Diligence

Deal making is glamorous; due diligence is not. A significant part of evaluating vendors is completing the due diligence. The objective is to do the work upfront to avoid the pain later.

Your due diligence should validate or invalidate vendor-supplied information on their processes, financials, experience, and performance, as well as examine the service provider itself. Due diligence should serve as a verification and analysis tool, providing assurance that the vendor meets your company's needs.

Due diligence helps companies determine what the service provider can do right now as opposed to what it might do if given the business. Due diligence should confirm and assess all of the information supplied in the RFP and specifically evaluate the following information:

- Company profile, strategy, mission, and reputation;

- Financial status, including reviews of audited financial statements;

- Customer references from other companies that have outsourced similar processes to the vendor;

- Management qualifications, including criminal background checks;

- Process expertise, methodology, and effectiveness;

- Quality initiatives and certifications;

- Technology, infrastructure stability, and applications;

- Security and audit controls;

- Legal and regulatory compliance including any litigation;

- Use of subcontractors;

- Insurance; and

- Ability to meet disaster recovery and business continuity requirements.

Other important elements include information on employee policies, attrition, service attitudes, and management values. There should be a cultural fit between the vendor and your company.

Often, companies perform due diligence on one or more of the vendors that respond to the RFP. The length and formality of the due diligence process varies according to your company's previous experience with outsourcing, the time line for implementing outsourcing, the outsourcing risk, and your company's familiarity with the vendor.

The Vendor's Management Team

Get to know the management team. Many companies have emerged recently due to the demand for offshore resources. Familiarize yourself with the backgrounds of the management team members, their experience, areas of expertise, the culture they want to instill in the company, and their goals for the company. Also look at the vendor's financials to assess its ability to invest in further growth.

Make sure there is a fit between your company and the vendor's management team. According to Tim Lavin, senior vice president for operations at Ambergris Solutions, a leading Philippine-based provider of customer care, inbound sales, and technical support solutions, "There's a lot of companies offshore that are doing a wonderful job with delivering excellent service, but there's also a lot of companies that are jumping on the bandwagon. My advice would be to first check out the experience levels of the executives that are principle in the organization and ensure that they have credible backgrounds."[3]

The Vendor's References — Don't Trust, Verify!

It is not enough to develop an RFP, distribute it, evaluate the responses, and meet with the providers. The selection process should also include talking to existing vendor's customers. This means the RFP response must include account references with appropriate contact information.

You should normally require two to three references as part of the RFP response. Many companies request five to 10 references. We strongly urge companies to call the reference accounts.

Prior to the call, develop a list of questions so as not to lose your focus during the conversation. Keeping in mind these are reference accounts and are selected on the basis of a solid relationship with the vendor, do not hesitate to probe into possible problem areas.

If you are aware of the weaknesses in the vendor's existing relationships, you may be able to avoid these problems. Adequate time spent checking references and working through details will pay off with a good contract and amiable relationship.

Companies should also study the vendor's record with recent clients. Ask for detailed histories on the last three clients, then talk to the vendor and the client separately. Ask what went well and where there was room for improvement. Ask what lessons were learned and how they were applied. This will reveal whether the vendor is learning from experience, the importance of which is frequently underrated.

As Derek Holley, president of eTelecare, a Los Angeles–based company with operational contact centers in the Philippines, explains, "The whole idea behind evaluating outsourcers is to find the facts and not the story. If you look for stories, you'll end up hiring the company that has the best storytellers."[4]

In addition to checking references, evaluate project management competency, the level of success achieved, the quality and standards of work delivered, adherence to contract terms, and the communication process. Vendor differentiation is difficult, and many vendors make promises they are unable to keep. Careful due diligence to uncover potential surprises is your company's job and will be critical to the success of the relationship.

Site Visit: Look for Show-Stoppers

No contract should be signed without a site visit. Just as you would not hire an employee without interviewing them in person, you certainly should not hire a vendor without visiting them in person. Site visits help companies improve their understanding of the supplier's current and future capabilities and operations, as well as the local culture and sociopolitical climate.

Expect to spend a couple of days at the vendor site and sit down with as many people as possible: team leaders, project managers, customer service agents, and upper management. If you are outsourcing a call center or any function that entails the vendor's employees speaking directly with your prospects or customers, you will want to interview some of the staff that will work on your project.

Try to talk with agents and team leaders separate from upper management. Make sure that the story they tell you about culture and processes is consistent.

Before the site visits, you must prepare carefully. They often are hectic and are part of a multi-city evaluation tour, so questions can easily be forgotten if they are not documented beforehand. Your team should assess whether the vendor has the following components critical to outsourcing success:

- Employee recruiting and retention policies,

- Reliable and redundant infrastructure, and

- Experience with the exact process or task in question.

Make sure the vendor's facilities provide a comfortable working environment for employees, adequate capacity for growth, and up-to-date telecom equipment.

Employee Recruiting and Retention Policies

During the site visit, review the supplier's record in attracting talented staff. Sit in on a coaching session. Meet with employees one-on-one separate from their managers so they will be more at ease. Review the vendor's human resource processes and inquire about recruitment practices. Find out the success ratio: how many resumes the vendors receives and what percentage of applicants get hired. Will the vendor be able to scale up to meet your growth requirements?

Attrition has become a significant problem for offshore vendors, so look for vendors that are able to retain employees successfully. According to Krishnaswamy Subrahmaniam, president and CEO of Covansys India and Asia, "We have almost no attrition amongst our most experienced employees (those with ten to 15 years of experience), and very little turnover within our project management ranks (all of whom have seven to ten years in the industry). At the team lead level, however, where employees usually have about three to four years of experience, retention is often a challenge. That's where most of the churn takes place."[5]

Reliable and Redundant Infrastructure

Make sure to evaluate the vendor's technology. Has it implemented up-to-date software and hardware? Are the voice, data, and power systems reliable and redundant? If you are outsourcing your call center, this is a critical issue. Think about having thousands of your customers unable to reach the call center because of a power outage. Understanding the vendor's infrastructure is very important. As Deena Harapanahalli, founder of Opensegue Technology Partners, said, "In this business, milliseconds matter."[6]

Experience with Process or Task

A visit to a supplier's reference customer (or delivery center) is another way to help you evaluate relevant experience. Although the main purpose of the reference visit is to witness the kind of service the supplier has provided to a company similar to your own, the meeting can provide other useful insights.

The people you will meet will have gone through the same supplier selection process as you and will probably be keen to share some of their knowledge. Simply learning about their experience with the vendor and the mistakes they made can help you avoid some of the same pitfalls.

Vendor Strategies for Managing Attrition

Attrition can be a serious problem that dictates the success or failure of an outsourcing project. This is especially true for long-term or multiyear outsourcing contracts where the loss of key individuals can dramatically affect the ROI. During the selection process, it's important to understand abnormalities in attrition rates and the HR processes that the vendor has instituted to manage attrition effectively. How is it keeping the talent pipeline flowing?

While evaluating a new vendor or location, attrition rates must be benchmarked with normal industry average standards in that place and market segment. For example, call center reps tend to have higher attrition rates than engineers who do computer-aided-engineering.

A good hiring process, career path planning, performance-driven incentive planning, a productive, positive work environment, retention strategies, and several other HR tactics converge to make attrition a non-issue. You must look at the retention management processes while selecting a vendor, and ensure that they will apply to the people staffed on your project. Losing talented and capable people is costly. Even worse is losing key people on a project with no prospect of replacing them.

Vendors have used their creativity to find ways to keep employees, but many of their once novel approaches are now considered the norm. Examples for perks are transportation to and from work, free lunch and dinner, housing allowances, tuition assistance, health insurance for families, retention bonuses, and performance bonuses.

Once touted as having extremely low attrition rates, India is now struggling with the issue of employee retention. In tier-one cities such as Bangalore, attrition can be 60% or higher. Since companies are becoming more comfortable outsourcing to countries such as India, there has been an explosion of providers.

When you have an industry growing as fast as the BPO industry is, there is a great need for talented people. A lack of experienced managers in India has created much movement both within and across companies where people are being pushed up the supervisory chain.

Major drivers of high attrition rates include:

- Supply and demand of talent and services,

- Poor compensation,

- Bad working environment and poor work-life balance, and

- Incompatibility of skills with role and responsibility assigned.

Supply- and Demand-Driven Attrition
This type of attrition may be short-term or long-term depending upon the training and the education available in a region. How many schools, graduates, and training institutions does the destination have?

A good study of the total talent pool of a region (such as Ireland or China) can tell you whether you would encounter a scenario where attrition will adversely affect your business interests. Measuring the total capacity of a region is an important part of setting up your offshore facilities. It should be part of due diligence.

Compensation-Driven Attrition

This type of attrition is more likely to be a vendor-specific or a city-specific phenomenon. Industry benchmarks can help vendors bring low salaries in line with their competitors. Oppositely, new vendors in the same city (such as Bangalore) can drive the salary structure sky-high for the same skill sets, more than a competitive cost structure can justify.

It is not unusual for talented programmers to find a better-paying job before they step out of the hallways of their old company. The IT industry and major employers in the region may have to address this issue by enforcing collective 'no poaching' agreements or by learning to manage attrition due to artificially inflated compensation.

Bad Work Environment and Poor Work-Life Balance

Many outsourcing vendors based in low-cost countries have found that once their employees have attained a minimum common quality of life, they start to expect, perhaps not unreasonably, a better balance in their work-life. As individuals in developing countries realize economic growth, attrition rises, driven by longer working hours and bad working conditions.

Increasingly, service providers are trying to strike the right work-life balance by offering their employees flexible working hours, onsite baby-sitting facilities, company-sponsored transportation between the office and home, and subsidized or free meals. These benefits improve the work-life balance. Such measures can go a long way toward retaining employees.

Service providers are also offering incentives such as retention bonuses tied to the number of years that employees will stay. Other strategies include awarding performance bonuses related to service level achievements or linking with universities and offering master courses for employees at subsidized rates.

Incompatibility of Skills

In their hurry for growth, some vendors accept every possible project they can and staff employees on assignments they are unsuitable for, hoping the workers will learn on the job and survive. This strategy typically results immediately in a poor quality performance and later in higher attrition rates.

To mitigate this risk, many companies participate in the vendor's screening and filtering process for employees. The more effort vendors spend on hiring the right resources, the less attrition they will experience. Mature vendors should have reliable processes in place to optimize the skill sets of their employees.

The bottom line on site visits: Rather than just touring countries and having a few high-level meetings with vendors, companies must embark on site visits prepared to work. They must develop a strategy for site visits that includes an evaluation framework and set the formal meeting agenda themselves. The goal is to listen to what the vendor is telling you and use your powers of observation to see if what the vendor's people are promising you matches with what is happening at the site.

Test Pilot: Reality Testing

Once companies issue RFPs, receive and evaluate responses, and perform due diligence, they enter into contract negotiations with one or more of the service providers they have determined can best meet their needs. Often times; however, companies prefer to utilize a pilot project first, before moving forward with outsourcing a complete project.

A pilot project is one strategy that many companies use to ensure a proper fit between their company and the offshore vendor. A pilot allows you to critically review the vendor's project management process for efficiency and effectiveness.

It is important for your company to determine if project execution is completed within guidelines, if the deliverables are timely, and if the vendor has adhered to defined quality standards. This is an excellent way for your organization to check and recheck the facts before making a final decision regarding a vendor.

Depending on the scale and scope of the outsourced initiative, a pilot program may be a good idea. Companies can evaluate the actual benefits of outsourcing before jumping into a long-term relationship.

For instance, if your company plans to outsource 300 call centers agents, it is a good idea to start small and work out the kinks, along with the training programs, documentation, procedures, customized training materials, and technology, before completely scaling up the project. Most vendors offer a program in which about 30 agents are trained, and operations are executed on a pilot basis for two to three months.

Finalize the Decision

If you have followed all the steps outlined in the vendor selection methodology, then you are doing it right. You have taken your time and completed the necessary vendor due diligence. In addition, the pilot should have allowed you to get a taste of the vendor's skills and the confidence to proceed. You didn't just blindly jump in to a relationship like some other firms have. Now you are ready to decide whether you want to go with a single vendor or multiple vendors to diversify the risk.

Vendor Selection Pitfalls to Avoid

Outsourcing is a marathon, not a sprint. Selecting a vendor has always been hard, but, in recent years, it has become tougher than ever. The choices facing managers and the data requiring analysis have multiplied, while the time for analyzing them has been compressed. So take your time and do the necessary due diligence. Never quickly pick a vendor and jump in to outsourcing just to be the first or just because your competitor has already done so.

Outsourcing vendor selection is different from commodity sourcing. Far too often companies try to handle vendor selection through their established business processes and resources. They build teams that approach outsourcing vendor selection as they would approach any major purchasing relationship. Factors such as the timing of involvement, training of personnel, and performance measurement systems are typically not considered. Consequently, business outcomes take their toll when teams run out of time, when key data are missed, when gaps in skill or knowledge remain unfilled, and financial losses are incurred.

Poorly defined baseline metrics. Often, key metrics are missing. Without a compelling baseline scenario and a clear definition of functional needs and requirements, companies can easily select the wrong vendor (for example, a smaller provider incapable of scaling up for higher volumes) or the wrong outsourcing solution (for example, offshore instead of onshore or captive instead of third-party).

Inadequate skilled resources for site visits. Companies frequently don't have the in-house expertise to conduct effective site visits, so they seek help outside of the company. Consequently, they are faced with two different issues. The first issue relates to consultants who, by definition, are available for short periods of time with specialized skills. Consultants tend to be strong on process but limited on business process knowledge. The second issue concerns senior managers who go on tire-kicking exercises without getting into the details that make or break outsourcing projects. They must take with them process experts who can pick apart a vendor and still maintain objectivity.

We end this chapter with some outsourcing best and worst practices.

The Best-Practice Companies	The Worst-Practice Companies
Search for and benchmark information from multiple sources.	Listen to sales pitches and make decisions based on them.
Are analytical. They compare their current capabilities with the vendor's capabilities. (Value is only created if the outsourcer can complete the process better than you.)	Are ad hoc. They make offshoring decisions based on gut feelings and intuition.
Focus on the key questions in their RFPs.	Write 30-page RFPs that generate 150-page responses from vendors and are never read.
Choose high-quality providers and negotiate the lowest prices from them.	Choose the lowest-cost providers.
Align incentives so that both parties work toward a common goal.	Treat their vendors like hired help rather than true partners.

Table 7.1: Best and Worst Practices

Summary

After the long RFI/RFP process, you will receive incredible pressure from vendor sales reps and executives trying to convince you that they are the best service provider and that their "value/cost ratio" is the best in the industry. Don't cave into the pressure. Adopt a disciplined process to vendor selection and you will be okay.

Choosing a vendor to manage your business processes and applications is a big step. Making the final decision means signing a contract that clearly defines the performance measures, team size, team members, pricing policies, business continuity plans, and overall quality of work standards.

Chapter Eight

The Location Selection Decision

The location decision concerns companies seeking to locate, relocate, or expand their outsourcing operations. The location decision process encompasses the identification, analysis, evaluation, and selection of a site. This chapter provides you with a methodology for assessing the attractiveness of a location. It also examines the pros and cons of different nearshore and offshore destinations.

Introduction

Choosing where to locate operations is not a new problem. In fact, there is even an entire science called location theory devoted to it. Location theory addresses the questions of which economic activities are located where and why. It has become an integral part of economic geography, spatial economics, real estate management, and regional science.

Traditionally, the location of economic activities was determined by broader factors, such as the characteristics of a particular region or metropolitan area, or narrower ones, such as the traits of a zone or city block. With the advent of globalization, the Internet, and modern logistics, location theory is taking on a new significance as managers constantly evaluate what site is most feasible for delivering products and services to customers at the right price.

When managers consider nearshore or offshore options for third-party outsourcing or captive centers, one of the first things they wonder is if they should decide on the country first and the vendor second, or the vendor first and the country second. Some companies select the vendor and then worry about the location. Others settle on the country and then attempt to pick the best vendor (in the case of third-party outsourcing) or best city (in the case of captive centers) in that country.

Either way, managers have to understand how to decide which city and country is the right one for their operations. Which new (greenfield) location would maximize the returns for your company? Even those managers who have operations in an offshore location need to know how to undertake geographic diversification or consolidate business process operations to manage costs, increase productivity, and manage exchange rate fluctuations.

Choosing where to offshore — India, the Philippines, Hungary, or Canada — is an important, long-term decision that can determine the skills and competencies, based on culture, education, and language, that are available for your project. Other critical factors affecting the location decision are the physical infrastructure, corporate taxes, labor flexibility (unions, hire and fire laws), quality of life, ease of travel, government regulations, legal policies, and political stability.

In this chapter, we examine popular nearshore and offshore destinations and explore their positive and negative attributes. We also highlight up-and-coming countries that you many consider potential alternatives.

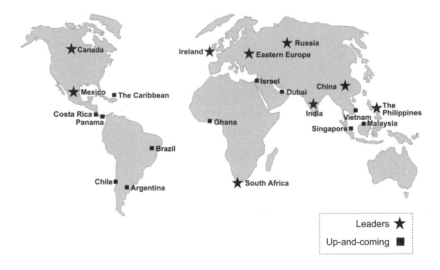

Figure 8.1: Top Outsourcing Locations

Structuring the Location Decision

Although vendors should be judged solely on their own merits, the fact remains that a supplier's country determines the makeup of its workforce and wage structure. Moreover, a nearshore or offshore vendor's expertise and language skills are largely the product of its country's educational system and business culture.

Virtually no detail is irrelevant in site selection. Geography, history, culture, language, and government policies contribute to the development and growth of every country's industries and, to some extent, labor productivity.

How should geographic and cultural issues influence companies' offshore decisions? At what point should the delivery model, cultural adaptability, and hourly labor rates of individual companies enter into decision processes? We answer these questions in the ensuing pages.

Workforce Attractiveness and Economics

One of the major drivers of global outsourcing is the promise of cost savings from labor arbitrage. Although it is not the only reason why companies seek to relocate their operations offshore, it is often the catalyst that first leads companies to explore outsourcing.

Labor arbitrage drives the cost savings. Compare the average salary of a U.S. IT professional at $80,000, to a programmer in India at $10,000–$15,000 or China at $6,000–$10,000. The salary of an average call center representative in India might range from $3,000–$6,000 fully loaded (including benefits, transportation, and cafeteria), while the salary of an average call center representative in the Philippines might range from $6,000–$10,000. With easy access to lower-cost resources, you can see why the economics are attractive.

Although cost savings may be the primary motive for global outsourcing, there are several other considerations companies need to take into account before signing on the dotted line. People are at the top of the list. The vendor's employees can make or break a project. Some of the critical attributes related to employee quality are language skills, technical skills, educational levels, cultural compatibility, and quality management programs (see Table 8.1).

Category	Includes
Labor	Size of labor pool, wages, skills and training, regulations
Cost savings	Costs that can be saved by utilizing this country
Language skills	Proficiency in English and other languages
Technical skills	Proficiency in IT tools, applications, and programming
Education	The quality of universities and colleges
Cultural compatibility	Compatibility of business practices and understanding of the American culture
Quality	ISO 9000, Six Sigma, CMM

Table 8.1: Location Decision Matrix — Workforce Attractiveness

Location Attractiveness and Risks

Table 8.2 summarizes the factors that need to be considered when assessing the attractiveness of a city or country.

Category	Includes
Infrastructure	Roads, electricity, telecom, and network stability
Stability (political, economic, medical)	Political concerns: stability of current regime
	War: loss caused by invasion, civil war, or revolution
	Strikes: loss caused by riots, strikes, or civil commotion
	Terrorism: loss caused by malicious damage or sabotage
	Medical concerns: ability to respond to medical emergencies
Legal environment	Copyright protection, intellectual property rights
	Reporting issues (accounting requirements, taxes)
Regulatory environment	Government action: loss caused by the implementation of any discriminatory law, order, decree, or regulation
	Loss caused by the imposition of an embargo
	Cancellation of licenses and permits
Travel convenience	Ease of travel by plane or car
Time zones	How well the time zones match

Table 8.2: Location Decision Matrix — Location Attractiveness and Risks

When companies think about sending processes or data offshore, they must contemplate the risks involved, such as the political, economic, and medical stability of a particular location. Other factors not to be overlooked are government regulations, taxes, and infrastructure.

Infrastructure — roads, electricity, and communications — is a huge consideration. Think about having your contact center set up in Bangalore, India, with thousands of calls coming in hourly. Power outages that occur for a few minutes every couple of hours are not good. In developed countries, availability of electricity is taken for granted. Rarely are companies confronted with power outages. The same cannot be said for developing countries. When your success is dependent on computers or telecommunications, infrastructure evaluation is critical.

Visa Restrictions

Part of your decision regarding onshore, offshore, or nearshore may be influenced by the vendor's ability to obtain visas for its workforce. After September 11, 2001, the United States overhauled its visa laws. Visa applications take longer to process, and applicants are required to submit more forms and pass more security clearances.

Typically, a non-U.S. citizen traveling to the United States for work will apply for a visa that falls under the H (temporary worker), L (intracompany transferee), or B-1 (business visitor) categories. For work such as knowledge transfer or training, workers could travel to the United States on a general business visa, but if they are doing any actual onsite work then they really are required to travel on H-1B or L-1 long-term visas that are more difficult to obtain.

In November 2004, U.S. Congress passed legislation aimed at reforming H-1B and L-1 visas. The bill states that up to 20,000 foreign nationals with master's or higher-level degrees from U.S. universities will be exempt from the H-1B cap, which stands at 58,200 for 2005. The H-1B visas are snapped up extraordinarily quickly and have prompted some high-tech companies to lobby Congress to increase the cap, which was once as high as 195,000.

The new visa restrictions are affecting offshore vendors that are trying to build up an onsite U.S. presence or provide a multishore business model for their clients.

The Methodology of Selection

The following location selection approach takes companies efficiently through the process of generating a short-list of locations and assessing the workforce and location attractiveness of the few remaining countries.

In the initial phases, companies carefully reduce their long list of locations, taking into account the key location drivers for the outsourcing process or task. The destinations on the long list are screened via Internet resources, in-house databases, and analyst reports, and scored based on the relevant workforce and location criteria.

This screening approach aims to eliminate locations that do not meet the strategic objectives of the company and to identify promising locations for further consideration. The objective at this stage is not to select one preferred place but to create a short-list.

The next step is to evaluate the country short-list. This should be done through fieldwork and interviews with similar operations and recruitment agents. The most important factors relate to the country resources, specifically people. The availability, quality, flexibility, and cost of staff are the main drivers for situating businesses at different locations and need to be carefully considered for short-listed cities.

Reviewing the quality, availability, productivity, and attrition rates of staff is crucial because labor is the biggest variable cost factor in outsourcing. Locations that were frequently selected for specific operations in the recent past (such as call centers in Dublin or programming in Bangalore) are coping with a labor shortage because too many companies are looking for the same skills. As a result, cost levels are increasing at a higher speed than desirable, staff turnover is rising, and recruitment times are expanding.

Evaluating short-listed city and country candidates is not an easy task. It is time-consuming and can be quite costly, depending on which locations are identified. Companies often attempt to cut short the process by relying on past data or desk research — a potential problem since location dynamics change constantly.

When trying to assess the risks and impact that locations have on the overall corporate performance, data from the past or from competitor choices don't provide enough insight. The dynamics in the business environment can only be understood by validation in the field.

The Top Nearshore Locations

In the following pages, we review the top and up-and-coming nearshore destinations for U.S. and European companies — Canada, Mexico, Ireland, Central and South America, the Caribbean, and Eastern Europe — and discuss the competitive advantages and challenges that each country or region faces.

Destination: Canada

With similar business standards and the same time zones and official language as the United States, Canada is a haven for U.S. companies that do not want to stray far from home. The Canadian centers for outsourcing include Halifax, Montreal, and Toronto.

Other areas of Canada are also trying to jump on the outsourcing bandwagon. The Exploits Centre for Information Technology Excellence (EXCITE) Corporation and the Near Shore Atlantic Initiative are promoting Newfoundland and Labrador, Canada's easternmost province, as an ideal destination for outsourcing. Stanley Singh, the director of EXCITE, states, "The region boasts high employee loyalty and retention rates because of the province's high quality of life and low cost of living."[1]

Because Canada is consistently billed as one of the safest nearshore destinations, many outsourcing firms are looking to establish a presence. EDS maintains about 7,000 employees in Canada and books roughly $1 billion in annual revenues there. Convergys has situated more than 11,000 employees throughout Canada including some in Newfoundland, Halifax, Winnipeg, Ottawa, and Edmonton.

Even Indian vendors are establishing a footprint in Canada as they look to give their customers a broader range of geographic options. Wipro opened a development center in Windsor, Ontario. The center will offer a complete range of services, from product design to business solutions and IT infrastructure services.

However, the country's reputation and proximity come at a price. Businesses that decide to outsource to Canada do not realize the cost benefits that they would if they ventured farther away to India, the Philippines, or China.

Competitive Advantages

The country has an excellent university system and comparatively inexpensive real estate. Labor rates are lower than those of the United States, and the exchange rate between Canada and the United States adds to their attractiveness. The cultural gap between Canada and Westernized countries such as the United Kingdom and the United States is minimal.

Category	Comments
Labor	Total population in 2004 was 32.5 million.
Cost savings	IT professionals earn an average annual salary of $63,502, compared to $81,061 in the United States.
Language skills	English and French are the official languages of Canada, and many people speak both.
Technical skills	Technical skills are excellent. Microsoft hires many engineers from the University of Waterloo.
Education	The university system is one of the best in the world.
Cultural compatibility	Canada has a rich, shared culture with both the United States and the United Kingdom.
Quality	Canada had 11,759 ISO 9000 certifications as of 2003.

Table 8.3: Canadian Workforce's Attractiveness and Economics[2]

Category	Comments
Infrastructure	Some infrastructure may be aging in major cities.
Stability	Canada has very little political and economic risk.
Legal environment	Strong legal system.
Regulatory environment	Federal and local governments are very supportive of foreign investment and outsourcing ventures. A member of NAFTA and the World Trade Organization (WTO).
Travel convenience	Toronto is a short, one-and-a-half-hour flight from New York. In some cases, outsourcing sites are near enough for U.S. company managers to drive to them.
Time zone	Canada has six time zones. Toronto and New York both follow eastern standard time (EST) and are five hours behind Greenwich mean time (GMT).

Table 8.4: Canada's Location Attractiveness and Risks

Challenges

Canada, while safe, may not satisfy some companies' hunger for cost savings. The country falls at the high end of the offshoring short-list, comparable to Ireland. U.S. companies looking to run a 24x7, "follow-the-sun" development operation also should not consider Canada since it matches up roughly with U.S. time zones. However, the minimized time difference allows easier project management as U.S. managers can easily reach their Canadian partners during normal business hours.

Gregg Scoresby, CEO of BPO firm Core3, states, "There is a level of market acceptance with India now that makes people less concerned about the benefits of nearshore. The costs are not as compelling in Canada. You may be able to save 25% versus the U.S., but in India you could save 50%, which is what our clients have experienced, with the same or better quality of service."[3]

Long-Term Outlook

Canada is becoming a popular nearshore destination. To remain competitive, it must promote itself more aggressively as a talented, nearshore option for U.S. firms and take steps to upgrade the aging infrastructure of its cities, roadways, airports, and borders.

Destination: Mexico

In the last decade or so, Mexico has undergone an enormous transformation, opening its closed economy, negotiating free trade agreements with many countries, and implementing more fiscally responsible policies since the peso imploded in 1994. Mexico's people are no longer dominated by one political party but instead live under a multiparty democracy.

The government has tried to make its actions more transparent, publishing the financial statements of state and local governments in the newspaper and on the Internet. In addition, Mexican government officials have tried to apply policies more consistently and not devise new ones with every administration change. All these events have combined to give Mexico a presence in the offshoring market.

Category	Comments
Labor	Total population in 2004 was 105 million. Mexico has excellent employee retention.
Cost savings	A call center agent earns $4.25 per hour.
Language skills	Large pool of English- and Spanish-speaking resources.
Technical skills	Only 2% of the population has university degrees, but good technical universities do exist.
Education	Mexico has an extensive system of 240 institutions of higher education (colleges and vocational/technical schools) and 69 universities. In the Monterrey area, educational levels tend to be above the national norm.
Cultural compatibility	Many Mexicans have spent time in the United States and understand the U.S.-Hispanic market.
Quality	Mexico had 1,935 ISO 9000 certifications in 2003.

Table 8.5: Mexican Workforce's Attractiveness and Economics[4]

Competitive Advantages

The most obvious advantage Mexico has, as a nearshore destination, is its location. For North American companies fearful of outsourcing processes to a provider located more than a day's flight away, Mexico is an interesting prospect. It appeals to companies that prefer not to rush to India but instead want to take advantage of a nearshore option.

Category	Comments
Infrastructure	Infrastructure is poor outside of the country's three technology parks in Monterrey, Apodaca, and Guadalajara. The electricity system, which is state controlled, will require a $100 billion infusion within a decade in order to meet growing demand.
Stability	The general political climate is relatively calm.
Legal environment	The Mexican legal system differs significantly from the U.S. system. For example, civil litigation is rare in Mexico because it's expensive and no punitive damages are awarded. Litigation in Mexico isn't practical unless a vital business objective is at stake.
Regulatory environment	Mexico is subject to the extensive guidelines of NAFTA, but Mexican customs regulations, product standards, and labor laws may offer pitfalls to unwary U.S. companies.
Travel convenience	Flying directly from New York to Mexico City takes five-and-a-half hours.
Time zone	Mexico takes up three different time zones. Mexico City is one hour behind EST and six hours behind GMT.

Table 8.6: Mexico's Location Attractiveness and Risks[5]

The country also offers competitive labor rates and a wealth of Spanish-speaking resources. As Spanish is one of the most widely spoken languages in the world (ranked with English, Mandarin Chinese, and Hindi) and one of the dominant two in the United States, this advantage is significant.

Challenges

Mexico's mid-1990s currency crisis puts the country in a precarious position. The country has only implemented fiscally responsible policies in the last few years, which means that the government cannot begin spending freely on education (the country battles high dropout rates) and infrastructure without risking its investment-grade rating. Without massive investments in the two, however, Mexico will lose out as a global outsourcing destination and receive only low-level work, such as basic call center operations.

The country has already watched the promises of NAFTA fade and the number of its manufacturing jobs dwindle as they were relocated to China. If Mexico doesn't secure outside funding to overhaul its educational system and infrastructure, the same fate could be in store for its BPO and IT services jobs.

Long-Term Outlook

Mexico has gained ground as a viable nearshore market. If the country continues on its stable economic course, remains immune to the currency crises of its South American neighbors, and improves its infrastructure and educational system, it could emerge as a top destination for outsourcing IT services and call center operations.

Destination: Ireland

Offshoring to Ireland is similar in many ways to outsourcing to Canada. Companies tend to select the two countries as offshoring destinations for the same reasons: increased stability and lowered risk.

Competitive Advantages

Ireland wisely invested in its educational system and is now reaping the rewards with an increasingly well-educated and growing workforce. However, the number of available technical graduates is limited to a few thousand annually, which can make the country more of an ideal destination for call center operations rather than software development. A solid infrastructure and educational system, increased cultural compatibility, and English proficiency also add to Ireland's attractiveness.

Category	Comments
Labor	Ireland's total population in 2004 was 4 million.
Cost savings	Programmers are paid $25,000–$40,000 per year. Customer service reps are paid an average salary of $31,466 yearly.
Language skills	English is the primary language, but many citizens learn other languages. Agents generally are fluent in two or more languages, which is critical for companies seeking to support European operations.
Technical skills	Ireland has invested in high-tech education but has only about 12,000 graduates in engineering, as well as computer and software engineering each year.
Education	The educational system is strong, but the number of graduates is limited at 35,000 graduates yearly.
Cultural compatibility	Ireland's cultural compatibility with other members of the European Union and the United States is very high.
Quality	Ireland had 1,645 ISO 9000 certifications as of 2003.

Table 8.7: Irish Workforce's Attractiveness and Economics[6]

Challenges

Ireland is one of the oldest players in offshoring. According to IDA Ireland, the Irish government agency responsible for the industrial development and investment of foreign companies in Ireland, more than 1,100 overseas companies have established operations on the Emerald Isle. With its membership to the European Union, Ireland has watched its economy outpace the rest of Europe and its labor force and wage rates increase, while unemployment decreased.

Large companies such as Dell monopolize much of the skilled, literate, but relatively small Irish workforce, and the cost savings advantage of offshoring to Ireland has dropped. Companies that send their back-office operations to Ireland may find it difficult to scale up due to the lack of low-cost labor.

Category	Comments
Infrastructure	Deregulated telecom market with more than 20 providers.
Stability	Low political risk.
Legal environment	The country joined the WTO on January 1995. Companies face little bureaucracy. Legal procedures are uncomplicated, inexpensive, and quick.
Regulatory environment	Ireland has a highly beneficial corporate tax environment. It offers a number of grants — for capital, R&D, training, and employment — to offset the costs of setting up operations. There is no local tax except on property.
Travel convenience	The nonstop flight from New York to Dublin takes six-and-a-half hours.
Time zone	All of Ireland follows GMT, which translates to Dublin being five hours ahead of EST.

Table 8.8: Ireland's Location Attractiveness and Risks

Long-Term Outlook

U.S. companies such as IBM and Microsoft have development centers in Ireland, which are increasing competition for labor and thus driving up the cost of labor. The talent and maturity of services in Ireland are very good, but you will need to pay more for such skills.

Other Nearshore Destinations: Countries on the Verge

Although Canada, Mexico, and Ireland may have more collective experience as nearshore destinations, other countries in Central and South America, the Caribbean, and Eastern Europe are fast gaining reputations as viable global outsourcing destinations.

Destination: South America. Brazil could topple one of the top nearshore locations with its enormous population if President da Silva and his team are successful in their agenda of maintaining economic stability by fighting inflation, instituting tax and pension reform, and maintaining strict fiscal discipline. Brazil's massive debts mean that the government has little funding to reinvest in the country's educational system or infrastructure.

Nearby, Argentina and Chile have both positioned themselves to benefit from the trend toward global outsourcing. Chile's costs are slightly higher than Argentina's. Geopolitically speaking, Chile is a less risky prospect than Argentina, which is still recovering from its 2001 economic collapse.

Argentina, however, has a larger pool of Spanish speakers and high-quality programmers, as well as a state-of-the-art telecommunications infrastructure and the same time zone as the East Coast of the United States. Several multinationals such as IBM, AOL, Marriott, and American Express have taken advantage of the local scenario to base call center operations there.

Destination: Central America. One of the clear advantages of Central American nearshore locations such as Costa Rica and Panama, like their southern counterparts, are the Spanish-speaking skills they offer. U.S. companies that require call center reps fluent in Spanish can look to Central and South America.

The Costa Rican outsourcing industry is preparing to step up its emerging IT expertise. Procter & Gamble (P&G), building on the $3 billion, 10-year IT outsourcing deal it signed with Hewlett-Packard in 2003, expanded the deal's scope to include business process outsourcing in Costa Rica. Intel has also made substantial investments in Costa Rica. Even India is taking notice of this rookie country. India's Minister of State for External Affairs, Rao Inderjit Singh, is establishing a regional IT training center in Costa Rica, at a cost of $2 million.

IT services providers in Costa Rica such as IsThmus are working hard to make U.S. companies' short-lists of nearshore vendors. IsThmus partnered with Vialogix, a Web development company based in North Carolina, to help it redesign the Web site of IT consulting firm Mariner. IsThmus and Vialogix combined their methodologies to manage the project, gather requirements, and design and code. By mixing onsite and nearshore resources, Mariner reduced the cost by 50%.

Andy Hilliard, COO of IsThmus, states, "Costa Rica has close economic ties to the United States and a strong education system, which produces high-quality professionals, while maintaining relative price parity with offshore options. In contrast to India or China, Costa Rica is safe, stable, easy to get to, and compatible with U.S. time zones. Many companies like that while their programmers are working, ours are too."[7]

Destination: The Caribbean. The Caribbean could emerge as a competitive nearshore force if call centers continue to crop up in Puerto Rico, Jamaica, the Dominican Republic, and other locations. The main obstacle to the Caribbean's success as an outsourcing destination is the high cost of connectivity and access. The Caribbean's primary benefits are its nearness to and its long trading history with the United States.

Destination: Eastern Europe. For Western Europe, nearshore means Eastern European countries such as Hungary, Bulgaria, Poland, Romania, Slovakia, Estonia, and the Czech Republic.

These countries possess some or all of the following: skilled software engineers; up-to-date infrastructure; increased ease of travel from Western Europe or the United States in comparison to India, China, or the Philippines; and low cultural gaps with Western European customers.

Within the EU accession states, Hungary enjoys advantages that can help leverage the offshore BPO trend such as proximity, availability of labor, legal tax framework, and cost differentials.

However, these countries have drawbacks in terms of size and the abundance of available labor. For instance, Romania produces only 5,000 university graduates in the software field.

The Top Offshore Locations

Many countries hope to get into the offshore game. Some have spent years preparing their infrastructure in anticipation of the offshore boom. In the following pages, we review the top offshore destinations for U.S and European companies — China, India, the Philippines, Russia, and South Africa — and discuss the competitive advantages and challenges of each country.

Destination: China

Since the late 1970s, China has been busy charting a course of economic reform. When the first Sino-foreign joint venture, the Beijing Aviation Food Company, was founded in 1980, no one was aware of the event's significance. Over the next two decades, over 250,000 businesses would follow Beijing Aviation Food's lead, bringing the previously isolated country welcome foreign investment, technology, and management expertise to nurture its growth.

Does history — or at least economic history — repeat itself? China has already proven itself adept at absorbing manufacturing jobs. Since 1992, more than 760,000 U.S. manufacturing jobs have moved to its shores according to the U.S.-China Security Review Commission. Now the question is whether China can position itself as an attractive destination for companies interested in offshoring. With its accession to the WTO, tapping its enormous, inexpensive labor force should become easier.

Competitive Advantages

China mirrors the India advantage in that it has a stable government and a highly educated, almost unlimited workforce. While companies worry that the talent pool will be used up in smaller nearby countries, such as the Philippines, that possibility does not exist for China.

The country's educational system produces as many, if not more, scientists and engineers as there are in the United States, and universities have seen their enrollments more than double in a few short years. In 2003, China's 35 software engineering colleges graduated more than 140,000 software engineers.

China has other competitive advantages. It is the seventh-largest economy in the world. The total value of goods and services has been growing at a double-digit rate for more than 20 years. It also has one of the world's largest domestic markets, with a population of 1.3 billion.

Category	Comments
Labor	In 2004, China had the world's largest population, 1.3 billion.
Cost savings	Entry-level programmers earn an average yearly salary of $6,000 – $10,000, depending on education level.
Language skills	Students aged eight and nine years old attending school in major Chinese cities are required to learn English. In addition, to ready itself for the 2008 Olympics in Beijing, the country is leading an intense effort to increase the population's proficiency in English.
Technical skills	China's universities graduate almost as many scientists and engineers as their U.S. counterparts do.
Education	University enrollment jumped from 1 million students in 1998 to 17 million students in 2003.
Cultural compatibility	China is allowing the import of more Western books and films in an effort to show it is becoming more tolerant and to comply with WTO guidelines. However, the government continues to regularly censor all media.
Quality	Few companies have attained CMM Level 5 certification, but several have reached CMM Levels 3 and 4. In 2003, China had 96,715 ISO 9000 certifications.

Table 8.9: Chinese Workforce's Attractiveness and Economics[8]

Not only is labor plentiful, it is inexpensive compared to many Asian countries, such as Malaysia, Thailand, Vietnam, Indonesia, and the Philippines. Moreover, the number of English-speaking graduates in the workforce, particularly crucial in software outsourcing, has doubled since 2000, to more than 24 million in 2004. The country's labor, environmental, and health and safety standards are also more relaxed than those of the United States.[9]

Challenges

The legal and business environments within China remain a challenge for many companies. Firms consistently cite "bureaucratic inertia, lack of transparency, inconsistent enforcement of the law, and strict regulatory control" as issues with which they regularly struggle.[10] Protection of intellectual property and enforcement of copyright laws are also serious problems in China. Many countries hoped that China's accession to the WTO would eventually lessen these obstacles.

On the IT outsourcing side, China has over 8,000 software-services providers, and almost three-quarters of them have fewer than 50 employees. The top ten IT services companies capture only about a 20% share of the market, compared with the 45% commanded by India's top ten. We anticipate a wave of consolidation as China gears up for software outsourcing and challenges India's domination.

Cultural compatibility is another issue businesses will face in China. For many years, the country's borders were effectively closed to outside influence, particularly Western influence, but recently more Western books, films, and music have been spotted on the shelves of China's stores. The pace of social change, however, continues to lag the pace of economic change.

Chinese service providers will also have to manage their talent much better. Most do little to develop their employees, and very few use stock options, training programs, or other incentives to retain talent.

Long-Term Outlook

China's status as a major world power means that its actions not only affect its citizens and communities but also the world's. Many multinationals, such as Home Depot, which is expanding into China, view the country as an integral part of their long-term growth strategies.

Category	Comments
Infrastructure	Infrastructure varies widely. It is best in the special economic zones that the country built to attract foreign investment.
Stability	China has been fighting pressure from the United States and the European Union to float its currency, the yuan, in an effort to make exports more attractive. Such a change could destabilize China and affect the world economy.
Legal environment	The Business Software Alliance estimates that China pirates, or installs without a license, 92% of its business software. It has the second-highest piracy rate in the world, following Vietnam, which has a 97% piracy rate. Microsoft battled China for three years over copyright infringement, and Cisco won a settlement from Huwaei, a Chinese communication equipment company, for wholesale infringement. Two recent amendments to copyright laws may signal China's willingness to take the issue more seriously.
Regulatory environment	WTO acceptance in December 2001 has led to China's relaxing many of its regulations. In addition, many foreign businesses situated in the special economic zones enjoy national and local tax reductions and tax holidays.
Travel convenience	Travelers flying from New York to Beijing arrive at their destination in about 19 hours (includes one stop).
Time zone	Despite its size, China operates on one time zone and is 13 hours ahead of EST and eight hours ahead of GMT.

Table 8.10: China's Location Attractiveness and Risks

However, there are some risks. A major disease outbreak, the collapse of China's banking industry, a change in its currency policy, or the growing gap between China's socioeconomic classes could have serious consequences for all, especially the companies that select China as an offshoring destination.

On the bright side, China's membership in the WTO should help to keep the country in line and eventually trickle down to reform the legal and business environment on a local level. The 2008 Olympic Games to be held in Beijing represent another positive for those considering China. Companies considering offshoring should see benefits in terms of better infrastructure and more English speakers.

Destination: India

Read any article on BPO, and chances are that India will be cited in the first few lines as one of the premier destinations for companies outsourcing business processes. India is already recognized as a haven for software development.

Offshoring in India began in 1985 when Texas Instruments established a captive R&D unit in Bangalore. India developed its outsourcing foothold by sticking to certain core IT capabilities such as application development and maintenance, database management, and packaged application customization. Sticking to the basics has paid off.

In the decade following, offshoring exploded in India, with many Fortune 1000 companies electing to set up wholly owned offshoring centers in India or to outsource work to external service providers based in India. Citibank, Motorola, Oracle, Apple, and Microsoft are just a few of the bigger names that have set up shop in the country.

Many of these corporations have established India-based, captive, back-office service centers. These multinationals have the process expertise, in-house demand, and patience to support major investments and multiyear transitions. They have witnessed cost savings of 40%–50% and quality that meets or beats industry benchmarks.

Competitive Advantages

India ranks high on several parameters such as quality, potential of talent pool, cost structure, overall process capability, educational systems, and major productivity gains. The country is home to the largest educated, English-speaking population in the world.

Recent, rapid improvements in telecom infrastructure, favorable government and tax incentives, increased investments in technical education, along with an abundant supply of programmers, engineers, and accounting talent have made India a hot spot for offshore initiatives. Within the country, some of the leading cities are Bangalore, Hyderabad, Mumbai, Chennai, New Delhi, Gurgaon, and Pune.

India has a 9–12 hour time difference with respect to the U.S. markets. This difference is useful in the case of BPO operations: It results in reduced turnaround times since processing services are performed during the night hours of developed countries. This means that a job submitted at 6 p.m. Pacific standard time (PST) reaches India at 6 a.m. (India's time) and is completed by 6 a.m. PST the following morning, enabling a 24x7 operation.

Category	Comments
Labor	Total population in 2004 was 1.1 billion.
Cost savings	India offers significant opportunities for labor arbitrage with labor costs 40%–50% lower than those of other countries. An Indian IT professional earns an average annual salary of $10,000–$15,000 (compared to $81,061 in the United States).
Language skills	An estimated 250–300 million of the total population speaks English.
Technical skills	India's workforce offers an extremely large pool of technical skills. The country's universities add 180,000 engineering graduates to its ranks annually. At the end of 2002, NASSCOM estimated that there were approximately 522,000 Indian software and IT services professionals.
Education	More than 6 million people are enrolled in the 200 universities, 5,000 colleges, and 100,000 secondary schools.
Cultural compatibility	Despite training in pop culture, a cultural gap still exists between Indian agents and Western customers.
Quality	When it comes to software development and process methodologies, all top-tier vendors are certified at CMM Level 5. India had 10,198 ISO 9000 certifications as of 2003.

Table 8.11: Indian Workforce's Attractiveness and Economics[11]

Challenges

Companies that select India as their offshoring destination will encounter challenges. The country's layers of bureaucracy and tricky regulatory environment are notorious. India's democracy is well-established, but religious and separatist violence does occur, and the possibility of war with Pakistan over Kashmir looms.

India also has resource challenges. Given the rapid growth of offshoring, there are very high attrition levels as companies poach each other's employees. Originally, attrition levels hovered at about 10%. Since the offshoring boom began, attrition rates have risen to 25%–60%. The problem is particularly acute in top-tier cities such as Bangalore and Chennai. Another problem is limited middle management strength. The resource pool consists of graduates excellent at entry-level jobs but with minimal skills for middle management.

Category	Comments
Infrastructure	Bottlenecks in telecommunications, transportation, and energy seriously limit the nation's economic growth and development. In some areas, electric power is erratic, and the telephone systems unreliable.
Stability	Although it is currently safe to travel to India, tensions between Pakistan and India continue. In addition, religious riots and labor strikes can disrupt BPO operations.
Legal environment	India has several rigorous laws designed to protect copyrights and intellectual property (IP) rights. Enforcement, however, of IP rights and patent protection is weak.
Regulatory environment	The Indian government allows total income tax exemption on export of BPO services under Sections 10A and 10B of the Income Tax Act. The current general corporate tax rate is 35% plus surcharge.
Travel convenience	Flying from New York to Bangalore, India, takes two days and includes two stops.
Time zone	India is 9 hours ahead of EST.

Table 8.12: India's Location Attractiveness and Risks

The Indian industry and government are proactively addressing some of these issues. Government officials are serving as advocates and sponsors for offshore investment by undertaking a range of policy changes to encourage the development of infrastructure. Begun in 1991, India's government restructuring program includes the liberalization of trade restrictions and foreign investment regulations, commitments to protect IP property rights, and a general loosening of state control over business practices.

Long-Term Outlook

India should remain an attractive option for companies desiring to outsource people-intensive processes, such as transaction processing or customer care. Its attractiveness will likely diminish as multinationals like IBM and smaller India-based vendors continue to compete for the same talent pool, thereby driving labor rates upward and increasing employee turnover. A 2004 study by HR company Hewitt found that Indian employees in software development and IT-enabled services enjoyed average salary increases in 2003 of almost 14%. It's not surprising why companies such as India-based Infosys have begun thinking about lower-cost talent outside of the country's borders.

Another option that Indian vendors are pursuing is moving out of the tier-one cities. Some India-based service providers have begun responding to the threat that China, Eastern Europe, and other low-cost regions pose by strategically focusing on tier-two and tier-three Indian cities such as Kochin and Kanpur. Srinivas Koneru, founder of Opensegue Technology Partners (OSTP), said, "We are offering a China price of our own and moving to tier-three cities that have lower labor and infrastructure costs."[12]

Other Indian companies are also moving to tier-two and tier-three cities. Wipro, MphasiS, and First Indian Corporation have all expressed interest in opening facilities in Mysore and Mangalore, while Gecis is busy building a call center in Jaipur that will house 1,800 employees.

Newer providers are also devising innovative pricing and delivery models that differ from traditional engagements in which a certain number of employees are dedicated solely to a single customer's project. One new model bills customers only for successful delivery, for example, if it satisfactorily completes the assigned task, such as improving the performance of a particular application.

Destination: The Philippines

The Philippines is one of India's closest competitors in providing BPO services. Leading global companies such as Procter & Gamble, Sykes Enterprises, Accenture, and ChevronTexaco are using the Philippines as a base for supporting business processes.

These processes include accounting and financial reporting, technical customer support, employee services, accounts payable, and travel management. Many companies have situated their Asia-Pacific shared services centers in cities such as Manila, Makati, Quezon City, Pasig City, Taguig, Pasay, Mandaluyong, Muntinlupa, and Las Pinas.

Competitive Advantages

A long U.S.-Philippine relationship has resulted in low language and cultural barriers between the two countries. Although Philippine BPO providers acknowledge India's head start in offshoring, they point out that Filipinos understand American consumers very well.

"The English language in the Philippines is almost second nature to a lot of our countrymen. The medium of instruction in universities and in business is English," according to Charina Quizon of Ambergris Solutions, a Philippine-based provider of customer care, inbound sales, and technical support solutions.[13] As a result, the Philippines is considered a good location for offshore call centers.

As of December 2004, an estimated 60-plus call centers with 40,000 total seats employing 50,000 people were operating in the Philippines. The country's call center revenues are thought to be $400–$480 million, with a projected growth rate of 100%.[14] Some notable companies include Convergys, Sykes, Teletech, Ambergris, eTelecare, APAC, ICT, and West.

There is a sizable Filipino workforce skilled in both technology and business processes. Average IT salaries range from $5,000–$15,000 per year. Average BPO salaries range from $3,000–$10,000 per year depending on experience.[15]

Category	Comments
Labor	Total population in 2004 was 86.2 million. Low employee turnover is an advantage.
Cost savings	Philippine call center workers start at $2.50 and may go as high as $5.00 (compared to U.S. rates of $8–$20).
Language skills	The Philippines has two official languages: Filipino and English. English is widely spoken.
Technical skills	The universities generate more than 15,000 technical graduates each year.
Education	Universities are considered quite good. More than 380,000 students graduate every year.
Cultural compatibility	Close ties exist with the United States.
Quality	The Philippines had 509 ISO 9000 certifications in 2003.

Table 8.13: The Philippine Workforce's Attractiveness and Economics[16]

Challenges

Political stability and corruption are the primary problems. Since the impeachment of former President Estrada on corruption charges, the country has devoted itself to attracting foreign investment, assigning several senior government officials to promote trade and foreign investment, and closely overseeing any disputes involving foreign investors to ensure they are treated fairly. In addition, President Arroyo has waged a campaign to rid the country of corruption, setting her sights on the customs and tax departments.[17]

The prospect of terrorism is a recurring problem. Muslim rebel groups advocating for an Islamic state in the southern Philippines have contributed to the country's instability by leading bombing and kidnapping attacks on civilians (although these attacks have been confined to a small region).

Category	Comments
Infrastructure	High-quality telecom infrastructure in major cities.
Stability	The country faced economic problems in the early 1990s including inflation, rising unemployment, and complaints of official corruption. A more stable political and economic environment has emerged in the last few years.
Legal environment	A member of the WTO since January 1995.
Regulatory environment	In 1991, the Philippines created special economic zones. Companies that set up operations in these zones may receive a tax holiday for up to six years.
Travel convenience	Travel time from London to Manila is approximately 15 hours and includes one stop. Travel time from New York City to Manila is about 21 hours and includes at least one stop.
Time zone	The Philippines is located within one time zone that is eight hours ahead of GMT and 13 hours ahead of EST.

Table 8.14: The Philippines' Location Attractiveness and Risks

Long-Term Outlook

The Philippine government must deliver on its promise of economic reform in order to sustain the country's positive momentum. It also must overhaul the tax system to bolster government revenues and further deregulate and privatize the economy.

Companies have expressed concerns that the Philippines has limited manpower, but that concern appears unwarranted. Several years ago, call centers remained concentrated in the metro Manila district, but companies have realized that an attractive labor force exists outside the capital and have set up operations in multiple cities.

The Philippines remains an attractive offshoring destination with the continued government incentives such as the four- to eight-year income tax holiday; tax and duty exemption on imported capital equipment; the deduction for training expenses up to 150%; and exemption from 10% input VAT on allowable local purchases of goods and services (for example, communication charges).

Destination: Russia

With an economic growth rate of about 7% in 2004 and investment-grade credit ratings from some of the international rating agencies, Russia has emerged from its economic upheaval of the late 1990s and built a reputation as an attractive offshore market, particularly for software development.

Russia's strength is its engineering and scientific talent. It has about 3,500 engineers for every 1 million people, nearly the same ratio as the United States.[18] To take advantage of this talent, companies such as Boeing, IBM, Dell, and Citibank have established a presence there.

Category	Comments
Labor	Total population in 2004 of 143.8 million. Employee retention is considered a problem in Russia.
Cost savings	Average cost for a programmer is $20 per hour.
Language skills	Significant language barriers exist between Russian-speaking workers and English-speaking customers.
Technical skills	Russia has approximately one million technically trained employees, more than China, Japan, or the United States, and three times as many as India.
Education	Worldwide, Russia has the third-largest pool of engineers, mathematicians, and scientists per capita. Many universities, mainly in the major cities — St. Petersburg, Moscow, and Novosibirsk — offer a steady stream of technical graduates.
Cultural compatibility	As a former communist country, the current generation of Russians does not have much cultural compatibility with Westerners.
Quality	Russia had 2,118 ISO 9000 certifications in 2003.

Table 8.15: Russian Workforce's Attractiveness and Economics[19]

Competitive Advantages

The immense pool of technically trained Russian employees is a huge draw for companies interested in offshoring software development. The technical skills of the Russian workforce go beyond basic programming and extend to complex engineering tasks. In fact, more people work in R&D in Russia than in any other country in the world.[20]

Along with Canada, Ireland, and Mexico, Russia markets its proximity to Europe and the United States as a distinct advantage over other offshoring countries. An eight-hour difference between the East Coast of the United States and Moscow means that firms can hand work off at the end of the business day to staff in Russia, who can have it ready the following morning. The advantage for European companies lies in being able to sync schedules with Russian workers.

Category	Comments
Infrastructure	Infrastructure is best in technology parks and major cities. Bandwidth costs are high.
Stability	Russia is a barely functional democracy.
Legal environment	The legal environment is weak and constantly in flux.
Regulatory environment	Russia is the only country of the top eight offshoring locations without membership in the WTO.
Travel convenience	A nonstop flight from New York to Moscow is nine hours.
Time zone	Russia spans 11 different time zones. The easternmost time zone is two hours ahead of GMT and the westernmost is 12 hours ahead of GMT.

Table 8.16: Russia's Location Attractiveness and Risks

Challenges

Critics of Russia argue that the bureaucracy needs to be downsized dramatically, regulations for banks need to be tightened, and reforms in the country's tax structure have to be completed. Skeptics point to the investigation of a major shareholder in one of the nation's top oil companies on fraud charges as evidence of the government's willingness to meddle when it suits its best interest.

Russia must reform its business practices to help make it a global offshore player. Its business practices are not as transparent as U.S. businesses may be used to, even with the spate of U.S. business scandals concerning hidden deals. Russian businesses eventually must adopt U.S. GAAP or other accounting standards used in Western countries.

There also are security concerns regarding Russia, despite the government's assertions that the war in Chechnya is over. A wave of suicide bombings and other acts of terrorism — several of which have occurred in the offshoring hub of Moscow — reinforce security as an issue. Lastly, companies that consider establishing offshore operations outside of major Russian cities may sacrifice sound infrastructure.

Long-Term Outlook

Russia's eventual acceptance to the WTO should enhance its attractiveness as an offshoring destination. Much rides on whether Putin continues to open up the Russian economy to foreign investment.

Destination: South Africa

South Africa has come a long way from its troubled past and is fast becoming known as an attractive offshore destination. The country has embraced foreign investment by opening all business sectors to investors and by placing limited restrictions on investments.

Competitive Advantages

Some U.K. and German companies view South Africa favorably because its time zone (two hours ahead of GMT) allows them to keep their offshoring operations in sync with their local operations. While the flight to South Africa from the United Kingdom is long, the lack of a significant time zone difference allows better coordination of offshore operations.

Companies also cite a diminished cultural gap between South Africans and U.K. or U.S. citizens. Alison Jones, director of European sales and operations for Source One Communications, a global offshore contact center solutions provider, explained her company's decision to open a contact center in South Africa this way: "Very often…when I phone an Indian call center there are accent problems. It is very scripted and false…. Whereas in South Africa, it's a lot more natural. The conversation flows better, and people are able to engage in conversations much easier, much more naturally."[21]

The favorable exchange rate is another advantage of offshoring in South Africa, although the rand has been gaining ground steadily on the U.S. dollar and the euro. In 2003 the average rand per dollar was 7.55, while in 2004 the average rand per dollar was 6.45.[22]

Challenges

South Africa began a privatization push of its state-owned enterprises in the late 1990s in an effort to secure much-needed outside funds. Although the telecommunications fixed-line monopoly in South Africa ended, rates are still not competitive, which drives costs up for businesses interested in setting up call center operations.

Category	Comments
Labor	In 2004, South Africa's total population was 42.7 million.
Cost savings	IT professionals in South Africa earn an annual salary of $35,951 (compared to $81,061 in the United States).
Language skills	South Africa has 11 official languages. Many South Africans speak English, and it is often used in business.
Technical skills	South Africa has six *technikons* (universities of technology), 11 traditional universities, and six comprehensive institutions.
Education	The South African university system consists of 23 universities graduating some 400,000 students. The quality of education is considered good.
Cultural compatibility	South Africa's British and German heritage makes it highly compatible with European companies.
Quality	South Africa had 2,537 ISO 9000 certifications in 2003.

Table 8.17: South African Workforce's Attractiveness and Economics[23]

The country faces uphill social and medical battles. AIDS has taken a severe toll on South Africa, with an estimated 11% of the population infected.[24] A 2003 World Bank study warned that the nation could face a "complete economic collapse" if it does not take steps to combat the disease, although government officials have called that claim unfounded and point to the steps they have taken to decrease the infection rate. In addition, South Africa has an extremely high crime rate. Both of these problems could translate to increased costs for employers in the form of healthcare and security.

Lastly, South Africa must confront its shortage of skilled employees, many of whom have left and sought work in other countries, such as the United Kingdom.

Category	Comments
Infrastructure	Roads, rail, air, and shipping are improving steadily. Gauteng province is the high-tech hub, with 70% of the high-tech workforce of South Africa.
Stability	South Africa has been a multiparty democracy since the lifting of apartheid.
Legal environment	The Competition Act of 1998 was developed to end anticompetitive practices and dominance. Companies have complained that South Africa enforces intellectual property and copyright laws loosely.
Regulatory environment	The taxation system is in a state of transition. Packages for investors in strategic industrial projects are available and entail tax allowances for approved investments.
Travel convenience	Direct flights to South Africa leaving from New York's JFK and arriving in Johannesburg take 15 hours.
Time zone	South Africa operates on one time zone — two hours ahead of GMT and seven hours ahead of EST.

Table 8.18: South Africa's Location Attractiveness and Risks

Long-Term Outlook

South Africa is a middle-income, developing country. It has an abundant supply of natural resources and well-developed financial, legal, communications, energy, and transport sectors.

Growth, however, has not been strong enough to cut into high unemployment, and daunting economic and social problems remain from the apartheid era, especially the issue of poverty and the lack of economic empowerment among the disadvantaged groups.

Other Offshore Destinations: Countries on the Verge

As the number of companies considering offshoring grows, so does the number of locations competing for their business. While India holds the largest market share and should continue to do so for years, several countries are looking to give India a run for its money. As offshore outsourcing has matured, established destinations like India are themselves sending work to China, the Philippines, and Vietnam in an effort to find talent and keep costs low.

In Asia, Singapore, Malaysia, and Vietnam serve as alternatives to the top offshore locations. The Middle East is also positioning itself aggressively as a must-evaluate option. Let's look at each of these up-and-coming offshore destinations.

Destination: The Middle East. Bahrain, Qatar, Kuwait, and the United Arab Emirates are developing successful technology outsourcing niches. Located in the center of Europe and Asia, Dubai has infrastructure to rival any European or North American city.

"The development of Dubai as an outsourcing destination through the Dubai Outsource Zone (DOZ) initiative is part of the larger knowledge economy vision of His Highness Sheikh Mohammed Bin Rashid Al Maktoum, Crown Prince of Dubai and UAE Defense Minister," said Ismail Al Naqi, director of the DOZ. "Dubai has unique advantages that can enable it to become one of the world's key outsourcing hubs. The DOZ initiative capitalizes on these advantages to provide companies a competitive, cost-effective location for basing global and regional outsourcing hubs. The DOZ offers 100% exemption from taxes, a multilingual, multiskilled workforce, government support services, state-of-the-art infrastructure, and other benefits."[25]

Many companies located there easily build multinational workforces, drawing from the people of 190 nationalities. Akash Arora, the chief technical architect and CEO of Netlink, says, "We relocated our headquarters from India to Dubai with the single belief that Dubai provides an ideal environment to work and play, thereby keeping our workforce in optimum shape to deliver to our global clients."[26]

Israel's dominance in the Middle East is being eclipsed due to the Arab-Israeli conflict. Israel was one of the primary destinations for offshore outsourcing until the prolonged clash with the Palestinians began. The country's labor pool, though small in comparison to players such as India or China, is quite technologically savvy. In particular, Israel has shown a talent for developing high-end systems, security software, and learning systems.

Destination: Malaysia. Malaysia's status as a choice offshore location is backed by a strong pro IT government, which has led to the development of the famous Multimedia Super Corridor (MSC). The MSC occupies a 15-kilometer by 50-kilometer corridor governed by innovative cyberlaws, policies, and practices to provide companies an ideal multimedia environment. Other positive factors include a largely English-speaking workforce and low real estate and labor costs. Malaysia has very sophisticated communications and IT infrastructure.

Destination: Singapore. Due to a government that encourages foreign investment by offering businesses big tax incentives, excellent telecom and IT infrastructure, and a culture heavily influenced by the West, Singapore has teetered on the edge of becoming a major offshore destination. A shortage of skilled IT workers and a lack of sufficient low-cost labor are the reasons why it hasn't become one of the top offshoring destinations.

Destination: Vietnam. Vietnam is surfacing as an offshore destination for software development and architecture. The country is politically and economically stable and, although poor, has invested heavily in educating its population. Typical pay is about $6,000 per year, high by local standards (Vietnam's gross domestic product is about $400 per capita). The cost of IT development in Vietnam is estimated to be 15% less than doing the work in India.[27]

Summary

Location is often a major cost and productivity factor. Managers considering global outsourcing must evaluate macroeconomic, demographic, and political issues of long-term significance. They must carefully weigh international trade issues, such as currency exchange risks, import-export quotas, and taxes. The availability of skilled labor; infrastructure support services; political, cultural, and legal concerns; and quality-of-life issues — all must be addressed before a significant investment in a new country is made.

Finally, it's important to note that location selection is not an exact science. Companies tend to learn from their experiences in site selection. Often, two or three sites that seem to have identical location profiles yield vastly different operational results. After looking at several existing sites, managers begin to see what makes a location good for their specific purposes. They find that an ideal location for a call center is not necessarily a promising location for a software development center.

The best approach to location selection is to analyze the demographic and performance characteristics of the firm's existing sites and select sites based on those factors most closely associated with superior operational results.

1.	A sustainable cost advantage
2.	Delivery methodologies such as software engineering processes and project management
3.	The caliber and quantity of resources
4.	The quality of the domestic market and its vertical expertise
5.	Technical and language skills
6.	Infrastructure reliability and availability
7.	Educational system
8.	Work ethic, culture, and quality of life
9.	Government commitment and support (taxes)
10.	Geopolitical stability considerations

Table 8.19: Summarizing the Top Ten Risks in Offshore Outsourcing

Chapter Nine

Setting up the Contractual Framework — MSA, SOW, and SLAs

Outsourcing relationships constantly evolve with the dynamics of the underlying business. To be successful, contracts must be carefully constructed to ensure that the business needs can be addressed efficiently, the risks identified, and the parties protected in case of dispute. This chapter outlines the different contractual elements of a global outsourcing relationship. These elements include the master services agreement (MSA), the statement of work (SOW), and the service level agreement (SLA).

Outsourcing Contract Terminology

This chapter will cover the numerous contract documents that will encompass the outsourcing agreement. Most of these documents will be used when outsourcing to a third-party vendor. Some agreements, especially those related to service levels, will be important to create even if companies are building captive centers.

The contract-related documents that encapsulate every outsourcing engagement include the following:

- **Master services agreement (MSA):** a broad agreement that establishes the high-level outsourcing relationship between two companies.

- **Statement of work (SOW):** a document that will help to keep the arrangement on track by clarifying your company's needs and the vendor's responsibilities. The SOW should define the scope and objectives of the services to be provided and include a time line and deliverables.

- **Service level agreement (SLA):** an agreement that defines minimum service level requirements and remedies for failure to meet standards in the contract. It is crucial to discuss key objectives and measurements of success. Without clearly defining key metrics in the beginning, confusion could arise about responsibilities, which, in worst-case scenarios, leads to finger-pointing and dissatisfaction. You must spend time on this step. Defining requirements upfront and carefully planning the SLA can save time and eliminate rework.

Figure 9.1 shows how these different documents are related.

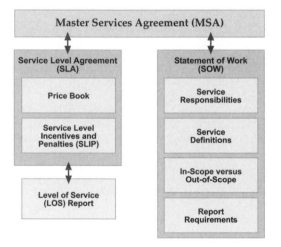

Figure 9.1: Types of Outsourcing Documents

Contracts Accurately Describe the Deal

Contract creation and negotiations are really projects within a project. All contractual documents are critical for the mutual understanding of what is expected from the vendor and the company. Many outsourcing agreements fail because the vendor is expecting to provide one level of service, while the customer is anticipating a totally different level.

For example, take a hypothetical outsourcing agreement for desktop support. Before Client A outsourced, its in-house IT staff had a service level to be onsite within two hours. When Client A outsourced to a third-party vendor, however, it agreed that vendor's technician would be onsite within six hours. You can see how unhappy Client A's employees would be when no one showed up for six hours to fix their problem. You can also understand why the vendor would be unhappy when employees starting complaining after two hours. It was a lose-lose situation.

Part of fixing the problem was creating service levels consistent with what the employees were used to receiving. The other part of the equation, and where Client A failed miserably, was to communicate the new levels of service to employees. We cover the importance of communication in Chapter 10.

Let's look at what should be included in the contractual framework that forms the backdrop of an outsourcing project, beginning with the master services agreement (MSA).

The Master Services Agreement

In early 2004, Royal Dutch/Shell Group entered into an information technology MSA with Wipro and IBM. The long-term outsourcing deal was estimated to be valued at over $1 billion. It was part of the oil giant's plan to save $850 million in IT spending by outsourcing IT operations to India and Malaysia. The company expects to cut between 1,900 and 2,800 jobs from the 9,300 strong IT workforce over the next few years due to the MSA.[1]

For large outsourcing deals, defining the right MSA is critical. When negotiating, make sure you have a strategic view of what you want to achieve and the goals that are important to you. Think about the incentives for both your company and the vendor. Make sure that anything that is important to you (meeting deadlines or getting your project operational as soon as possible) is part of the contract.

In the overall sourcing steps, the MSA follows vendor and country selection. The RFP and the vendor's response can be used as inputs to this process. The agreement acts as a legally binding document that defines all aspects of the outsourcing relationship.

An MSA is not specific to any project but rather it is generic in nature. It is a fairly comprehensive legal document, largely prepared by your legal and sourcing team, that specifies the rules of the game — collaborative vision, strategic goals, policies, planning, duration, quality, intellectual property rights, people poaching rules, and other expectations.

For the MSA to work, it has to be fair to both parties, so your company should try to understand what is important to the vendor. When both companies understand each other's goals, they have the basis for a sound relationship. Figure 9.2 illustrates the three basic building blocks for constructing an MSA — general, financial, and legal.

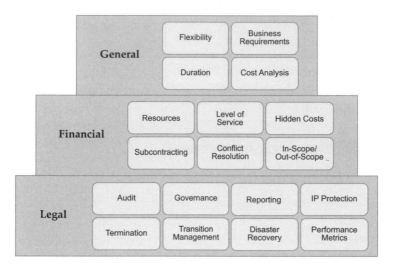

Figure 9.2: Building Blocks for a Master Services Agreement

The General Master Services Agreement Framework

Price, quality, and deadlines are not the only things that need to be negotiated. There are other aspects of a good outsourcing contract.

Length and Flexibility

Outsourcing agreements, especially BPO ones, are often long-term — one year, three years, or even 10 years — so the contract needs to be flexible enough to change with the times. Expect significant revisions to your BPO contract every two years as you may want to expand or limit the scope of your project or accommodate new risks and technologies.

Dispute Resolution

What if a vendor fails to perform its duties? As is expected, many outsourcing relationships periodically encounter problems that can stem from unclear requirements or missed metrics. Your company should have provisions for a dispute resolution process that attempts to resolve problems in an expeditious manner, as well as a provision for continuation of services during the conflict period. Be sure to document the procedures for reporting and resolving problems.

Duration, Expiration, and Renewal

Explicitly define the duration of the contract and spell out the terms under which it will expire or the terms under which it can be renewed. You need to consider the type of technology and the state of the market when negotiating the appropriate length of the contract and its renewal. While there can be benefits to long-term outsourcing contracts, for projects such as IT, certain technologies may be subject to rapid change and a shorter-term contract may prove beneficial.

Similarly, your company needs to specify when you will notify the vendor of your intent not to renew the contract prior to expiration. It is better to require a formal renewal in writing rather than specifying conditions for automatic renewal.

For peak cost savings, try to coordinate the expiration dates of contracts for other related services (such as telecommunications, infrastructure costs, programming, and network support) so that they coincide. You can minimize the risk of terminating a contract early and incurring penalties as a result of the termination of another related contract.

Termination

Does your contract have consensual termination or renegotiation stipulations? Does your contract have hostile termination or insourcing stipulations? Are you protected? How do you or the vendor initiate termination? What fees apply in the event of termination?

You need to make sure your contract has an 'out-clause' in case you are unhappy with the vendor. The extent and flexibility of termination rights can vary depending upon the service. The contract should define aspects such as termination rights for a variety of conditions, including change in control (acquisition or merger), change in vendor location, substantial increase in cost, repeated failure to meet service levels, inability to provide critical services, bankruptcy, company closure, and insolvency.

A large U.S. telecom company that outsourced its call center to a midsize Canadian vendor had to think about the issue of termination. At first, they were a big fish in a small pond and were treated very well by the vendor. Unfortunately for the telecom corporation, the vendor was acquired by a very large outsourcing firm, and the telecom company became a small fish in a big pond. Service levels dropped, reporting deteriorated, and the telecom company grew dissatisfied with the vendor's performance. Fortunately, it wrote a clause in its agreement that allowed it to cancel the contract in the event of a vendor merger or acquisition.

Exit or escape clauses are necessary to minimize risk. The contract should establish notification and time frame requirements and provide for the prompt return of your company's data upon termination. Any costs reimbursements incurred by your company for early termination should be clearly stated. You need to know: What's our walk-away price?

Performance Improvement Metrics

Define the cost reductions with the vendor. Will savings come from people reduction (make sure to define which people) or re-engineered processes (make sure to specify which processes). Document and understand the details and do not accept generalities. Do not allow the outsourcer to only define metrics for the first year and gloss over improvements for the remaining years of the contract. Add achievable improvements every year and change your baseline as you go. Build a review process into the contract that will encourage comparing your presents costs and savings with what the vendor originally promised.

Service Scope and Definitions

The MSA should clearly articulate the scope and definitions of the services including:

- Descriptions of services to be performed by vendor, including support, maintenance, or training of employees.

- Time frames for implementation of services.

- Obligations of the company outsourcing.

- Your company's rights in modifying existing services.

- Guidelines for adding new or different services.

- Guidelines for contract renegotiation.

Often a company will start with a limited scope for the outsourcing project. As it becomes more comfortable outsourcing, it increases the project's scope. A good example of a gradual scope escalation model is Best Buy, a $15 billion specialty retailer headquartered in Minnesota. Best Buy's offshore experience began in November 1999 when it outsourced some application system management to Tata Consultancy Services (TCS), based in India. Since 1999, the relationship has expanded, with TCS providing Best Buy services in the areas of application development, maintenance, performance engineering, and deployment.

Audit Framework

The MSA should specify the types of audit reports the company will receive during the length of the outsourcing engagement including financial, performance, or security reviews. The contract should specify the audit frequency and any fees for obtaining the audits. Depending on the size and duration of the outsourcing contract, along with the potential risk assessment, your company will need to decide if it can rely on internal audits or if there is a need for external audits and reviews.

For companies outsourcing to offshore or nearshore vendors, your contract should contain additional security provisions. Your contract should specify periodic control reviews, which may include intrusion detection, reviews of technology security such as the firewall configuration, and internal employee security checks. You should request regular reports on the findings of these audit checks to ensure vendor compliance.

Operational Details

The MSA should also incorporate provisions that address the following controls:

- Compliance with applicable regulatory requirements.

- Notification requirements and approval rights for any material changes to services, systems, controls, key project personnel, and service locations.

- Clearly defined payment cycle and terms — the period within which you make the payment after receiving the invoice (such as 30 days). Vendors can be paid after they reach milestones, or they can be paid regularly on a weekly or monthly basis.

- Insurance coverage maintained by the service provider.

Contingency Plans

The MSA should state the vendor's responsibility for backup schedule and information protection, including technology, customer files, and disaster recovery plans. The vendor should provide the contingency plan, which outlines the required operating procedures in the event of business disruption and includes provisions for business recovery time frames.

With offshore and nearshore outsourcing, there are additional concerns regarding contingency plans. The infrastructure in countries such as India or Panama is not as reliable as it is in the United States; therefore, offshoring requires paying more attention to disaster recovery. You need to have in writing what the vendor will do if a power outage or natural disaster occurs, how long the vendor will be down, and what the backup plan is.

Assignment and Subcontracting

Your company should include in the contract provisions a section that prohibits assignment of the contract to a third party without your consent. Assignment provisions should also reflect notification requirements for any changes to subcontractors.

Some outsourcing vendors may work with third parties to deliver services. To provide accountability, your company should formally designate the primary contracting vendor. The MSA should specify that the primary contracting vendor is responsible for the services in the contract regardless of which service provider completes the work. Your MSA should also include notification and approval procedures regarding changes to the vendor's subcontractors.

The Financial Master Services Agreement Framework

How much will outsourcing cost you? This phase of the contract negotiations strives to ensure that the contract is being executed within the approved cost parameters. It consists of pricing, pricing methods, price stability, and hidden costs.

The contract should fully describe the calculation of fees for in-scope services, including recurring services, as well as any charges based upon volume of activity or for out-of-scope services.

Contracts should also address the responsibility and additional cost for procurement of required hardware and software. Any conditions under which the cost structure may be changed should be specified in detail, including limits on any cost increases.

Pricing

Outsourcing arrangements with vendors can run from thousands of dollars to millions of dollars over the course of a multiyear agreement, depending on the size and complexity of the contract. When the relationship involves the vendor purchasing assets, such as infrastructure or data centers, hiring staff, or integrating client facilities, the service provider makes a substantial investment. Accordingly, price setting itself is both complex and iterative.

Pricing Methods

There are several choices when it comes to pricing an outsourcing project. Familiarize yourself with vendor pricing and margins, look at all options, and choose the most appropriate one for the specific contract.

Contracts can be written on a fixed-price or variable-price basis. With fixed-price engagements, the vendor assumes the risk of absorbing cost variability. When set too low, fixed-price arrangements diminish the vendor's flexibility and motivation to respond to changing business conditions or emerging technologies. While variable pricing allows for increased risk sharing, it may also create misunderstandings if costs exceed expectations, especially if scope and accountability are poorly defined. Tata Consultancy Services estimated that for the first nine months of 2004, 56.3% of its international revenues came from fixed-price, fixed-time contracts, while 43.7% were attributed to T&M contracts.

Several different pricing methods follow.

- **Fixed price.** The cost is the same for each billing period for the entire contract length so you know exactly what the bill is each month, with no hidden charges. However, if the scope of the project is not adequately defined at the beginning of the contract, then out-of-scope services will cost more and will often be very expensive. For example, if a vendor has a contract billed at $10,000 per month for software maintenance and your company wanted to add an additional system, then you would be charged more for that additional service since it would be out-of-scope.

- **Unit pricing.** The vendor sets a rate for a specific level of service and you pay based on usage of that service. For example, if you outsource your call center and pay $7 per call and receive 10,000 calls per month, you would pay $70,000 for that month.

- **Cost plus.** The vendor receives payment for its actual costs, plus a predetermined profit margin that is usually a percentage of actual costs. For example, if an ITO vendor develops software at a cost of $10,000 and the contract specifies a 10% markup, then you pay $11,000.

- **Variable pricing.** The vendor establishes the price of the service based on a variable such as system availability or average handle time (AHT), defined as the average time from when a rep accepts a call to when the rep is ready to accept the next call, or the talk time plus the time to wrap up the call. Say a call center vendor establishes the price based on AHT. It bills $7.00, $7.50, or $8.00 per call for service levels of 80% answered in 2, 3, or 4 minutes AHT, respectively. If the AHT is 80% in 3 minutes for that billing period, you would pay $7.50 per call.

- **Incentive-based pricing.** Incentives encourage the vendor to perform above the SLA by offering a bonus. This pricing plan can also require the vendor to pay a penalty for not performing at an agreed-upon service level. For example, you hire an ITO to build a software program. The vendor agrees to do so within three months for $30,000. If the program is ready within two months, you will pay an additional $10,000, but if the vendor fails to meet the 90-day deadline, then you will only pay $20,000.

Price Stability

In long-term outsourcing arrangements, it is important to understand the price stability. Vendors typically include a provision in the contract that will increase costs in the future either by a specified percentage or per unit. Some vendors may increase their prices by more than 30% per year, so you need to ensure that you discuss the annual percentage rise before signing the contract. Some may also identify circumstances under which price reductions might be warranted, such as decreases in hardware or telecommunication costs.

Hidden Costs

Some vendors advertise low-labor costs while promoting their services until they get you to sign the contract. Later they produce an invoice with billing for separate services like documentation, overtime, or project management. Make sure you discuss hidden costs with the outsourcing vendor and ensure all costs are documented in your contract.

A word of caution about comparing vendor quotes: Make sure you are comparing apples to apples. One telecom company evaluating different vendor proposals started to read the fine print and found numerous hidden charges in one proposal. The vendor charged $.15 per minute extra for use of its ACD and $1,500 extra per month for the T1. During ramp-up, most vendors do not charge for the longer handling times that occur but price on a cost-per-call basis. This vendor was also going to charge for the longer handling times, thus making the telecom company pay for training its reps.

Even if companies do a good job of estimating vendor costs, they may still fall short when estimating their internal costs. An often-overlooked expense of global outsourcing is the required investment in management time and travel. Project management takes on new complexity with offshore work and can eat up money and management time while sinking quality if it's not done right. You should reserve 5%–15% of your total budget for the internal management team to oversee the outsourced process. Depending on the location, travel costs can quickly accumulate and tend to be underestimated.

The Legal Master Services Agreement Framework

Warranties, liability, and confidentiality are a few of the legal issues that you will need to address. Some of the most important issues include protecting your trade secrets (processes, source code) and intellectual property (IP). You must also be aware of local regulations, such as labor and taxation laws.

You must ensure your contract is in accordance with generally accepted accounting principles (GAAP) and regulatory reporting requirements. Also, before signing the contract, make sure you understand how you will enforce your contract rights from the United States and the chosen offshore or nearshore country.

Data Security and Privacy

The MSA should detail the vendor's responsibility for ensuring the security and confidentiality of data, hardware, and software applications. The agreement should prohibit the vendor and its employees (or subcontractors) from using or disclosing your information, except to deliver the contracted services.

The security and privacy policies have to be especially robust in scenarios where customer data is being accessed. The importance of customer data privacy was brought to the forefront by the front page news involving ChoicePoint and LexisNexis. If the vendor receives personal customer information, any breaches in security must be escalated immediately. The vendor must report when, where, how and why the problem occurred, the impact, and the corrective actions initiated.

Ownership and License Agreements

Who maintains ownership of information? Is the ownership of data or source code clearly defined? The contract should contain the ownership rights to and allowable use of your company's data, hardware, software, documentation, and intellectual property. Your company must retain ownership of your data.

Other intellectual property rights may include your company's name and logo, trademarked or copyrighted material, domain names, Web sites, and software code developed by the outsourcing vendor.

Liability Damages

Poor performance in terms of product quality or delivery slippages will result in erosion or customer loss. Your MSA must protect against any damage to your business interests. Specific terms and conditions for handling damages due to the violation of agreed-upon delivery conditions must be handled through the specific SLA or the project contract.

In practice, however, serious violations do not normally occur intentionally, although hardly any public data on this topic exist. Bad project management or lack of ownership is more likely to be the reason for poor delivery, which should have been recognized upfront anyway if companies are executing their global outsourcing strategies properly.

Your legal team should be cognizant of the laws in the country where your company is outsourcing including: customs, export import, child labor, hiring and labor protection, and others. For example, custom regulations may delay delivery of hardware needed to set up your testing infrastructure in a global location, thus leading to an unexpected delay.

If your company is from the United Kingdom, the TUPE (transfer of undertaking and protection of employees) regulations will drive the process for the vendor, almost mandating it to hire your employees and offer them a job at their global locations. Unawareness of such legal regulations may cause delayed delivery of your project goals.

Large corporations are generally equipped with sufficient legal staff to protect their business interests. However, small companies considering outsourcing must rely on indirect legal risk mitigation strategies. They should look for a proven track record, take extra care in developing agreements, and make sure that there are suitable contract termination clauses to protect them against any unforeseen performance issues.

Indemnification and Limitation of Liability

Indemnification clauses are especially important in outsourcing contracts. They must ensure that the nearshore or offshore vendor does not hold your company accountable for liabilities from its own negligence. Care must be taken in the wording of the contract to ensure that you will not be held liable for claims in a foreign country as a result of the vendor's actions.

Limiting the amount of liability is something that many vendors would be especially sensitive about. So in every outsourcing contract, assess whether the liability amount is sufficient enough to cover the potential loss if the vendor fails to perform its obligations as specified in the contract.

Regulatory Compliance

Ensure that the MSA includes a section stating that the outsourcing service provider will comply with regulatory rules and requirements. The contract should also indicate that the vendor agrees to present accurate regulatory information based on the processes or products outsourced and level of service it supports.

The bottom line: At the end of this phase of the sourcing relationship, you should have negotiated a general term sheet, pricing, and other financial details, as well as the overarching legal framework. You should have worked with the appropriate legal counsel to negotiate and structure the contract. This will help you avoid a common misstep, namely, the contract is drafted hastily and problems arise from a relationship that is not well thought out before the deal is sealed.

Statement of Work

An MSA between a vendor and its client usually describes the whole project and the broad legal framework. A statement of work (SOW) is a document that details the generic services, service responsibilities, units of measure, and pricing for each service.

The SOW answers the questions of what the vendor will support, what the client is responsible for, what the time frames are, and how the service will be billed. Some important details to cover in your SOW are:

- Service responsibilities,
- Service definitions,
- In-scope versus out-of-scope, and
- Report requirements.

Service Responsibilities

Understanding the responsibilities of both the client and the vendor is critical in an outsourcing relationship. Often companies will create a responsibilities matrix that clearly spells out who will be responsible for what function (see Table 9.1).

Service Function	Responsible
Business requirements definition	Client
Project management	Client/Vendor
Testing	Vendor
Deployment	Vendor
Quality assurance	Vendor
LOS reporting	Vendor

Table 9.1: Responsibilities Matrix

Service Definitions

Although it sounds simplistic, documenting the definitions of the services that will be provided is necessary. Why? It is important that both your company and the vendor are using common terminology to define relevant terms such as system uptime or call handling time. The SOW should include a section dedicated to service definitions.

Sample definitions for a call center engagement might include:

- First call problem resolution ratio: the number of calls answered for which the ticket is closed on the first customer contact and without escalation to tier two, expressed as a percentage of all calls answered.

- Average call handle time: the average time from when a rep accepts a call offered until the rep is ready to accept the next call offered.

- Average speed of answer: the average length of time that a call offered is kept waiting for the rep.

- Call center availability: the amount of time during which the call center is available via telephone, expressed as a percentage of the maximum time available during that same time period.

Once the services are defined, you must spell out exactly what services the vendor will perform. It is better to have too much defined rather than leave operational details vague. Some issues to consider are:

- **Geographic regions.** Will all of your company's countries and locations fall under the contract, or will certain locations be excluded?

- **Period of operations.** The SOW needs to define the business hours when the service will be offered. Normal business hours have to be delineated, such as Monday through Friday between 8:00 a.m. EST and 5:00 p.m. EST, excluding holidays (which also need to be listed).

- **Languages.** Even details such as which languages will be supported should be clearly defined. For call centers, clients usually get to select two languages that are supported during normal business hours and one language that is supported after business hours.

Examples of detailed services for a call center outsourcing engagement might be:

- Vendor ABC will respond to calls offered, twenty-four hours a day, seven days a week (24x7).

- By 9:00 a.m. EST, Vendor ABC will electronically send a daily call statistics report that compares actual service levels to expected service levels for the preceding day for calls offered, calls answered, calls abandoned, average speed of answer, answer speed ratio, and abandon rate.

The SOW also defines service levels terminology such as:

- **Availability:** the time a specific service is available for use by the client's employees or customers. Availability is measured in time periods such as 24x7 or the previously described "normal business hours."

- **Reliability:** the percentage of committed time a particular service is operable and available to the client's employees or customers. Reliability is calculated by dividing the total time the service was operable (uptime) by the total time the service was committed to be available for use (availability). The resulting number is expressed as a percentage of the total availability (for example, 98% or 99.99% availability).

- **Earned value:** the percentage of completion for a project. Take a software project where the coding completion is based on a plus and minus scale. A 10% difference would indicate that corrective action would need to be taken.

In-Scope versus Out-of-Scope

The SOW typically defines what services are in-scope and what services are out-of-scope. The term "in-scope" refers to functions, processes, locations, or current third-party agreements that will be covered by the vendor and are part of the outsourcing agreement. The term "out-of-scope" indicates services that are not included in the agreement and can be written into the SLA for an additional cost.

Although this step seems very basic, it is often the cause of much dissatisfaction with outsourcing. Clients usually want to list many services as in-scope, but the truth is that the more services that are included and the higher the level of service stipulated, the more outsourcing will cost your company. For example, if the client chooses a two-hour response time over a six-hour response time, obviously that choice will cost more (see Figure 9.3).

Say a telecom company outsources the call center technical support for its Internet service. Customer calls about browser problems with their Internet service would likely be regarded as in-scope, while calls about other topics such as viruses or spyware would be labeled out-of-scope. The vendor would not support out-of-scope calls.

Report Requirements

Contractual terms should include the frequency and type of reports your company will receive, such as satisfaction surveys, level of service reports, performance reports, control audits, financial statements, security, and testing reports.

The level of service (LOS) report evaluates the vendor's conformance with the agreed-upon service levels as specified in the SLA. We discuss the LOS report in Chapter 12. The SOW should also outline the procedures and costs for obtaining custom reports.

Service Level Agreement

The service level agreement, or SLA, outlines the baseline requirements for the outsourced service, defines performance levels, and establishes incentives and penalties for hitting or missing the defined service levels. For example, in a contract involving a credit-card company outsourcing debt collection, the SLA may contain performance criteria such as:

- Number of calls made per week;

- Time it takes for the debt to be collected;

- Percentage of total debt successfully collected; and

- Complaints received about the outsourcing company's services.

SLAs are generally part of agreements covering major sourcing initiatives or large programs (covering a number of projects) under the broad umbrella MSA. The purpose of the SLA is to protect your company against vendor performance failures by documenting provisions in the contract regarding incentives, penalties, and contract cancellations.

Service levels are one of those areas that are highly discussed but rarely defined well. Firms can use a plethora of different metrics to define service level requirements, but knowing which metrics are most critical to the overall success of the company is the most important part of establishing an SLA.

The Metrics of a Service Level Agreement

Your sourcing team should develop the SLA by first identifying the significant metrics. For example, if you are designing an SLA for inbound or outbound call centers, the metrics can be performance related, such as abandon rate, average call handling time, processing error rates, or system uptime, or organizational, such as employee attrition.

As defined in the SOW, the SLA is defined in terms of availability, reliability, or value created. When defining availability, focus on the time periods that are most important to your company's operations.

For example, if a critical application is unavailable 2% of the time, this may or may not directly affect your company. Ideally, that 2% unavailability should be during off peak hours and used for tasks such as maintenance or error corrections. If that 2% occurs during critical operating hours, it has the potential to cost your company a significant amount of money and hurt customer satisfaction. So when you are defining your SLA metrics, consider elements such as time of day and peak hours.

Although the specific performance metrics will vary with the type of services outsourced, some generic issues to consider include:

- Availability, reliability, and timeliness of services including uptime.

- Confidentiality, security, and integrity of data.

- Security standards compliance, including vulnerability.

- Business continuity compliance such as the vendor's contractual responsibility for backup, record retention, data protection, and the maintenance of disaster recovery and business recovery time frames.

- Change control procedures and requirements.

Once you have identified the metrics, you have to figure out how to measure them. You also need to determine the frequency of the measurements and an acceptable range of results, such as plus/minus 10%, to determine when the SLA is violated.

Designing a Service Level Agreement

Unfortunately, designing a detailed SLA during the negotiating phase is difficult, especially for offshore contracts, so typically the SLAs are constructed in two phases. The preliminary SLA in the contract negotiation phase defines the level of performance the vendor promises to deliver and your rights if they fail to do so.

This SLA and key performance indicators (KPIs) are refined during the transition phase. KPIs are metrics that directly measure how well the vendor is meeting its goals. They are finalized at the end of the transition period, although they may be re-examined at a future date if new processes or technologies are implemented.

Effective SLAs identify the expected results and the measures by which both parties will evaluate performance. It is important to write down what the vendor is expected to deliver, as well as the roles and responsibilities of both parties. Avoid statements such as "to be defined or agreed upon later" at all costs. Do not leave anything undocumented. If the vendor says it was not in the SLA, you can safely assume that there will be an extra cost associated with getting that task completed.

A well-designed SLA describes the start and end dates for the service, the schedule for reviewing performance, and the documentation to be used in measuring the service. Other important questions to be answered in the SLA include:

- What types of service levels are customers and end users expecting?

- How will you measure the service level? Will it be user satisfaction surveys, errors in work, or automated software methods such as system availability?

- What is the measurement period? Is it daily (24x7 or 9 to 6), weekly, or monthly?

- What is the minimum quality of work? What are the provisions and penalties for over- and underperformance?

- What is the escalation process for issue resolution?

An SLA should always be mutually agreeable to you and the vendor. Both parties should discuss the requirements and desired outcomes and negotiate an SLA that can be implemented with attainable goals.

SLAs often lack effective performance penalties and incentives. Be certain to attach specific penalties for performance levels that were not met, such as hold time for customers or problem resolution time. Remember that you cannot measure what you cannot define, so if it is not clearly defined in the SLA, then there will be no way to measure the performance of the vendor.

According to Tim Barry, vice president of outsourcing at Keane, "When outsourcing deals have problems, it's typically because client and supplier expectations regarding performance and service levels are misaligned. Regardless of the type of outsourcing deal, it's critical that both parties create and approve statements of work and service level agreements that support the client's business needs."[2]

Your SLA should measure whether or not a provider is delivering the needed results. This step refines the cost and value of each metric and defines the reporting process, and the process for changing metrics. Metrics should be unambiguous. Document contract terms for failures to deliver or penalties for missed metrics. Do not wait until after you sign the contract to agree upon the cost of each metric.

Service Level Incentives and Penalties

It is one thing to document the service expectations, and another for those expectations to be delivered. The service level incentives and penalties (SLIP) reiterates the service expectations and specifies:

- Incentives for exceeding the service levels or
- Penalties for missing the required levels.

By including both incentives and penalties for the vendor, there is an upside for improving performance and a downside for reducing adequate customer satisfaction.

A service level variance (SLV) is a deviation from the documented level of service. If an SLV occurs, then root cause analysis of why the problem occurred must happen, and corrective actions must be taken. Defined criteria such as quantity, frequency, and customer impact will determine the corrective process. SLVs do not normally apply to all metrics, only to those that the company needs to ensure are monitored regularly and that could have a potential negative impact if not met.

Often problems will be coded so as to ascertain the severity and impact on service levels. Each code will also have a resolution target. Let's look at a couple of examples in IT infrastructure outsourcing.

- Code 1: an emergency situation defined as a critical work stoppage during normal business hours that affects a large number of employees or customers, such as a network outage or a virus infecting multiple users. A code 1 would need to be resolved within four hours.

- Code 2: a major service disruption where groups of customers or employees are unable to operate, such as an isolated software outage. A code 2 would need to be resolved in six hours.

- Code 3: a minor service disruption where there is no work stoppage and a workaround for the problem is available. An example would be a printer is not working properly, but another printer is available. A code 3 would need to be resolved within 24 hours.

- Code 4: a condition where there is no work impact, such as an inquiry about a new software package. A code 4 would need to be resolved in five business days.

So what happens if things go wrong? SLA noncompliance does happen. It is important that the SLA defines noncompliance penalties. Vendors may offer free services or contract extensions, but these benefits often are not what clients want as they are the least desirable forms of restitution. Consider placing in your agreement the option to terminate the contract without penalties or financial restitution if SLA noncompliance happens.

Canceling the contract usually is not what the vendor or client wants; it is more of a last resort. Implementing communication and escalation procedures for the times when service levels are not being met is critical.

Frequently we hear from clients who are unhappy with their vendors and are convinced that they are not getting the level of service they are paying for. Vendors typically respond that they are meeting all service targets specified in the contract. This scenario illustrates a disconnect (he said, she said) that often characterizes SLAs in outsourcing deals.

There is a fine balance between service levels and cost. Both the vendor and the client need to be happy with the balance (see Figure 9.3). We cannot stress enough the importance of defining service levels carefully.

Clients are dumbfounded when service level targets for a critical metric have been met, but their systems weren't available when the customers needed them.

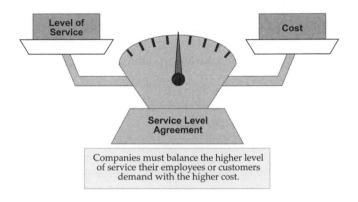

Figure 9.3: Level of Service and Cost Tradeoff

Careful development of penalty and incentive programs is valuable, as long as both your company and the vendor has a way to win (you, if they exceed expectations, and them, if they receive a performance-based bonus). Although helpful for managing vendor performance, penalties and incentives require careful monitoring. Make sure that the vendor's achieving the incentive is worthwhile for your company.

For example, say you hire a Chinese software firm to create a database application due in November for your Christmas campaign. If they finish it in October, then they get a bonus. The problem is that you really do not need it until November. The incentive is not a good fit for your company and adds no value for the additional benefit you gave the vendor. The SLIP clearly communicates priorities and defines how each organization will be measured.

Renegotiating Contracts

Companies renegotiate contracts with vendors all the time. One key thing to remember before renegotiating is to study the vendor's cost structure — not the pricing, but the cost structure. There are several ways to understand the mechanics that drives cost.

- Build your own cost model,

- Run a pilot before you negotiate or sign a major contract, or

- Gather industry data or other market-research data.

After you understand the vendor's approximate cost structure, it's time to tie in your short- and long-term strategy to the negotiating process. From now on, negotiating a sourcing contract should be like handling any other business deal.

Contracting Pitfalls to Avoid

Short-term thinking. Drawing up a legal framework before launching a global outsourcing project is similar to drafting a prenuptial agreement before marriage. Although some would argue that a prenup means that the marriage is doomed to fail, if there is a lot at risk, it is essential to involve a legal document. The same legal precautions need to be taken before signing a multiyear global outsourcing agreement.

Haggling over price. There are no winners in outsourcing negotiations. When you're making a one-time purchase at a garage sale, you or the seller might be tempted to take advantage of one another and haggle over the price. But with outsourcing, the client and the vendor must live together after the deal, so it doesn't make sense to try to "beat" anyone during negotiations. You want to agree on a great MSA, without causing the vendor to be resentful, which can result in mediocre service.

Hurrying the process. Your project managers will be keen to expedite the outsourcing project, while your legal team will delay the process while honing contractual details. Remember that your legal team is simply doing its job to support the business and mitigate outside risks. At the same time, the team should understand that they are there to support the business and not erect unnecessary barriers.

Adverse clauses. Companies looking to outsource should not sign contracts with conditions that may adversely affect them. Such contract stipulations may include unreasonable extended terms (over 10 years) for services, significant cost increases after the first two or three years, or substantial cancellation penalties.

Trading short-term benefits for long-term pricing. Practices such as low first-year costs in exchange for higher future support and maintenance costs may not be in the best interest of your company. For a 10-year contract, the short-term cost benefits you receive will be made up by the vendor when it charges a premium for the services in years two through nine. These types of agreements, with excessive fees on the back end, may hurt your company's chances for long-term success.

Summary

The importance of preparing and negotiating well-written legal contracts cannot be dismissed. Time spent on contracts and SLAs during negotiations will save much confusion and unhappiness later.

Contracts protect against bad intentions, poor execution, and unforeseen risk. Often what happens after the contract is signed differs markedly from what was promised during the courtship period (RFP and vendor selection phases). Horror stories from companies that have outsourced and expected a level of service only to be disappointed abound. Don't let your company be one of them.

One telecom company learned the importance of comprehensive contracts when it outsourced part of its call center operations to a large Canadian customer care company with 15,000 reps worldwide. The company selected the vendor because it demonstrated during the selection process that it was dedicated to helping clients.

The reality was quite different. Several times within the span of a year, the vendor called the telecom company when a snowstorm hit and stated that it could not take any calls that night because buses and taxis were not running and reps could not make it into work. The vendor said that the calls would have to be rerouted to the telecom company. In one instance, the vendor relayed the bad news by calling the customer's call center manager at home late one Sunday evening.

Ironically, the telecom company is located in upstate New York, which probably had just as much snow as Canada. Needless to say, the telecom company is searching for a new vendor. The moral of the story is to anticipate some of these unforeseen circumstances in your contract and look long and hard at the vendor's client retention, customer satisfaction rates, and exit clauses before you sign on the dotted line.

A good understanding of the different agreements discussed — the MSA, SOW, and SLA — and knowledge of the vendor's cost structure are essential to signing good contracts. This is hands-on work to be done by your business, sourcing and legal team. Your constant objective is to minimize risk and ensure satisfactory outcomes.

1. Define the important service levels to measure.	Decide which service levels are important to measure on a regular basis.
2. Define how you will measure each service level.	Clearly define each service level and what it means. If the server is available, what exactly does this mean. Is it available 24x7 or simply from 9:00–5:00? Is it EST or another time zone?
3. Define how you will report each measurement.	Define the reporting format and data that the vendor will be required to provide to you. For each report, define the frequency of the report (daily, weekly, monthly, or yearly).
4. Define performance improvement levels.	Long-term agreements should have key performance indicators and service level increases that the vendor will be expected to implement.
5. Define any incentives.	Define the metrics for exceptional performance and the bonus amount the vendor will be paid.
6. Define any penalties.	Make sure to define the metrics that would be considered instances where the vendor has failed in performance and specify the appropriate and expected monetary credit.
7. Define any termination criteria.	When can the contract be cancelled? The SLA should state specific examples that are justification for the breach (such as a repeated severe service failure) of contract.

Table 9.2: Summarizing the Top Seven Critical Issues in an SLA

We have reached the end of the sourcing section, which explained the decisions necessary for outsourcing business processes. To recap, Chapter 6 focused on creating effective RFIs and RFPs. Chapter 7 examined the complex process of vendor selection. Chapter 8 studied the countries that offer a superior outsourcing destination. Lastly, this chapter presented tips for contract negotiations and SLA creation.

Our objective for the fourth section of the book, execution, Chapters 10 through 13, is to help you conquer some of the tough execution details by delving into transition management, governance, and performance improvement.

Chapter Ten

Transition Management

After the contract is signed, transition management is a major driver of the success or failure of your outsourcing project. Well-executed transitions require a systematic approach to people, process, and technology issues. This chapter outlines the key aspects of transition: knowledge transfer, quality management, communication, and employee management.

What Is Transition Management?

Transition management is the first major execution activity you will face after completing sourcing-related activities. In the simplest terms, transition management centers on transferring internal control of people and processes to an external party. The aim of transition management is to quickly launch the outsourcing project. Too often, organizations rest after the deal is signed, and its value rapidly declines.

Consider the case of Hewlett-Packard and Procter & Gamble: The two companies signed a $3 billion global outsourcing contract on August 1, 2003. Only 94 days elapsed between the RFP and the signed contract. The result was a 10,000-page contract and about 3,700 tasks to transition. With a contract of this magnitude, transition management was a huge issue. The two firms agreed on a "where is, as is" strategy in which HP initially just put P&G's technology operations and workers on its books. So in the first 90 days, HP began absorbing P&G's three data centers in Cincinnati, Singapore, and Brussels, 2,000 of its employees, as well as its network infrastructure and technical contracts.[1]

Transition management is a joint responsibility. The service provider is responsible for supervising the overall transition program, while your company is responsible for overseeing the participation of your team in data gathering and requirements definition, gap analysis, knowledge sharing, and readiness assessment.

In addition, you have to lead change management within the organization, oversee stakeholder communications (internal and external), and ensure senior managers are involved to address transition issues. The vendor supplies the resources and methodology to assess your operations, define gaps, and develop a migration strategy.

Elements of Transition Management

Transition management can be specifically defined as the detailed preparation, analysis, and documentation of all relevant processes, tasks, workflows, functions, people, and technologies.

People transition: The assets relating to the outsourced services, including the employees, are transferred to the service provider. The scale depends on the contract size. The number of countries the firm operates in also complicates the people transition, as different labor laws apply. Typically, if employees will be moving to the vendor, the usual process of interviews, job offers, and acceptance periods follows. It may be necessary to devise retention plans for key employees, in addition to severance plans and reassignment programs for affected staff. The people phase of the transition is often a major focus of leadership.

Process transition: The business activity (process or task) being done in-house is transferred to the external vendor (or the offshore captive center). A team that includes staff from both your company and the vendor supervises the process transition, which takes a significant amount of planning and time. Job shadowing is often conducted so that the vendor's employees can see firsthand how the process is currently being executed. During this phase, current process flows and steps are reviewed and updated, and new documentation is assembled. Process transition is part of knowledge transfer.

Technology and facilities transition: The technology — proprietary or packaged applications, infrastructure, and data centers — associated with the outsourced process is also moved to the service provider. As with the process transition, the technology transition constitutes part of knowledge transfer. Issues such as hardware assets, software licenses, maintenance agreements, hosting, LANs, WANs, and telecom need to be reviewed and may be included in the transition. You and the vendor will need to agree who is accountable for each of these items to ensure roles and responsibilities are clear.

The task of figuring out what determines a successful outsourcing transition is up to you. For the process transition, is it no angry calls from customers? For the people transition, is it providing adequate compensation, job security, and employee benefits? For the technology transition, is it no downtime? Transition management entails thinking through what will make a transition flawless and ensuring these elements are in your plan. So the main activities of transition management include dealing with employee issues, communicating what is happening, making sure knowledge is not lost, and making sure everything goes smoothly.

Structured Approach to Transition Management

Transition management can occur smoothly with proper upfront planning and attention to details as one BPO solutions company illustrates. The vendor took over the accounts payable process for a large international provider of food, agricultural, and risk management products and services. Within 60 days, the vendor had migrated all the North American payables functions to its Delhi, India, service center. The vendor was operating at the same level of productivity that the company was operating at in the United States within 60 days. The payback period was about 20 days, with the company saving more than 50% and realizing a quality increase of almost 10%. The vendor thought the excellent results stemmed from the highly structured and managed transition process.

Daniel Wittner, senior vice president of sales at Zenta Group, a BPO company headquartered in Pennsylvania with five facilities in India, explains, "The biggest issue during transition is having a plan and making sure you have executive sponsorship from the client. The client needs a sponsor who says this is what we're going to do and here's our time line. To be successful, you have to execute crisply offshore, and that means having a defined project plan that covers all the key aspects, including the technology that you will need."[2]

A structured approach to people, process, and technology issues leads to a transition management plan with four key components: employee transition management, knowledge transfer, internal and external communication management, and ongoing process quality management.

Employee Transition Management

The human factor can greatly affect the outcome of operations, especially as outsourcing revolves around people and processes, not just technology. For the project to work, internal resources must be a willing part of the process. This takes some effort if employees' positions are at risk.

Communications apprise all employees within your company of your outsourcing intentions and the reasons behind them. Employees want to know what is happening, why, and how it affects them. Problems occur when leadership does not inform middle management and lower-level employees of their intentions. When business units are not kept informed, they become frustrated, and the vendor transition slows.

Too often, outsourcing is treated like a dark secret, and corporate rumor mills breed fear and distrust. Companies must step forward and clearly state their objectives, such as to save costs, become more competitive, give customers better service, or provide a better return for stockholders. Your employees must understand why their company is putting so much effort into launching and managing an outsourcing initiative.

Managing employee communication can be the difference between a successful transition with limited disruptions and shattered morale among the remaining employees. Ron Glickman, CIO at DFS Group, a subsidiary of Louis Vuitton Moet Hennessy, advises companies to move fast to spread the word once a decision to outsource has been made.

DFS Group outsourced to Cognizant, a major IT services firm with an offshore presence, and eliminated three out of four IT jobs inside DFS. There was discontent among those who lost their jobs, but Glickman's goal was to avoid turning the process into an unproductive waiting game with staff wondering who would be laid off next. According to Glickman, "Moving as quickly as possible with the change process helps minimize morale issues. Speed is really important."[3] DFS reduced the tension by making sure employees were aware of what was happening and were paid bonuses for staying on through the transition.

The business model you have selected will dictate the issues that need to be part of employee management. Utilizing a captive center entails much different tasks than outsourcing to a third-party vendor. We will look into these two business models and discuss the different sensitive issues that make up employee management.

Utilizing a Third-Party Vendor

When outsourcing to a third-party vendor, there is an extra step that companies must address: how to handle the employees who currently manage the processes selected for outsourcing. In the past, many vendors such as IBM or EDS would absorb the customer's employees into their organizations as part of the deal. With offshore business models, absorption is not as prevalent a tactic. So, with nearshore and offshore outsourcing, companies must make the tough decision about what to do with current employees: redeploy, transfer, or let go.

The sensitive subjects of redeployment or other staff options should be included as part of the transition costs, as it may involve severance payments and possible employment court settlements if it is not handled correctly. Expenses for retention and severance plans are generally handled by the client.

Your employees should be your primary focus during transition management. Many of those affected by outsourcing attribute their dissatisfaction to poor communication. The communication effort should begin before any vendor employees show up. You must have a strategy for letting all employees know, especially those who may be at risk of losing their jobs, the reasons for outsourcing and the transition process that is going to occur. It will not be an easy task, but it is a necessary one.

Companies underestimate the importance of the human side of offshoring. According to Ilya Billig, a former marketing vice president at LUXOFT, a Russian software company, "Companies need to communicate by clearly stating the goals, the course of actions that will be taken not to lose people or how many people may lose jobs, and what people can do to avoid losing jobs. That is the most important thing to do for any company that is considering outsourcing. The companies need to be very honest...[and] open in their outsourcing approach."[4]

It is important to maintain business continuity during the period between when an offshore initiative is announced and when it is implemented. A Fortune 500 firm that laid off almost all of its IT staff, employees, and contractors in favor of outsourcing found out the impact of poor transition planning. It immediately let go its contractors and gave employees three month's notice. Interestingly, a fire in the data center a few nights later caused a complete outage of the servers located there.

Management requested that all soon-to-be-terminated employees show up that weekend to fix the problem. Most, however, decided to stay home, causing severe business continuity problems.

Staffing and Transitioning a Captive Center

In addition to deciding what to do with employees working on the processes to be outsourced, there are other issues that companies setting up nearshore or offshore captive centers have to address, such as interviewing, hiring and retaining employees, and scaling up.

Pay close attention to the hiring issues in your captive center. As managers, we all know how hard it is to attract and retain qualified employees in our own countries. It is even more difficult in nearshore or offshore locations. Many of these countries, such as India, have watched the number of BPO providers explode, and competition for talent is fierce, similar to the dot-com era when startups were struggling to find enough IT people. Depending on your captive center's location, you may face some of these problems.

Another critical transition issue is staffing ratios. During transition, there are periods of low productivity. For instance, as you ramp up the offshore center, you might have one person onshore and two people offshore for the same task. As the offshore team learns and becomes more productive, especially with repetitive tasks, the offshore ratio will revert back to onshore productivity levels.

Knowledge Transfer

Knowledge transfer is the task of bringing the vendor's employees up to speed on your procedures and processes. Before you can begin transferring knowledge, you have to establish what knowledge has to remain in-house and what should be transferred. Job shadowing may be a solution to help train the vendor's employees for day-to-day operations.

Consider the case of Otis Elevator, the world's largest manufacturer of elevators headquartered in Connecticut. In 2001, Otis moved from a project-by-project service delivery model to having Wipro set up a dedicated offshore development and maintenance center in Bangalore, India. This dedicated center had a permanent team that only worked on Otis application development and maintenance projects.

An effective transition plan was a priority for Otis. According to David Wood, director of systems development at Otis, "The first big issue was knowledge transfer. We were sitting on a large inventory of applications built by a variety of vendors." Wood and the Wipro project leader spent a month developing a transition plan that included writing technical documentation that outlined file-naming standards, hardware, and software specifications; creating a high-level project plan; identifying the best onshore and offshore managers; and providing opportunities for knowledge transfer, such as job shadowing. "The transition period requires bringing a few people who will eventually be working offshore onsite to go through the application, get an understanding of it, and create the documentation that's required," says Wood.[5]

Otis spent $420,000 on the transition and didn't recoup that investment and start saving money for a year. Wood estimates Otis is saving $1.4 million a year on application development and maintenance, a nice complement to the annual $7 million it has been saving by using its own captive development center in Pune, India.

The time allotted for knowledge transfer should not be underestimated. The moment the project begins, staffing can start. It usually takes about one to two months to get the employee numbers ramped up, followed by one to two months to train the individuals. Once the employee starts, the learning curve stands at about three to four months. It takes another one to two months for the employee to reach peak performance. All in all, you could be looking at six to ten months for the project to stabilize and process improvements to occur. The time line varies according to how complicated the project is.

The offshore transition can take as little as six weeks. That's how long it took HCL to fully transfer the support activities of one of its customers, a network infrastructure equipment company, to its offshore offices. Three months elapsed, however, before HCL was able to implement the tools, trouble ticket system, and support processes that the customer's prior vendor had used. According to HCL, the network equipment company realized a 60% cost reduction when it switched from relying on a U.S. service provider to signing up with HCL.[6]

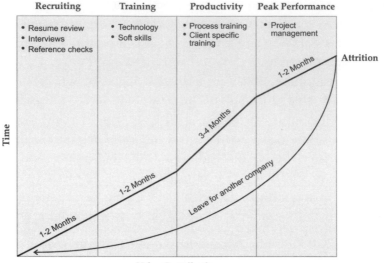

Figure 10.1: The Value Contribution Curve

Ambergris Solutions is a leading Philippine-based provider of customer care, inbound sales, and technical support solutions. One of its clients, a Fortune 100 computer manufacturer, is using 300 Ambergris agents to answer customer billing inquiries, communicate order status and shipping information, accept additional orders for spare parts and peripherals as well as order changes, set up returns transactions, and handle complaints. It took the two companies seven weeks and three days from when their partnership began to integrate the first call. After the 90-day initial ramp period, Ambergris had a service level of 86%, bypassing the target of 80%, and an average handle time of 6.54 minutes in comparison to the target of 7.5 minutes.[7]

Knowledge Transfer Kickoff

A proper knowledge transfer is essential to ensure that the vendor fully understands your requirements and that no gap exists between your expectations and its delivery. Typically, knowledge transfer includes a small vendor team coming to your site and learning about your people, product, processes, and tools.

Details of this training must be planned well and its duration tightly controlled. All aspects of the meeting, such as security badges for the vendor team and working laptops and e-mail accounts should be set up prior to the team's arrival, so that productivity won't be hindered once the contingent arrives. Figure 10.2 illustrates a representative training plan for an outsourcing project.

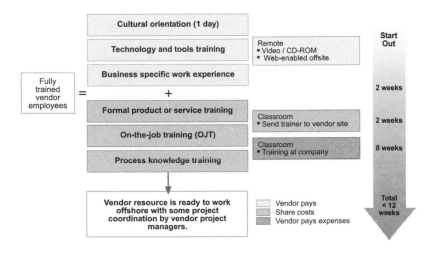

Figure 10.2: A Representative Knowledge Transfer (Initial Training) Plan

Train the Trainer

A huge part of transition management is getting the vendor team ready to take over the processes. Training entire teams of people is expensive and time-consuming, so often vendors will send a small transition team to your company's location to understand the process, map it, and get ready to transition it offshore.

The transition team then will return to the vendor's location and bring the rest of the staff up to speed through a train-the-trainer program. This type of program educates a few individuals in a formal classroom setting or one-on-one with experts, then leverages them to train other team members. This approach can contain training costs.

The other option many companies use is to send an expert from their company to the offshore location that is responsible for explaining how the process works and training the vendor staff.

The Importance of Training

Whether you are implementing a captive center or utilizing a third-party vendor, training employees is a critical component of transition management. Different levels of training will need to occur, such as:

- Process training: how to handle a customer or technical support call and what types of escalation procedures to follow.

- Technical training: how to use tools, applications, or proprietary software.

- Company specific training: how to achieve brand-specific messaging and consistent interactions with high-value customers.

- Responsibility based training: how to train people based on their role. For example, call center reps need training in listening and accent neutralization.

A formal training process is exceedingly important. If you are implementing a captive center, make sure to implement a training management process. If you are outsourcing to a third-party vendor, review what training process their employees have to go through before they start representing your company. Also have an idea of what training is critical for supporting your processes so that you can make sure the vendor's employees are receiving the proper training.

Accent neutralization or accent reduction classes may compose part of the training process if offshore employees interact directly with your customers either at call centers or through other means. As one of the "faces" of your company, it's critical that these employees possess outstanding language skills. While they may be able to read and write in the particular language with ease, they often lack confidence when it comes to speaking. Companies such as Atlanta Accent Management (AAM) have sprung up to train employees in correct pronunciation. Says Johanna Chapman, a speech language pathologist with AAM, "Just as a speaker of a second language was trained in grammar, semantics, and vocabulary, they can also be trained in the area of pronunciation, word stress, intonation, rhythm, and rate."[8]

Companies expect employees such as call center agents to complete accent neutralization training but often overlook the vendor's IT staff.

The COO of one BPO company we interviewed stated that one of the biggest challenges his company faced was communicating with the vendor's IT staff supporting his call center operation.

Documentation

Knowledge transfer also involves technology transfer and documentation. If the vendor will be assuming licenses or operations of client-owned applications or infrastructure, then all in-scope systems must be identified and documented. Maintenance agreements, hosting, and telecom may be part of the transition. Make sure the vendor has documented training manuals and escalation procedures for recurring problems.

Data Protection

With the FTC reporting more than 500,000 reports of identity theft in 2003 alone, information security and customer privacy are of paramount importance to consumers and the companies with which they do business. Make sure you understand the implications for sending data to a captive center or service provider. For example, if your company wanted to outsource testing for a software application, the first thing to do would be to avoid testing with real data and work as much as possible with dummy data — false names, social security numbers, addresses, etc.

Companies take a risk whenever they send sensitive customer data or proprietary information outside their walls. The obvious difference between sending data to a U.S.-based company and one located in another country is that the two nations will have different data security laws. To mitigate client concerns, some offshore providers, such as Infosys, sign all contracts under the legal jurisdiction of the country in which their clients are based.

Communication Management

Communication management describes the processes required to enable appropriate and timely generation, collection, and dissemination of outsourcing information between the internal and external teams.

In third-party outsourcing, communication refers to the day-to-day interactions between you and the vendor. You will need to develop a communication plan that addresses issues such as the time difference between different locations, the language and cultural differences, whether videoconferencing capabilities exist, and when to schedule status meetings. Such a plan should specify how often you communicate, what is on the agenda, who will initiate the discussion, how the meeting will take place, and who should be involved.

Richard Jones, CTO of mortgage lender Countrywide Financial, first gained experience working with offshore outsourcers before Y2K. The CTO thinks that poor operational communication is the most common reason work sent offshore fails to meet project specifications. "To make communications tight, you need to have an onshore element," he says.[9] Countrywide turned to Keane for its application development work. Keane's onshore presence allowed Countrywide IT managers to better communicate project requirements to the vendor.

Communication grows more complicated as more parties, countries, and time zones are involved. We recently worked on a project for a California company with a presence in India. Scheduling a status meeting and coordinating East Coast, West Coast, and Indian time zones added a layer of complexity to what should have been a straightforward task. When working offshore, simple problems become exacerbated. Having the processes and experienced management in place to address such issues quickly guarantees you greater success.

The Nuances of Communication

Differences in style and corporate culture don't preclude effective outsourcing relationships. Such differences, however, must be addressed, lest they lead to serious conflict.

The impact of your communications will vary among the members of your global team due to the subtly different cultural interpretations of the same words. Communication requires a new dimension when it comes to global outsourcing, and using straightforward words may not be enough. You must combine them with the proper context and a written example or a template, and validate the main points of your message by confirming them in a positive question-answer form. Tools such as videoconferencing or PowerPoint slides can aid communication.

One company figured out the value of direct communication while on a conference call with its vendor's technical reps. The company was explaining the IP address that needed to be entered from the vendor's location in India. The company kept stating the IP address as 125.79.10.89, but after the Indian vendor typed in the address, it always failed. The company finally e-mailed the IP address to the vendor, and it worked fine. The problem? The company was saying 1, 2, 5, dot, 7, 9, etc., but in India, dot means zero, so the vendor was entering 125079010089, and, of course, this IP address did not work. Simple communication can become complicated very quickly when offshoring.

Communication in Various Countries

When a project is behind schedule or off track, there are different ways to convey the same message.

- In America, employees are used to hearing "things are messed up here" or "we need to fix it" during the first few minutes of the project review. It's considered a normal way to raise project issues so resolutions can be found.

- When you are in England reviewing the same project, you would encounter the art of the "read between the lines" strategy. You might listen to the first 30 minutes of discussion thinking that the project was a little behind but it would bounce back. When it was time to go, however you would discover differently when the project leader quietly approached you and whispered that the project was indeed messed up.

- The Chinese way of communicating is different again. A Chinese professional would likely give only brief reasons for the delay and no detailed explanation as to why it happened. You might have to learn to live with that uncertainty until your services were delivered.

- In India, it is considered impolite to relay harsh realities until it's absolutely necessary. Many Indian teams will acknowledge good project progress until almost the eleventh hour, that is, when you specifically ask for the delivery of the product and find the reality is not what you thought, thus triggering the crisis management mode. However, you would also likely see the same very team rise to the occasion and finish it on time. Once again, it is not about delivery, but the different way cultures communicate the same news.

Creating an Effective Communication Plan

The key aspects of developing and executing a practical and effective communication plan are:

- Understanding communication styles,

- Setting up a regular call schedule,

- Utilizing tools for better communication,

- Taking advantage of instant messaging, e-mail, and chat sessions,

- Instituting periodic project reviews, and

- Providing face-to-face feedback, rewards, and recognition.

Understanding Communication Styles

You and the outsourcer share the responsibility for the success of the outsourced environment. Your company sets the tone for the relationship, and the outsourcer responds to it. Miscommunications can fuel a breakdown in trust that threatens the relationship. Say your company is detail-oriented and asks your new vendor a long list of questions, and the vendor reacts defensively. Your company thinks the vendor is unprepared, while the outsourcer feels attacked. The truth is that the individual communication styles are different. In this instance, a better understanding by each party of the other's approach could have defused the perceived conflict.

Setting up a Regular Call Schedule

How many times do you talk to your colleagues sitting in the next cube or office? Similarly, talking to your global team, even if they are sitting in China, Russia, or India, is necessary for outsourcing success. The message: Simple, short communications tremendously boost the productivity of your global team. Encourage it. It supplies team members with a way to demonstrate interest and ownership in the project's outcome and to recognize problems before they escalate.

Project managers and key leaders must talk to their counterparts on a daily basis — at least a few minutes at the start of the day and then again towards the end. Others should do so on an as needed basis. Further, a 30-minute weekly or biweekly conference call with a majority of the teams on either side will help drive synergy.

Utilizing Tools for Better Communication

Encourage the extensive use of e-collaboration tools and technologies among team members. Electronic communications cost little and are a great way to keep all team members informed. With the emergence of offshoring, they have become a valuable tool for connecting teams on different continents.

More communication, however, is not necessarily better. Simple, succinct communications repeated several times to drive home messages without ambiguity are best. Further, successful global businesses do not rely on frequent global travel. Catching a plane to solve a problem or review a project in person is not cost-effective. In fact, it breeds knowledge experts whose experience is difficult to teach, and it invariably leads to higher attrition rates with little knowledge transfer.

Of course, some key members of your transition team should visit to get to know the vendor's (or your captive center's) project leaders, key players, and infrastructure. Thereafter, you should think of those employees as sitting next to your own staff and as an extension of your team. One tip: It helps to put an organizational chart of the vendor team with photographs on the desks of your teammates so that they can better relate to them during conference calls or videoconferencing.

Taking Advantage of Instant Messaging, E-Mail, and Chat

Instant messenger service, e-mail, and organized chat sessions within and with your teams are enormously powerful ways to compensate for reduced face time. Flexibility with communication times and vehicles is required from both your company and the third-party vendor or captive center employees. Gregg Scoresby, CEO of Core3, a leading provider of BPO solutions, agrees, "I was not a huge instant-messenger fan prior to having an offshore experience, and, now I'm on instant messenger at five every morning and ten every night."[10]

Instituting Periodic Project Reviews

Building reporting templates for project reviews distributed at every milestone achieved is an efficient, cost-effective way to continuously communicate project status to all concerned. Use these opportunities to give recognition to lower-level team members who have contributed in achieving that particular milestone. This builds your talent pipeline and mitigates attrition. Effective communication is a very powerful strategy to retain talent at both ends.

Providing Feedback, Rewards, and Recognition

Holding kick-off meetings; communicating major feedback, corrective actions, or project changes; distributing rewards and recognition; and wrapping a project are all good instances to communicate face-to-face. Leverage these occasions to strengthen relationships and build talent in line with your company culture.

Third-party call monitoring vendors such as Witness Systems, HyperQuality, and J.Lodge can help overextended companies provide valuable feedback to call center agents. Seattle-based HyperQuality will evaluate recorded phone calls, as well as e-mails and Web-based chat sessions. Typically HyperQuality will listen to and score one call for each agent every eight hours and compile a daily report. Call monitors rate agents based on their efficiency, cross-selling abilities, conversational skills, and ability to placate upset customers. Agents who outperform may receive awards ranging from cash bonuses and time off to gift certificates and gear. For example, Alaska Airlines, a HyperQuality client, rewards agents who handle 12–14 calls hourly and consistently achieve excellent call evaluations with a $225 quarterly bonus.

Process Quality Management

Quality management describes the processes required for making sure that the vendor is fulfilling the business objectives in the contract for which the outsourcing project was undertaken. It consists of certifications and quality assurance and controls. The goal is to make sure that the services you're providing to customers, partners, and employees remain high-quality during transition.

Quality Controls

In January 2003, Delta Air Lines moved part of its reservations call center to service centers owned by Wipro Spectramind in India. Dedicated voice and data connections tie Wipro's Mumbai, India, operations to Delta's U.S. operations. Initially, the airline was concerned about quality since it could lose revenues if customers were frustrated with the offshore service provider, so it decided to monitor operator performance remotely.

To control quality that is thousands of miles away, Delta uses contact center management software from Witness Systems, which captures voice and screen data from individual agent workstations that can be viewed in real time or archived. "It's a tremendous coaching tool, and nobody knows when they're being monitored," says John Jacobi, a vice president in Delta's technology unit.[11]

Certifications

To guarantee quality, many companies are emphasizing certifications such as ISO 9001. Possessing these certifications puts many companies at ease because they know that the quality of the vendor's work is high. The vendors are expected to deploy consistent, high-quality processes for analysis, design, development, quality assurance, reporting, project monitoring, and management.

Many offshore vendors tout certification such as ISO 9001 or Six Sigma as a stamp of quality. These certifications can help companies ensure that the vendor has established proper documentation methods and processes. Many companies view outsourcing as a loss of control of processes. With certifications, you can actually increase control. Compliance with laws such as Sarbanes-Oxley makes sure vendors have proper document and control testing in place.

Among IT services providers, the Capability Maturity Model, or CMM, assessment published by the Software Engineering Institute at Carnegie Mellon has proven to be the quality management standard of choice for the software industry. A company that has been assessed at CMM Level 5, the highest maturity level for any software process, should consistently deliver and deploy high-quality software.

Eric Rongley, CEO of Bleum, one of China's leading offshore software developers, believes that the Indian service providers early to adopt CMM first fueled the movement of outsourcing software development to India. The certification bolstered the confidence of otherwise hesitant multinationals. Bleum was assessed at CMM Level 4 in 2004 and is working toward Level 5 status in 2005.[12] Companies evaluating vendors based on their certifications should note that The Software Engineering Institute ended CMM training in 2003 and intends to replace CMM with CMMI, or Capability Maturity Model Integration.

Executing a Transition Plan

Developing a transition plan should be one of the first tasks tackled during project execution. It starts with mapping the workflow of the complete project. Transitioning outsourcing work happens to be the first phase of that. Your global project manager and the transition team must live by this project plan. A project transition plan can be created with software tools like Microsoft Project.

Mapping Current Workflows

Develop an accurate 'as is' process workflow. Identify the touch points on the workflow path. Capture who does what at each stage of the workflow and list their key skills. Label potential hand-off points or milestones. Start the mapping process by looking at existing documents that may be part of your quality manual. Validate further by conducting surveys, interviews, and random process flow checks.

The objective is to develop an accurate map. If no prior documents exist, this may be a good opportunity to develop robust process designs. Take care to interview the most experienced people in your company. They are typically busy, so plan early so you get on their calendar. An accurate workflow becomes a powerful tool for effective outsourcing.

Visibility into the Project Plan

At the very minimum, the schedule for the project shows tasks, time lines, milestones, and resource allocation. In addition, you can develop a more granular document that captures daily time sheets, financials, equipment usage, review reports, follow-up action item flow, and other key project parameters.

You also need to make sure you give the new outsourcing relationship a chance. Transition management takes time. For example, it could take about eight to 12 months before a call center stabilizes and improvements start to show. Companies need to ask how long the transition management process will last so they can be prepared.

Gregg Scoresby, the Core3 CEO, says "Although this sounds obvious, the most risk, and the rockiest time in an outsourcing relationship, is in the transition period. The good news is that with careful planning and coordination between the vendor and your company, transition management can happen smoothly." Scoresby added, "And most issues that occur in the transition period can be addressed through more effective planning and more frequent, defined, structured communication, as well."[13]

Quality Reviews During Transition

Senior management will require an overview of the project's progress, so periodic high-level business program reviews and quality reviews must be held to align changes in the business environment to reprioritize resources and mitigate other risks. Don't let your teams get bogged down preparing for these presentations. Encourage them to use already available information contained in project management tools rather than prepare cosmetic PowerPoint pitches for these reviews. Well-designed templates for these reviews can save team members much time.

The service level agreements and incentive and penalty clauses often act as the guideposts in quality reviews. Incentives and penalties should motivate both you and the vendor. Both parties should collaborate in setting goals and working to reach them. Consistently communicating these goals to every level of both organizations is essential.

Trust and communication are needed to effectively align your company with the vendor's, and to provide meaningful incentives for the vendor to invest in value initiatives. You must work together to build effective bridges to facilitate escalation and resolution of issues.

Summary

Building a core transition team to manage the transfer of the people, processes, technology, and associated knowledge is the essential foundation for successful execution. Suitably selected and trained project managers with global mind-sets must lead each project. These project managers function as competitive differentiators for your company.

Transition management means building the right teams at both ends, conducting training to impart essential global project management skills, and completing the necessary knowledge transfer to effectively transition and manage the sourcing work.

Transition management also means building a strong bridge between the supplier and the receiver, even if it is for just one project. Tossing the outsourcing work over the fence does not work efficiently and generally leads to poor results.

You and the vendor must listen to one another, share results, and collaborate in the development of continuous improvement plans. Statistics only tell one part of the story; perception is the only reality. Manage perceptions, be responsive, and be seen as responsive.

1.	Select the best and brightest employees for your transition team
2.	Spend time developing the transition plan
3.	Make sure communication issues are well planned and defined
4.	Communicate with employees effectively
5.	Carefully review the SLA and define quality metrics to measure success
6.	Produce a workflow diagram of current end-to-end processes
7.	Define infrastructure requirements and possible transition issues
8.	Decide how knowledge transfer will occur (train-the-trainer, onsite, etc.)
9.	Set up regular communication meetings (define medium, frequency, who should be on the call, etc.)
10.	Define reporting templates and frequency

Table 10.1: Summarizing the Top Ten Critical Issues in Transition Management

Chapter Eleven

Governance and Global Program Management

Governance refers to the ongoing decisions organizations make after signing the deal and managing the transition. These operational decisions help companies better manage the provider on a daily basis. This chapter illustrates the governance framework (global project management, relationship management, and communication management) needed to lower the risk of outsourcing. The stakes are high with global outsourcing, so setting up the right governance structures is taking on a sense of urgency.

What Is Outsourcing Governance?

Many global outsourcing engagements fail to deliver on promises of transformation and cost benefits. Research indicates that one-third to one-half of companies that outsource fail to achieve the benefits they expect. Are such failures inevitable? The answer is no — if organizations pay more attention to outsourcing governance.

Governance encapsulates the oversight and management of the entire outsourcing relationship. Although governance is viewed as the less glamorous, "behind the scenes" part of outsourcing, it can make or break a project. Often the reality of managing projects and people that aren't right outside your office door is not understood until it is upon you.

A successful relationship requires that both your company and the vendor recognize and accept specific roles. In outsourcing, the vendor's role is to deliver efficiency — skills, people, processes, measurement, and accountability. Your responsibility is effectiveness — understanding and communicating the correct actions for the organization, which requires business knowledge, awareness of corporate culture, relationship management, and risk mitigation.

Moving to a global outsourcing model requires that your company becomes a facilitator, negotiator, and program manager, while the vendor becomes the process expert and implementer. These roles allow both parties to focus on their core competencies.

Levels of Governance

Typically when best-practice companies begin an outsourcing engagement, they set up a PMO (program management office) that controls all aspects of the project— communications, risk management, and financials. This PMO, which has decision-making authority, interacts with the PMO on the vendor's side.

Within the PMO, you have to establish the three levels of a governance relationship (see Table 11.1):

1. The strategic level, often the executive steering committee, aligns the processes, projects, and goals with business requirements. It also directs the client and vendor's relationship.

2. In complex organizations, you have program offices that are tasked with making tactical decisions on program costs, project priorities, project milestones, expected ROI, and risk management.

3. The operational level, often called the project office, handles the day-to-day management of offshore projects to ensure that processes are running smoothly. The employees on this level handle the change process and issue resolution, as well as the actual day-to-day contractual relationship.

Reporting needs to occur at all levels with a combined scorecard that can be reviewed at the executive and operational manager levels so that any red flags can be resolved quickly. For both the strategic and operational levels, you will need to clearly define the roles and responsibilities for each team member and then identify the competencies for each person.

Steering Committee	Program Office	Project Office
▪ Define overall strategy ▪ Establish IT, business, HR, legal, audit, and compliance support ▪ Provide necessary funding ▪ Charter program management office ▪ Report to board	▪ Vendor evaluation ▪ Relationship management ▪ Process selection ▪ Best practices benchmarking ▪ Staff retraining and redeployment plan ▪ Communications ▪ Performance reporting	▪ Weekly check-ins ▪ Quarterly operations review ▪ Biyearly site visits ▪ SLA monitoring ▪ Document internal processes for further improvements

Table 11.1: Three Levels of Governance

Case Study: Governance in the Real World

Let's look at the governance structure established by a large multinational bank (client) and a global HR service provider.

In this example, the contract was set up so that governance was carried out through committees and teams with representatives from each firm. The contract stipulated the formation of only two committees, instead of the three we outlined earlier.

- Executive steering committee

- Operations management team

Executive Steering Committee

This committee was created to generally oversee the performance of each party's obligations under the master services agreement (MSA). It was not involved in the day-to-day management of the agreement or the services specified in the statement of work (SOW).

The executive steering committee consisted of the account managers and two other individuals selected by each party. The group met a minimum of once a month or more if necessary.

The responsibilities of the executive steering committee included:

- Reviewing and authorizing high-level technical, financial, and resource plans.

- Evaluating reports and recommendations approved by the operations management team.

- Annually assessing recommendations and providing authorization for: 1) service levels for the previous 12 months; 2) adjustment of service levels; 3) changes in pricing; 4) client satisfaction surveys and service level results; 5) implementation of the MSA and the achievement of key milestones and deliverables; and 6) change orders.

- Reviewing the relationship issues arising out of the MSA.

- Resolving disputes and concerns regarding replacement of key personnel.

- Providing guidance to the operations management team for performance improvement and submitting recommendations on issues affecting the relationships between the parties.

Operations Management Team

This team handled day-to-day management and was headed by a client account manager. It comprised service delivery managers and other individuals selected by each party. The responsibilities and authority of the operations management team spanned:

- Supervising the overall performance of the parties' respective roles and responsibilities under the agreement.

- Reviewing the implementation progress of the agreement, with an emphasis on the achievement of key milestones and deliverables.

- Implementing risk management and providing an analysis for review by the executive steering committee.

- Assessing the service delivery and transition management activities and the associated contract management reports supplied by the vendor teams.

- Approving changes to reports.

- Annually evaluating and making recommendations to the executive steering committee on the following items: KPIs and service levels based on previous 12 months; proposed changes to KPIs and service levels; client satisfaction surveys; and service adjustments.

- Studying the executive steering committee's suggestions related to the services or agreement and initiating appropriate actions.

- Implementing technical, financial and resource plans.

- Giving advice to the service delivery teams on performance improvement and making recommendations directly to the client and the service provider.

Critical Roles in Both Committees

The client's account manager, the client's service delivery manager, the vendor's account manager, and the vendor's delivery manager were the principal players governing the global outsourcing relationship.

The Client's Account Manager

This manager directed the service provider relationship. Specific responsibilities included:

- Developing and maintaining high-level relationships with the vendor.

- Acting as the principal point of contact for the service provider.

- Attending review meetings as required by the agreement.

- Proposing and creating new prospective services, in conjunction with the service provider.

- Managing change control and signing change orders.

- Resolving disputes between the client and the service provider.

- Monitoring customer satisfaction and identifying opportunities for service improvements.

- Overseeing the transition plan.

The Client's Service Delivery Manager

This manager handled the day-to-day management of service delivery and guaranteed the fulfillment of client responsibilities. Specific assignments entailed:

- Planning, allocating, and monitoring work undertaken.

- Attending review meetings required by the agreement.

- Providing the reports stipulated in the agreement.

- Ensuring that appropriate operational and quality control procedures were in use.

- Managing and resolving glitches and client complaints relating to operational activities.

The Service Provider's Account Manager

This individual managed the client account. Specific tasks included:

- Developing and maintaining high-level relationships with the client.

- Attending the required review meetings.

- Proposing and developing new prospective services, in conjunction with the client.

- Supervising the change control on behalf of the service provider and signing change orders.

- Handling disputes between the client and the service provider.

- Working closely with the client account manager to ensure service quality in conformance with the agreement.

- Monitoring customer satisfaction and identifying opportunities for development or improvement to the services.

- Overseeing the transition plan.

The Service Provider's Delivery Manager

This employee was charged with seeing that the day-to-day operational delivery of services met the service levels. Specific responsibilities encompassed:

- Planning and monitoring work undertaken in relation to the services.

- Attending the required review meetings.

- Receiving reports discussed in the agreement.

- Ensuring that appropriate operational and quality control procedures were in use.

- Coping with client complaints related to the operational activities of the service provider.

Elements of Governance

This discussion of one actual outsourcing engagement's governance structure was meant to illustrate the management and administrative resources necessary to coordinate onsite and offshore resources. These firms worked hard to avoid the common trap of governance: developing overly complex structures that create redundant roles and responsibilities.

As you can see from the responsibilities stated for the account and delivery managers, the key activities fell into four major areas: day-to-day project management, relationship management, change management, and operational risk management. Let's look at each in more detail.

Operational Project Management

Often in initial planning, many executives underestimate the cost of project management, and some do not even consider it in their initial cost-benefit ROI models. Our experience tells us that when you outsource a major business process, you should allot between 5% and 15% of your budget for managing that process. If the process is strategic or transformational in nature, your global outsourcing project management costs could rise to 20%.

Why Is Project Management So Difficult?

Building a global outsourcing partnership requires effort and delicate handling by management. Any business model that distributes work across multiple locations involves many hand-offs and requires close coordination to manage service levels. It's difficult enough managing a project onsite; that difficulty is amplified when a project spans countries with different time zones, work cultures, and communication styles.

In outsourcing, even if the vendor handles daily project management, client account managers still have to communicate with, collaborate with, and monitor the vendor. The distance between the client and the vendor puts a greater importance on day-to-day project management to ensure deadlines are being met and reporting is timely and accurate. Structured communication processes will decrease risk and increase efficiency, as Chapter 10 discussed.

Client account and delivery managers must allow for cultural and time differences even with simple tasks, such as sending e-mail or following up. Let's say it is 6:30 p.m. PST on a Monday and you are in San Francisco, while your vendor is in Bangalore, India. Your vendor says that she will get back to you tomorrow. If it is 6:30 p.m. PST, then tomorrow may be Tuesday for you, but in Bangalore, it was 8:00 a.m. on Tuesday, so tomorrow means Wednesday. Because of the potential for misunderstandings, onshore project managers need to prepare their own staff for working with offshore vendors.

The secret to successful project execution is to first understand the building blocks involved and then submit each of them to a level of rigor that your short-term and long-term sourcing goals justify. Since the level of severity also depends on the size and nature of each project, you should break down the outsourcing plan into suitably sized projects. Second, it is important to understand the elements of global project management (GPM) needed to manage each phase.

Essential Elements of Global Project Management

Good outsourcing execution is tightly coupled to your organization's global project management (GPM) skills. There is more to GPM than the well-known area of traditional project management (PM) discussed by universities, companies that make project management software, or institutions like PMI or SEI.[1]

This chapter discusses the different aspects of GPM essential for outsourcing. GPM is increasingly being recognized as a requisite skill for competing in the global marketplace and preventing delivery and schedule slippages. GPM also involves issues pertaining to local sourcing that require a good grasp of local and state infrastructure, language issues, rules, and regulations.

Some companies have started formal training in GPM already. Do your project managers have what it takes to become global project managers? What differentiates successful global project managers from successful local ones? What additional skills are needed? It is important that you include GPM upfront in your outsourcing plan and that it evolves with maturity and volume.

The critical steps of developing a GPM capability are:

- Selecting project leaders with a global mind-set.

- Understanding GPM skills — what makes it succeed or fail.

- Implementing a global project management training program.

Select Project Managers with a Global Mind-set

More often than not, companies fail when they execute outsourcing strategies because they pick the wrong project managers. New initiatives that are strategically tied to company growth necessitate top talent with a global growth mind-set.

How do best-practice firms select such project leaders? Initially, they take a practical approach that isn't overly dependent on the HR department. With experience, they gradually develop a mature HR process for selecting project leaders. Simply relying on HR from day one is not likely to work.

Instead of having HR select managers for you, ask for volunteers from your own team first, interview them (even if they already work for you), and identify the individuals whose integrity is beyond a doubt, breathe company values, and have a demonstrated track record. Even though HR will be an integral part of the selection process, it's your job as a business leader to pick the project leaders.

The employees chosen must be able to translate the company's strategic growth or cost management vision. To assess their fit with GPM, ask them why they are interested in this role. Selecting from the pool of employees who were former nationals of the vendor country can be a good starting point. These employees may be naturalized U.S. citizens who have absorbed the company culture and values and would like to return to their native country for some reason.

Dell, American Express, P&G, and Intel increasingly are making a GPM assignment a part of the career growth process. They realize that the new generation of global project leaders will become their most important talent pipeline in a globally competitive marketplace.

Understanding Global Project Management Skills

What will make global project managers succeed or fail? For one, their ability to apply good project management techniques in a different region, while abiding by the local rules and not compromising their company. Table 11.2 lists the 10 responsibilities of strong global project managers.

Developing a Global Project Management Program

The need for a GPM program depends upon the number of projects, the size of your organization, and the critical mass of talent that you may require going forward. Cost, needs, and strategy must strike a balance here. You do have to train your global project managers, but you do not have to invest in a full-blown training program if there will just be one or two managers for the next few years.

The simplest training program may entail having the selected GPM candidates obtain traditional PMI certification and then conducting an internal course specific to your outsourcing needs. The employees should possess some knowledge of country-specific export-import rules, labor laws, taxation, safety and compliance, the geopolitical environment, cultural awareness, and accent familiarization as applicable. Supplementary training needs can be better understood by visiting vendor locations and leveraging help from companies specializing in teaching employees about global culture.

Examine Your Contract	Know your contract fully and manage the project based on the service levels and definitions specified in the MSA.
Manage Contract Scope	Specifically define services as in-scope or out-of-scope. Scope creep will hurt project delivery and costs, as well as your credibility as a GPM.
Own the Project	Outsourcing does not mean giving away all ownership. Even if the vendor is responsible for delivery, a lack of ownership at your company will negatively affect the project.
Manage the Relationship	Act hands-on and own the relationship for successful transition and execution.
Monitor Financials	Monitor costs for in-scope and out-of-scope services. Stay on top of your budget.
Review Reports	Review all reports regularly as they will alert you if problems with the project occur.
Manage Resources	Maintain a detailed human resources plan so you know where your costs lie.
Monitor the Execution Plan	Check your execution plan to ensure it contains time lines, deliverables, roles, responsibilities, and performance details.
Check Time Lines	Monitor the execution plan and make sure the project remains on schedule.
Develop an Exit Strategy	Make sure to have an exit strategy and termination agreement.

Table 11.2: The Ten Key Responsibilities of a Global Project Manager

Oppositely, you may develop your own full-fledged training program if your company is large enough. As an alternate, formal programs covering the entire range of GPM training are cropping up to meet the growing market demand. A formal program may take weeks to complete, so it has to be tied to career growth and the planning process.

Building a Governance Team — The Bridge

A good governance team is not one-sided. It is like the two pillars of a suspension bridge that hold up the structure and act as the gatekeepers for the flow of information, products, and deliveries during the project lifecycle. Team members must talk to each other just as if they were sitting in adjacent cubes, except that the cubes are now separated by geographical distance. Figure 11.1 illustrates this point.

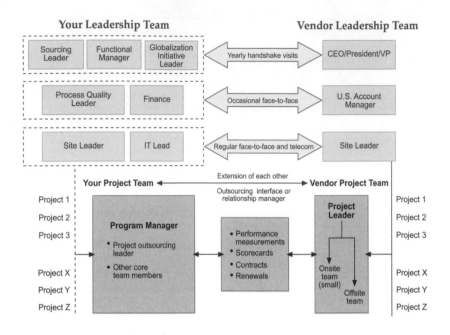

Figure 11.1: Governance Team Structure

Relationship Management

What is relationship management? Relationship management is building a true partnership between the vendor and outsourcer through communication. It is built on confidence and trust, which sustain it through negotiations and become the foundation for the successful delivery of services.

New Skills Needed — From Doing to Steering

Transitioning from doing to managing is often more difficult than it appears. There is almost always a skill change required at the management level. Instead of running operations, the role suddenly transitions to manage the outsourcer using effective communication skills and business process knowledge.

Why are new skills required? The problem is that pure technical or process expertise doesn't necessarily translate into business process management knowledge. The person running your in-house call center may not be the best person to manage your offshore call center. This misalignment is a cause of many outsourcing problems. It is especially a problem in deals that aim to achieve strategic value quickly. If your employees are unprepared to tackle the new relationship management challenges that outsourcing requires, the project risk increases exponentially.

Steering the relationship will require relinquishing the day-to-day operations and focusing instead on managing the outsourcing relationship. It may require learning new skills, especially for those employees that were in operational roles. The time and the cost required for this training should be addressed in the outsourcing planning process.

New Processes Needed

A global outsourcing project may require new organizational processes to manage the ongoing relationship between team members. Relationship management is necessary to compensate for the loss of direct interaction between stakeholders, managers, and team members.

Without these interactions, the project manager must allocate dedicated resources to maintain appropriate levels of communication and coordination. Regular formal and informal communication in the form of teleconferences, videoconferences, and e-mail exchanges is essential for success. Don't underestimate the difficulties of remote management and time differences.

Sony Electronics initially struggled to get offshore call center employees to understand the service demands of U.S. customers. Sony outsourced call center functions to India and the Philippines. Maureen Read, vice president and general manager of Sony's customer service center, says she regularly visits the Indian call center and spends a lot of time explaining Sony's customer service philosophy. "I learned early on that you cannot expect an Indian company to teach their Indian employees how to [understand] Americans," she says. Read says that with customer service in particular, people from your company have to provide "an ongoing influx of American viewpoints."[2]

In long-term, complex engagements, both parties should have relationship managers. These individuals ensure that issues are resolved appropriately. Your relationship manager should have liaison skills, organizational knowledge, business case expertise, analytical skills, and a good reputation. They should also be senior enough to make decisions within defined boundaries without waiting for approval.

Change Management

Change management is a vital activity for every project office and manager. The general rule of thumb says that competition or shifting consumer preferences render a significant amount of process design obsolete every five years. Change management works to ensure that standardized procedures are used for efficient, prompt handling of all changes — technology, process, and contracts.

Operational Changes

Managing the change process safeguards against companies and vendors disagreeing over what the vendor is providing. Once operations begin, change management needs to monitor change orders and work orders. Without this strict process, confusion and redundancy of work may occur.

Technology driven changes tend to occur mid-contract. The rapid pace of technology change adds to the challenge of global outsourcing and requires an equally swift ability to adapt.

Given the likelihood of technology changes, one area that will have to be amended is the scope of the contract. You need to define in your contract how changes in service scope or content will happen. You will also need to think about the process for changing the SLAs and contract.

How can you modify the agreement to be more responsive to your needs? What threshold operating levels should trigger the change process? What must be done to change the agreement? What are the limitations on change posed, for example, by the economics, term, or technology requirements of the outsourcing relationship?

Business is unpredictable, which is why you and the vendor need to establish an efficient process for handling project adjustments. Unisys, the global IT services company, had provided help desk support for a large pharmaceutical company for approximately two years when the pharmaceutical company suddenly asked Unisys to dramatically ramp up its coverage within a month's time. Unisys went from providing support services from 6 a.m. to 6 p.m. Monday through Friday to offering full-scale 24x7x365 support. According to Unisys, it was able to accommodate the request by "making the best possible use of resources."[3]

Striving to reach low-cost milestones also tends to drive contract and SLA changes. According to Sanjay Kumar, CEO of vCustomer, "Once companies reach a certain threshold in terms of cost savings, they should be shifting their focus to quality and process improvement. Companies should be focusing their efforts on telling vendors to deliver a higher level both in quality as well as service delivery metrics. Strategically, companies should be building in an incentive for the vendors who do deliver on the quality and process improvements."[4]

Many vendors are attempting to differentiate themselves by emphasizing their change management processes. Consider the case of Burlington Northern Santa Fe Railway (BNSF), which offshored some software development to Infosys in Bangalore, India. According to Jeff Campbell, vice president of technology services and CIO at BNSF, "Communication and collaboration are key to success. Infosys was world-class in change control and methods of delivery. They have a program office at our headquarters. They have full-time people here that manage the flow through methodology and communications."[5] Can you say the same about your vendor?

Plan for change early. Change management strategies often evolve as an afterthought after a project hits potholes. Many outsourcing deals are completed at breakneck speed by management hoping to achieve immediate short-term benefits. We call this the "let's get it out the door and then we will worry about change management later" approach to outsourcing.

Leading Change — The People Dimension

Change management supports outsourcing initiatives through leadership and communication. Note that change management, as defined here, is leadership change management and is different than the change process that accompanies the actual operations.

How does leadership-driven change work? The effort should begin before any vendor is involved. There must be a communication strategy to ensure employees, especially those who may be at risk of losing their job, understand the outsourcing reasons and feel they will be treated fairly. This is not easy. If your organization does not have the professional staff to support this effort, outside resources may be necessary.

The hard part is keeping different constituencies happy, given their separate interests and needs. The change management process must account for every group. The internal groups include employees, HR leadership, and senior and line management. External groups could encompass financial analysts, shareholders, and unions/works councils. The internal program should work in tandem with the provider's program to ensure clarity and consistency of message.

Bidirectional, ongoing dialog is important to the success of any global outsourcing project. It is through dialog that changes to business processes can be quickly identified as beneficial or detrimental to the other business processes and the ultimate success of the company.

Understanding and communicating the impacts of even the smallest process changes can help companies achieve substantial benefits rapidly. Conversely, non- or miscommunication of small changes can have detrimental, rippling effects within the company.

Risk Management

Companies should implement a comprehensive risk management process to govern their outsourcing relationships. The process should include ongoing risk and threat assessment, intellectual property (IP) handling, vendor financial and operational risk, and service monitoring. Outsourced relationships should be subject to the same risk management, security, privacy, and other policies that would be expected if the company were conducting the activities in-house.

Risk and Business Threat Assessment

Outsourced services can increase operational risks. Operational risk may be caused by fraud, error, or the inability to manage customer information. It may affect your company's reputation, security, or have legal implications.

Company risk. Errors in processes that directly affect customers can significantly harm the reputation of your company. For example, a company outsourced its call center to a Canadian vendor. The company ran a special promotion and when customers ran to the phone to place orders, the call center reps were unaware of the product and could not sell it. Not only did the company lose money, but the reputation of the company was damaged in the eyes of their customers.

Security risk. In outsourcing, inadequate management experience can lead to a lack of understanding key risks. In August 2004, Jolly Technologies halted all activities at its Indian R&D center after an employee e-mailed herself copies of source code using an online Yahoo account. The company, which produces labeling and card software for the printing industry, reported that portions of the source code and confidential design documents relating to one of its key products had been stolen by the recently hired software engineer. The center had only been running for three months. Jolly reported that the engineer had used her Yahoo e-mail account, which now allows 100MB of free storage space, to upload and ship the copied files out of the research facility.[6]

Legal risk. Outsourced activities that fail to comply with regulatory requirements can result in legal problems. In the case of HIPAA, the Healthcare Insurance Portability and Accountability Act, unauthorized disclosure of confidential patient information can expose healthcare organizations to civil or criminal penalties or litigation. A single violation can result in a civil penalty of $100, while multiple violations can lead to fines of as much as $25,000. If the provider is thought to have wrongfully disclosed consumer health information, the consequences of their actions increase: the fines may rise to $250,000 and be accompanied by a sentence of up to ten years in prison. Given the compliance risk, Kaiser Permanente covered its bases when it sent programming work to India by performing a great deal of due diligence upfront and by not sending any data overseas.[7]

Intellectual property (IP) protection is rapidly becoming the biggest risk facing global outsourcing, especially in the IT industry. The majority of U.S.-based software companies require their employees to sign an employment agreement that prohibits them from carrying or transferring in any way the company's source code out of a development facility. In

India and China, although the vendors or captive centers may require employees to sign similar agreements, the sluggish Indian and Chinese legal systems and the absence of IP laws make it difficult to enforce such agreements.

The Magnitude of the Risk

The magnitude of risk associated with outsourcing is comprised of the process outsourced, the location, and the vendor, as well as the service provider's people, processes, and technology. Your company should consider the factors that follow when evaluating the quantity of risk in your outsourcing decision.

- Risks pertaining to the process outsourced: sensitivity of data accessed by the vendor; volume of transactions; and criticality to company's business.

- Risks pertaining to the vendor: financial stability; business continuity; experience with the process outsourced; reliance on subcontractors; and country factors such as IP laws and geopolitical stability.

- Risks pertaining to the service provider's people, processes, and technology used: management and other employee attrition; scalability to accommodate growth; redundancy and reliability of communication lines and infrastructure; and security.

Risk Management Assessment and Adjustment

Over the course of a contract, things change. Risk management describes the processes concerned with identifying, analyzing, and responding to outsourcing partnership risks. It consists of ongoing risk assessment, impact analysis, and risk mitigation mechanisms. You should use detailed scenarios to attempt to understand new or potential risks and develop procedures and contingencies to mitigate them.

Why is this necessary? The goal for companies today is to achieve a state of business continuity in which critical business processes are always functioning and mission-critical services are always available. In light of geopolitical instability, business continuity is becoming an important subject for companies that are offshoring.

To attain and sustain business continuity, companies must engineer availability, security, and reliability into every process. Companies must examine existing processes with offshore exposure to determine the criticality of such processes and the completeness of business continuity plans.

Companies should create scenarios that focus on contingencies for situations in which political, social, or military emergencies develop. The probability of such an event occurring is low, but the potential impact can be significant. Many CTOs are asking vendors about their disaster recovery and backup plans.

There are some standard issues that should be addressed such as business continuity, data recovery, and data security, as well as some things unique to overseas work such as data privacy and intellectual property rights. Insurance coverage may need to go beyond standard liability to insure potential disruptions.

Security

Security is the most often cited concern among companies that are considering global outsourcing. Problems with security — a breach that fosters customer distrust or a catastrophic event that affects data, processes, and customers — can cost companies money and credibility.

As identify theft and corporate fraud become more prevalent in the United States, companies have to wonder if offshore or nearshore outsourcing is truly more risky. Take the example that happened in 2005 to 145,000 U.S. consumers who had their data stolen from ChoicePoint. Atlanta-based ChoicePoint maintains and sells background files on almost every U.S. citizen. Criminals tricked the company by posing as legitimate businesses to gain access to databases that contained information including names, addresses, social security numbers, and credit reports. A Nigerian man living in California was found guilty of one count of unlawful use of personal data in February 2005 and sentenced to 16 months in state prison.

This example reiterates that security should be a concern for every company — insourced, outsourced, onshore, nearshore, or offshore. Often times though, offshore vendors must make an extra effort to prove their security measures. When discussing security with vendors, ask about three aspects: physical, training, and legal.

Physical. Look at the building security and who has access to come into the facility and when. Is there key card access to enter the building, their suite, or even specific offices? What about data security? Are there controls in place that limit who has access to what data? One company we spoke to only allows the project manager access to all of the files. The remaining team members have access only to the files they need.

What about printing information? Are there printers all over the office or in one specific location? Bleum, a leading China-based provider of software outsourcing services, has a secure printer room with no wastebaskets and only shredders to dispose of the printouts when employees are done with them. The room only has yellow paper in it, so it's clear when customer data has been printed and obvious if an employee is walking around with customer data outside the printer room. The company's secure server rooms also require fingerprint access.

Training. It is critical that employees understand the importance of information security. Make sure the vendor has training procedures in place that emphasize security.

Legal. Many U.S. companies ask workers to fill out employment contracts and undergo background checks before they are hired. Outsourcing vendors should have these same policies in place.

As Eric Rongley, the CEO of Bleum, says, "It does not matter where the center is located, it is the security procedures you have in place. Trust the company, not the country."

Outsourcing Governance Maturity Models

Governance models change as your outsourcing maturity increases. How do you go from starting your first outsourcing project to becoming a world-class organization that leverages global resources effectively? Essentially, the governance models reflect the structure of your team, and the rules in managing the ever-changing relationship between you and your vendors' people, process, and tools. What is the right governance model for you at any given time?

One way to handle a fluid issue is to deconstruct it — break down the ever-changing outsourcing relationship into easily identifiable and manageable steps, and then scale your organization to manage that step accordingly.

Following are five stages of the outsourcing maturity curve that need to be handled by somewhat different operational governance models.

- Basic vendor relationship management.

- Project-specific (labor arbitrage driven) relationship management.

- Consolidated business processes relationship management.

- Managing global synergy — managing across regions, products, and processes.

- Strategic councils — managing relations across businesses.

Figure 11.2 shows the strategic relationship between the maturity curve and the governance models.

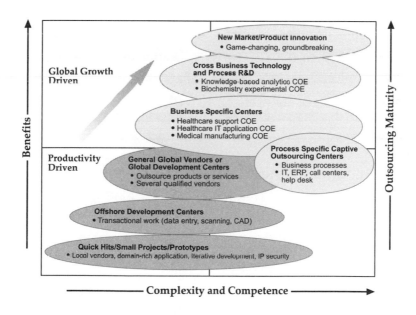

Figure 11.2: Maturity Stages of Outsourcing and Governance Models

Basic Vendor Relationship Management

The responsibility of establishing the vendor relationship must lie with your company's sourcing team. Your sourcing leader must lead — working with your legal, finance, technology, IT, and HR teams — the development of the process of identifying suitable vendors, qualifying them as an approved source of supply at a local or global level, and signing a master services agreement (MSA) that covers the basic framework of a working relationship over a mutually agreed-upon period of time.

MSAs, described in Chapter 9, includes, among other things: a high-level organizational commitment, accountability guidelines, compliance framework, security and privacy of data, legal process guidelines, safety issues, resource attrition, poaching guidelines, quality standards, and delivery agreement goals.

Your sourcing leader and the MSA should be your starting point for any outsourcing activity. If you have not established either, then you should pull someone from your team on a special assignment or hire a consultant to lay this foundation. All other agreements, such as the SLA or specific project contracts, logically flow from the MSA.

Operationally, depending upon the size and maturity of your company's outsourcing initiative, a team can then be put in place to manage the respective relationship. For example, if there is only one project in your company that requires an external vendor, then the respective project manager could be responsible for vendor relationship management and project execution.

Project Specific Relationship Management

The project manager must ensure that the relationship abides by the specific SLA or project contract and stays within the overall bounds of the MSA. Regular communications between your company and the vendor, periodic feedback, acceptable performance metrics, timely payments, and other efforts to drive customer satisfaction are the building blocks for an effective governance model. Figure 11.3 depicts the organizational structure for project specific relationship management.

The best-practice vendors understand that exceeding customer expectations stated in the SLA is in their economic best interest. They make a concentrated effort to understand the customer expectations correctly upfront.

On your end, there are a few simple actions you can complete to make sure the project is on track, adjusting them for specific domain and project circumstances.

- Make it personal. Gather expectations during face-to-face kick-off meetings and validate them during mid-project reviews.

- Conduct simple surveys with customers as a pulse check. It should not take more than three minutes. Look into bad feedback. Do not try to ignore feedback by rationalizing it statistically. It is a symptom of a problem you should understand and fix.

- Set up an outside-in customer expectation scorecard that asks what customers want (not recommended for a short-term project of less than six months).

- Gather feedback at the end of the project (minimize surprises).

- Respond to change requests, compensating for any errors or oversight. No excuses.

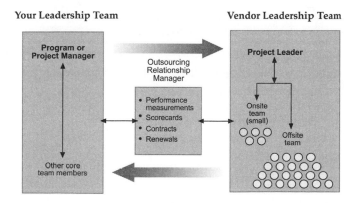

Figure 11.3: Project Specific Relationship Management

Consolidated BPO Relationship Management

Consolidated BPO relationship management builds on project specific relationship management. Here, several projects may exist, but they largely pertain to one business process or a set of processes being executed by one vendor or, in some cases, multiple vendors to either mitigate risk or cover different regions more effectively.

The building blocks for the governance model are the same as those of project specific relationship management, but with two managers staffed on the initiative as opposed to one. Figure 11.4 shows the governance model for this multiproject setting.

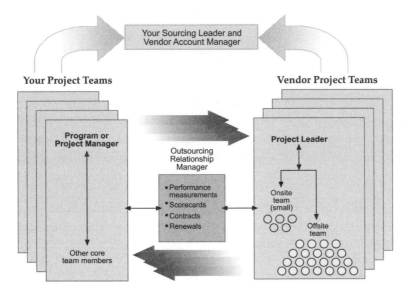

Figure 11.4: Consolidated BPO Relationship Management

Managing Global Synergy

In large-scale outsourcing engagements, global synergy between two large firms becomes critical. One question you will need to answer is if your outsourcing relationships can survive cultural incompatibility. Let's say your company culture is buttoned-down and conservative, while the outsourcer's style leans toward t-shirts and ping-pong matches during meeting breaks or vice versa. Will you be able to work well together?

Issues of work style can and should be overcome if compelling reasons exist for two firms to work together. That said, these differences should be recognized, addressed, and managed. Don't dismiss them as trivial.

Roles and Responsibilities of Strategic Councils

The movement towards multivendor relationship management across outsourced services is growing. Managing these relationships affects the entire organization. Having qualified people on both your side and the vendor's side is critical. Making sure everyone understands what their responsibilities are is another important step in governance.

At the strategic level, your organization must hire or develop account executives that have a laser-sharp focus on ongoing projects. They monitor service levels on a monthly basis and resolve relationship issues. The vendors, similarly, must designate executives responsible for strategy and setting the direction of the relationship.

At the tactical level, you need controller or operational managers that are responsible for the delivery of services. An equivalent tactical role exists for the vendor side. This employee is responsible for the process and focuses on day-to-day operations.

As outsourcing migrates from "handle my mess for less" to business transformation, changes in organizational roles and responsibilities are inevitable.

Summary

Governance centers on companies spending the time to manage vendor relationships. Effective governance is a function of two things: 1) the maturity of your outsourcing initiative and 2) the internal and external mix of people, process, and tools.

If your company harbors an "outsource and forget it" mind-set, success will likely elude you. You have to ensure the vendor is managing processes in a manner consistent with the direction of your firm — that they act as an extension of your company. Although outsourcing does free up time to focus on other pressing issues, you still need to be involved in the day-to-day governance process.

The seven principles listed in Table 11.3 provide a framework for effective governance.

Relationship Management	Actively build the outsourcing relationship.
Hands-on Management	Manage project resources and activities while anticipating risks.
Open Communication	Enable formal and informal communication and encourage information flow between all project team members.
Integrated Governance	Designate governance a vital and active part of the outsourcing project.
Risk Management	Identify and manage risks through all phases of the project.
Monitoring	Define and design reporting: meeting agendas, meeting schedules, performance reports, dashboard reports, and reporting schedules.
Teamwork	Utilize the talents, skills, and knowledge of each team member.

Table 11.3: Seven Principles of Effective Governance

Chapter Twelve

Performance Monitoring and Improvement

Imagine the following scenario: You have multiple business process outsourcing projects under a variety of business models and a diverse complexity of contracts and service level agreements governed by teams residing in several locations. How do your senior managers establish a performance monitoring and measurement framework that will help them supervise these disparate projects? What are the elements of this framework? This chapter discusses how your company can apply Six Sigma to monitoring and improving the performance of outsourcing initiatives.

Outsourcing Performance Management

In 2001, General Motors (GM), seeking greater cost reductions and control, entered into a ten-year agreement with Affiliated Computer Services (ACS) to outsource some of its F&A functions for North America and Europe. ACS services GM from centers in Arizona, Jamaica, and Spain. In order to ensure the quality of ACS's work, GM monitors the service level agreements, desk procedures, internal and external audits, onsite quality assurance teams, segregation of duties, and delegation of authority.

Performance monitoring and measurement is regarded as a core but often overlooked part of global outsourcing. With organizations outsourcing different aspects of their operations, vendors participating in sourcing deals, users and governance teams residing in separate locations, and activities occurring 24x7, it's a challenge to coordinate interactions, manage performance, monitor contract terms, and track financial metrics. A disciplined, continuous improvement program is a "need to have" for outsourcing success.

What Is Performance Management?

Performance management entails identifying metrics that lead to real improvements. Results-oriented global outsourcing requires a focused, collaborative approach to performance monitoring that holds each team accountable for meeting its commitments. A carefully architected process that establishes shared goals, defines measurements, and aligns incentive programs provides the overarching framework for a successful approach to outsourcing.

Imagine that you are explaining some problems with your outsourcing project to your CIO or CEO. Do you want to A) look hapless with no supporting data, or B) have sufficient metrics on hand that can identify the problem's source, so you know what to fix and can articulate a plan? The answer is B.

With implementation under way, your attention must turn to monitoring performance and ensuring accountability for results. Monitoring involves measuring, communicating, and being accountable. Monitoring means tracking, documenting, and reporting information to the right people in order to support the decision-making process.

Some of the key questions your company has to answer include the following:

- What is important to measure? Establish performance benchmarks and key performance indicators (KPIs) that clearly align with your company's outsourcing strategy and specific objectives — cost reduction, time to market, process variation, or customer satisfaction.

- What is important for your customers? Determine the baseline requirements, establish performance metrics, and cost measurements.

- How can you do better? Identify, design, and implement improvement opportunities through process redesign or re-engineering or team morale or productivity enhancers.

- What is the penalty for failing to meet goals?

- What is the reward for meeting goals?

- What processes and software will the vendor use to monitor performance? As part of your due diligence, you may want to inquire whether the vendor has performance monitoring software in place.

Performance Monitoring for Offshore Call Centers

Monitoring offshore agents to guarantee that they are providing the best possible service is a growing business. Witness Systems is one of the providers of remote workforce optimization software. Call center firms — West, Wipro Spectramind, and Spherion — are among Witness Systems' outsourcing clients. According to Wipro, after implementing Witness Systems' eQuality suite, customer satisfaction rose by 9%, call handling times decreased by 30%, and the productivity of agents and supervisors increased.

Performance monitoring software helps companies record, evaluate, and analyze customer service interactions quickly. You can establish business rules to trigger recording of the multimedia customer interactions deemed critical to your organization's operating performance such as "no-sale" or "dissatisfied customers." Storing and retrieving these offshore agent-customer interactions allows for future evaluation, coaching, training, and reporting.

ETelecare Global Solutions, a Los Angeles-based call center organization, implemented a four-part performance monitoring program that relies on performance targets, weekly evaluations, and ongoing coaching by call center supervisors to improve agent performance. ETelecare also monitors and assesses at least 20 transactions per agent per month.

Performance Metrics for Transaction Offshoring

To help your company determine which performance metrics to track, let's look at an example of how offshore insurance claims processing works. Consider the case of ICICI OneSource, a BPO player specializing in transaction processing. ICICI OneSource worked with a leading U.K. motor insurance company to provide inbound customer service and sales for motor insurance. Specifically, ICICI OneSource processed policies, sold breakdown insurance, and e-mailed quotations to clients.

Key factors in the project's success were call quality and hitting sales targets. Agents handling the insurer's customers lowered the average handle time (from a target of less than five minutes to an actual average of 3.47 minutes); decreased the average wrap time (from a target of less than one minute to an actual average of .21 minutes); increased the number of calls answered in less than ten seconds (from a target of 90 to an actual average of 96); and reduced the abandon ratio (from a target of less than 4% to an actual average of 2.3%).

Estimated annual savings for the U.K. insurer stand at $1 million.[1] The value of performance monitoring and management can be directly correlated to a tangible return on investment (ROI).

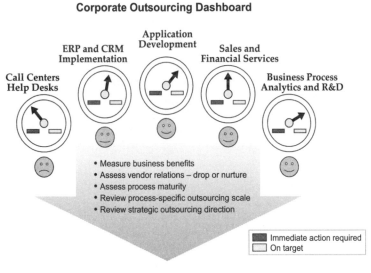

Figure 12.1: Performance Dashboard

Best Practices in Performance Monitoring

In order to better understand performance monitoring, let's look at some best-practice examples of process audits and quantitative metrics.

Process Audits

By developing the right mechanisms to measure, analyze, and disseminate information to the correct people both at your company and the vendor's, you will create data that leaders can use for managing the outsourcing project and for reporting purposes.

It is always a good idea to put into place audit controls such as:

- Are SLA deadlines being met and adhered to?

- Is reporting timely and accurate?

- Is the quality of work consistent with the defined SLAs?

- Is the number of people on the project accurate?

- Does the vendor have valid software licenses in place?

Auditing takes time, but it works to ensure that the vendor is doing the right thing most of the time. For example, DHL Worldwide Express outsourced development and maintenance work to Infosys. At DHL, a project manager audits the time sheets from the vendor and rolls the figure into an invoice, which has to be audited against the overall project and then funneled to finance for payment. Ron Kifer, a vice president at DHL, said, "We knew there would be invoicing and auditing, but we didn't fully appreciate the due diligence and time it would require."[2]

Many companies use a dashboard (or scorecard) report to summarize SLA metrics. The dashboard report highlights what is going well and what needs to be escalated. A color-coded system of red, green, and yellow allows managers to see problems in red that need to be resolved immediately or areas that are green that do not require action. The scorecard is discussed in more detail later in the chapter.

Quantitative Metrics and Process Benchmarking

Metrics drive insight. Insight can help eliminate inefficiencies. In other words, process measures can lead to performance changes. The best way to measure performance is quantitatively. Qualitative assessments are too fuzzy to use when planning business growth.[3] Once you have the quantitative performance data, you can always translate it into a qualitative assessment of the vendor's performance.

Surprisingly, many companies that outsource do not have a good way to calculate the actual costs or productivity benefits of their outsourcing initiatives. When asked, companies usually give answers based on labor arbitrage benefits, but not much beyond that, hardly an inclusive or accurate measurement.

All costs, including productivity, customer response time, training, and quality, must be factored in to determine the true benefits of an outsourcing project. You need to look at the real cost of outsourcing and the related performance parameters. Your benefits from outsourcing may increase even more if you measure the vendor's performance, as well as your own.

Before we discuss performance improvement more, let's take a step back. Outsourcing a bad process is not going to save you much money, even if the savings are driven by labor arbitrage. In all likelihood, it will hurt you since you will have to pay to fix the poor-quality process. If you cannot fix your own process, do not expect the vendor to immediately deliver more productive results. A better approach is for your company to attempt to fix the process first and baseline the benefits. Completing this task should give you upfront productivity benefits even before you outsource.

Relative to quantitative metrics, it is common for companies to find fault with vendor quality, such as errors in a software application, even if they do not have their own metrics in place. If you have not established metrics for your internal processes, such as software development, you will have a hard time figuring out the productivity benefits of outsourcing. Baselining your own performance will help you understand your internal process kinks and enable better vendor performance monitoring.

Designing a Quantitative Performance Metric

Metrics can act like a double-edged sword. Badly designed metrics drive bad behavior, so setting up optimal ones is integral to your best results. Performance monitoring should function as a means for contract fulfillment and driving the right vendor behavior.

To design a quantitative performance metric, you need to dive into the details of the specific project contract and the associated SLA. Prepare a comprehensive list of all parameters that must be measured, bearing in mind that tracking every parameter can be costly and even impossible as the processes or the infrastructure may not exist. Therefore, it becomes imperative to roll up all the potential parameters into higher-level indicators that are easily measured. Select these high-level criteria in a way that ensures delays or poor quality can be communicated to a designated team member for quick follow-up.

Always start with good quality data; less is better, but it should be of good quality. Drill down that data further as you evolve in your ability to measure without overburdening the system. Always keep the cost-benefit aspect of measuring data in mind. Do not measure things that add little value. Setting up a good metric is very important. More often than not, companies set up metrics incorrectly and encourage the wrong behavior. Some common high-level measurements include:

- Time and material (milestone based contractual measurements)

- Quality requirements (payment per bug fix)

- Customer satisfaction (survey or scorecard based)

- Delivery slippage (penalty for delay per day or week)

- Cost overrun (timely but over the budgeted expenditure)

Performance Improvement Using Six Sigma

Improving your outsourcing project requires focusing on the underlying processes. Process improvement refers to a strategy of finding solutions to eliminate the root causes of problems or errors in your company's processes, or if outsourcing, in the vendor's processes.

Process improvement revolves around adding lasting value. One of the challenges in BPO is to transform processes for the better. Process improvements can occur through several methods, including economies of scale, labor arbitrage, or outsourcing to lower-cost nearshore or offshore locations. Other ways to achieve process improvements include:

- Reducing the number of steps in the process;

- Increasing the number of successful cycles of the process;

- Decreasing the errors;

- Shortening the process time;

- Lowering the number of touch points; or

- Trimming the number of decisions required.

Many companies start by outsourcing processes "as is," or basically "take my mess and automate it for less." They prefer to wait until processes are transitioned and things settle down before re-engineering and streamlining processes using methods such as Six Sigma.

Six Sigma hinges on improving what is important or critical to the quality (CTQ). It relies on data, facts, and statistics to identify and correct process defects. For instance, in call centers, Six Sigma methods can help when developing new decision trees, changing the orders of the screens, and altering the decision rules so that calls do not have to be escalated. By eliminating steps in processes or changing the agent scripts, calls can be resolved faster.

Six Sigma–based process improvement starts with understanding the as-is and the to-be states so that you can articulate process goals. Tools such as the performance dashboard can help you identify improvement opportunities. Process improvement fixes problems by eliminating the causes of variation, but leaving the process intact. In Six Sigma, improvement teams employ the five-step process of DMAIC:

- Define the problem and the requirements.

- Measure the defects and process operation.

- Analyze the data and discover the causes of the problem.

- Improve the process to remove the causes of the defect.

- Control the process to make sure the defects do not reoccur.

Define — Problem or Failure Identification

Communication, monitoring, and reporting of SLA metrics is an ongoing responsibility that should be taken seriously (see Chapters 9 and 10). Some questions to answer are: How is performance monitored and reported? How are targets established? Who is responsible for reporting? What is the schedule for client reviews? What are the time frame, content, and format of standard reporting? When and how are exceptions to be reported? What are the escalation procedures?

The SLA simply sets up a framework for operations. In order for it to work effectively in the real world, procedures must be in place to identify problems or failures before they occur. By identifying ways in which a process, product, or service change might cause unintended problems, appropriate countermeasures can be developed.

The typical steps for problem identification follow.

- Brainstorm the potential problems (poor service quality, low customer satisfaction, excessive system downtime) and then describe them and their possible impact.

- Identify the possible causes of the problems.

- Develop a rating scale that will help the team understand the problems' potential risks. For each one, identify the severity of its impact and its occurrence in order to figure out what controls your company has in place to handle the problems.

- Discuss how to eliminate the causes of the problems and reduce their impact, as well as their chance of occurring.

- Assign responsibility for the action items defined in the previous steps, along with due dates for completion. Decide on a follow-up date to meet and review the action list.

Measure — Customer Satisfaction

The most reliable indicator of service performance improvement for outsourced projects such as call centers or technical support is client satisfaction. Many companies that outsource front-line processes are extremely concerned with customer satisfaction, so multiple ways of gauging customer satisfaction exist. Many vendors hire outside firms to conduct independent surveys to find out what the satisfaction level is at various points in the year.

Customer Surveys

Some vendors who handle customers' calls will place them in an auto response survey after the call has ended, offering the individuals the chance to offer feedback on the interaction. This automated method provides instant data that can be collated on a daily or weekly basis. It can be cheaper than having live agents conduct the survey, faster than paper surveys, and not as limiting as e-mailed ones, which count on customers having access to the Internet.

If the vendor doesn't offer this service, companies can still gather valuable feedback by asking agents to transfer the call to an outside party, such as Versay, which can host and run the survey with its proprietary software Versay Survey 1.0 and later report the data in whatever format the company prefers (summary reports, batch, or uploaded in real time to the Web).

Convergys has developed an offering called CyberSurvey, which evaluates service through Web-based surveys that respondents can access through a URL within an e-mail or a Web site pop-up window. Convergys also will warn companies immediately of poor customer satisfaction scores or service inadequacies through a program called SOS (Service Opportunity Solution) Performance Alerts.

The Level of Service Report

The best source of performance data is the level of service, or LOS, report. The LOS provides for periodic performance reports on metrics that it defines such as employee or customer satisfaction. LOS reports evaluate the vendor's conformance with the agreed-upon service levels as specified in the SLA. LOS reports also offer a way to continuously improve process delivery. Weekly and monthly reports will help your company understand and measure how well the vendor is performing.

The LOS contains the metrics and service level information for the engagement. The LOS discusses what the performance criteria are, how well the vendor is performing the service, how often reporting will occur, and what incentives and penalties the vendor will realize for service level variances.

Common service level metrics include percent system uptime, deadlines for completing batch processing, or number of processing errors. Industry standards for service levels may provide a reference point. Your company should periodically review overall performance standards to ensure consistency with your goals and objectives.

Table 12.1 offers an example of how an LOS for a call center outsourcing project might read.

Service Measure	Commitment	Frequency of Measure
Average speed of answer	240 seconds	Monthly
Call center availability	100%	Monthly
First call problem resolution ratio	80%	Monthly
Average call handle time	10 minutes	Daily, weekly, monthly

Table 12.1: Service Levels

Analyze — Improvement Measurements

So far, you have found the data, mined it, and converted it into useful information. Now you are ready to analyze the data to either understand root causes or hopefully gain insights. The focus is on detailed analysis of improvement actions.

Improvement actions typically fall into two categories:

- Realizing immediate productivity or cost saving benefits or

- Moving up the maturity curve with a vendor

For the same job content, you should expect lower labor or contract rates from your vendor year over year. The reduction in rates should keep falling commensurate with at least the same percentage points of productivity improvements expected of your own staff.

If vendors have to compete in a global economy as part of your extended team, they must be challenged to adopt the same productivity gains that occur in developed countries. Some countries, historically and culturally, are not used to seeing salaries reduced even if the economy gets tougher or if the same skills become abundant elsewhere. Many continue to offer the same "raises" to their employees as they did five or ten years ago.

We think global competition will drive those vendors out of business. Their cost structures must align with changing business dynamics and the comparable performance delivery culture. Continuous performance improvement is the only constant in a sustainable service delivery business model. It is no wonder then that new outsourcing destinations are popping up daily and that many more will follow.

Another level of performance improvement occurs as vendors become more mature. With enough technology and product knowledge, they can transition into offering higher-level services at the same prices, which triggers another level of outsourcing to the vendor.

Customer Analytics

In the area of call centers, customer analytics has surfaced as an emerging area for analyzing the root cause of client dissatisfaction. Once organizations know why individuals are not happy with their customer service interaction, they can make changes either to the process or to the rep's training, so improvements can be made quickly and proactively. Companies can also use analytics to identify successful marketing strategies and predict the future behavior of customers.

Teletech, a customer management provider with 33,000 employees based in 65 different global service centers, is a big user of customer analytics. For one healthcare client, the company combined contact center data with customer defection data to develop a profile of customers likely to defect. The profile tracked data such as how often the client had phoned and how much money the person had been denied. If the company received a call from someone who fit the profile, Teletech transferred the caller to a "save desk," staffed by an agent trained for such situations.[4]

Improve — Change the Design or Penalize

Your analysis should highlight areas for improvement. One European healthcare company took immediate action after reviewing customer service data. First it reallocated supervisors' time to coaching agents instead of managing information systems. Second it expanded training by sending agents to visit client locations, in this case, hospitals, in order to better understand the caller's point of view. Three months after the healthcare company launched the program, employee productivity shot up by 23%, while 93% of calls were answered in 10 seconds, and the abandonment rate dwindled to 1%.

Incentives and Penalties

Putting into place incentives to motivate providers to exceed performance requirements (for example, exceed the number of hardware installations) is one side of performance management. The other side is applying penalties to prompt providers to meet performance requirements.

Analyzing performance data helps companies:

- Assess penalties for failure to perform as required by individual service as well as aggregate service levels.

- Apply penalties in the form of credit to the client.

- Increase penalties for recurring deficient performance.

- Retain a percentage of the provider's pay for a particular service until performance requirements are met.

- Refund the penalty if the provider returns to agreed-upon performance levels within a designated period.

- Ensure the provider will cover costs, but not profit, when a particular performance requirement is not met.

Rewards and Recognition

The improvements don't always have to stem from training or correcting certain processes. Giving individual rewards or group recognition can also achieve results. Motivated employees equal better service and productivity.

Rewards and recognition assume increasing importance for a remote, extended team, but outsourcing stakeholders often neglect these areas and don't leverage them for performance monitoring and enhancement. They should be part of your collective strategy for talent retention and knowledge transition.

Cultural sensitivity can do wonders here. Although cash awards would generally never be refused, there are societies where several other forms of recognition may have a better motivational impact. It is important that you and your HR staff understand that. The key is not to forget anyone who should be rewarded. It is hard to drive granularity among individual performances, especially because cultural and communication barriers may not bring out the real contributors on several occasions. Group trophies, institutional awards, and team plaques are useful symbolic gestures for generating teamwork across global frontiers. Individual awards should be given when it absolutely makes sense.

Improving Synergy Across Processes, Products, and Vendors

As your company gains experience with outsourcing and you start leading projects that cut across various products, processes, and global locations, the need arises to drive synergy across all the teams, sharing best practices and processes among teams and locations.

Vendor award and best-practice conferences and other interactions between the entire sourcing team are useful for increasing synergy. A biannual vendor conference is a good idea for starters. Vendors benefit from them too, and a new maturity of relationship management can evolve from them. Some industry analyst firms offer similar conferences for vendors or conduct summits with various participants to drive synergy and help them share best practices, study trends, and gather research data for their own consulting services growth.

Control — Continuous Learning and Recalibration

The core activity in learning and adjustment is constantly looking for ways to benchmark processes and change them if problems are unearthed.

If you are outsourcing offshore or nearshore, the physical distance between you and the operations might necessitate frequent site visits to gather performance improvement data. The questions you want to constantly think about include:

- Results: How much did my organization save from outsourcing? What is the total cost versus total benefit?

- Control: Which outsourcing operations, data, or activities are not performing according to plan?

- Strategic: How is our current business model — captive center, sole sourcing, or multisourcing — performing?

- Adjustments: Are the metrics and measures aligned with the strategic business changes that have occurred?

Answering these questions with detailed data allows you to recalibrate your strategy.

Performance Monitoring in Action: Outsourcing Testing

In this section we look at a detailed case study of Perfect Products Software (PPS), which decided to outsource error, or bug, fixing while developing a new software application so that its internal employees could focus on other high-end areas of product design: architecture, quality assurance, user experience, and system integration.

The company thought it was "wasting" its best programmers on bug fixing and decided it would be good to save their costly time for other challenging projects. So the intent and overall goals were strategically right, but we will see in the following two scenarios whether and how the company could really benefit from this outsourcing experience.

The first scenario shows how outsourcing with incorrect metrics can drive wrong behavior, while the second scenario tells you how outsourcing should be done with performance metrics and proper process design.

Scenario One: Outsourcing with Incorrect Metrics

The PPS application involved the development of an automated online bank loan mortgage process. The SLA detailed the outsourcing work arrangement, and the vendor was to be paid on a per-error fix basis. Given the tremendous amount of IT talent the vendor had, it really was simple enough to do, so everyone thought.

Process Landscape

A loose process was agreed upon, and a corresponding framework was set up to send and receive all bug reports and their fixes through a commonly accessible FTP server (Figure 12.2).

- PPS did not give serious thought to the severity levels of the bugs. It assumed that most errors would be easily fixed since the vendor was certified at CMM Level 4. PPS also thought that any bug fixing would not require much domain knowledge.

- Neither PPS nor the vendor considered a clear hand-off process necessary for each error arising during the application development process. The two companies agreed that as PPS discovered the errors it would put them on the server for the vendor to pick up and fix. There was no defined format to describe errors, so a free format was used. The vendor mimicked PPS's development environment, but they were not identical.

- Neither company considered onsite training necessary.

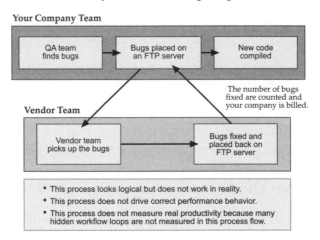

Simple Work Flow for Bug Fixing

Your Company Team

| QA team finds bugs | Bugs placed on an FTP server | New code compiled |

The number of bugs fixed are counted and your company is billed.

Vendor Team

| Vendor team picks up the bugs | Bugs fixed and placed back on FTP server |

- This process looks logical but does not work in reality.
- This process does not drive correct performance behavior.
- This process does not measure real productivity because many hidden workflow loops are not measured in this process flow.

Figure 12.2: Bug Fix Process Map and Metrics (First Scenario)

Metrics (or the Lack of Them)

A record was maintained for shipping and receipt of the errors or the fixes, so that payment could be made for completed work done. Therefore, the only metric was "bugs shipped and fixes received."

Without a clear tracing process or a rigorously mapped workflow for the software development process that showed bug severity or hand-offs between the two teams, this project soon took a very wrong turn.

Results

Let's take a step-by-step look at what happened in the first scenario for a typical bug fix process:

- The vendor looked at the pending error list, picked up the top one, and sent a short e-mail to the PPS project manager asking who he should talk to understand the real problem.

- The PPS project manager talked to the technical leader in his group to find out who would be the best person for the vendor to talk to. Eventually, the PPS project manager determined the vendor should speak with the person who first created the error report. The PPS project manager finally tracked down the bug report creator and responded to the vendor.

- The vendor and the bug report creator talked. At the end of the day, it took them longer to the fix the error than it would have for the bug report creator to address it. Further, the PPS employee lost time interacting with the vendor and the touch points in handling the problem increased. However, everyone was happy that at least now the vendor was somewhat trained in PPS's application.

- A similar scene was enfolding with another error and another member of the PPS team. Gradually, many of the team members became busy helping out the "low-cost" bug fixers.

- Due to the increased touch points, accumulated extra time to fix each bug, and hidden training time, the project fell behind schedule. The blame for schedule delivery largely lay with the outsourcing team and its bug fixing process.

- When the vendor's payments were delayed it produced the e-mail chains and the data to prove that the delays were inherent in the software development process.

In summary, PPS and the vendor had an unsuccessful, unproductive outsourcing experience. The root causes of their problems stemmed from neglecting process design and setting up the wrong metric to measure performance.

Scenario Two: Outsourcing with the Correct Metrics

A detailed as-is process map of PPS's current software development process was prepared (see Figure 12.3). The two companies experienced the following:

- The companies discovered that some of PPS's key programmers reported bugs differently. A simple spreadsheet process to track "who created the bug" was developed. It became apparent that PPS should have invested in more rigorous tools, but didn't because it considered its programmers to be very good and regarded such expenditures as unnecessary.

- PPS tried to stabilize the process and discussed how to map the error-fixing process with the vendor. PPS and the vendor began tracking time spent on bug fixing at both ends.

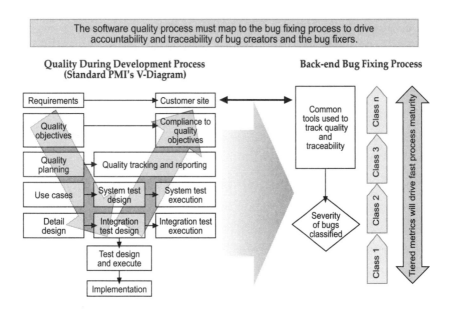

Figure 12.3: Software Development Process (Second Scenario)

Results

Even simple steps to improve the software development process led to a change in PPS's work culture. Process design and metric creation resulted in productivity.

- The project manager observed a significant drop in bugs over the next few weeks. The severity of errors became easier to identify. Only less severe bugs were included in the SLA to be fixed by the vendor.

- PPS decided to measure the vendor's performance by the number of bugs fixed and the time it took to fix the less severe ones. A 10% productivity clause was included in the contract — if the vendor excelled it would be rewarded but if it exceeded a defined time period to fix a bug, then it would have to forego the payment for that bug. Overall product delivery was not to be compromised in any case and was covered by a penalty clause in the SLA and SLIP.

- The vendor agreed to send its core team of lead bug fixers for a short domain-knowledge training course to PPS's U.S. headquarters to meet with the development team. This led to a faster cycle time for product development.

- To create an initial incentive for reducing errors, the PPS project manager instituted a new reward scheme for internal employees. The "wall of fame" installed in the PPS hallways listed the names of the best programmers who had the least amount of errors.

- Internal and external productivity became more measurable and a culture of excellence became more visible.

Metrics

A simple scorecard was created to measure performance. Project managers mutually reviewed the scorecard on a biweekly basis (assuming project duration was greater than six months). It was e-mailed to everyone on the project team every two weeks.

The scorecard reduced the project review time as long as the card showed 'green.' It was easy to read and to get a quick pulse of the project. Gradually, the performance measurements became an accepted practice, and the scorecards were placed on the company portal. They were assumed to be green, unless a red flag popped up. This system led to an increase in the maturity of the outsourcing process.

Summary

Quantitative measurements through performance scorecards are an effective way to monitor outsourcing projects. Care should be taken to monitor only high-quality, measurable data. The primary objective of establishing metrics is to drive the right behavior rather than get bogged down by detailed numbers that don't add value. Further, your strategic decisions should be based on the qualitative assessment of the quantitative performance scorecards.

Imposing a new outsourcing strategy that doesn't include a rigorous data-driven performance metric will result in a costly learning experience for your business.

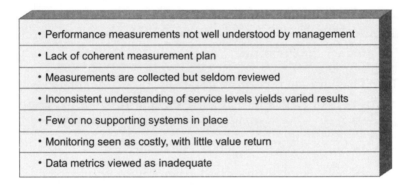

- Performance measurements not well understood by management
- Lack of coherent measurement plan
- Measurements are collected but seldom reviewed
- Inconsistent understanding of service levels yields varied results
- Few or no supporting systems in place
- Monitoring seen as costly, with little value return
- Data metrics viewed as inadequate

Table 12.2: Common Problems in Performance Management

Final Thoughts on Global Outsourcing

We would be remiss if we did not discuss the last steps of any outsourcing project — change and exit strategies. Companies are executing change and exit strategies as nearshore and offshore outsourcing matures. The change strategy centers on the fact that conditions fluctuate (labor arbitrage may not work anymore) and that your company has to adjust to them. They are altering or exiting outsourcing deals for numerous reasons, from poor service and concerns about risk to customer backlash.

Some businesses are even electing to bring outsourced operations back in house or onshore as JPMorgan and Dell have done. In September 2004, JPMorgan, the second-largest U.S. bank with approximately $1 trillion in assets, decided to cancel the $5 billion outsourcing megadeal it signed with IBM in 2002. Dell transferred technical support for corporate customers of its notebook computers to its U.S. call centers from company-owned facilities in India due to customer complaints about poor service.

Political pressure also can cause organizations to terminate outsourcing contracts. Indiana's Department of Workforce Development cancelled a $15.4 million application development outsourcing contract with TCS America, the U.S. subsidiary of India's Tata Consultancy Services, amid complaints from state workers and politicians.

Knowing when to enter into global outsourcing is a choice your company should examine carefully. Just as important is knowing when it makes sense to exit a country or separate from a vendor.

Timing the Exit

It's hard to think of exiting an outsourcing relationship as long as the benefits continue to accrue and it aligns with the company growth strategy. However, after a while, outsourcing projects reach a commodity stage at which it's possible for several vendors to deliver the same service or product without any significant differentiation. The processes grow to be repeatable, automated, and so well-known that outsourcing execution becomes a commodity skill. Further, new technology adds only incremental benefits. Cost (for example, programmer cost per hour) and competitive pricing remain as the only criteria for choosing one vendor or team over another.

The real question then becomes whether your company should take ownership of the process or project or continue buying it from a company as a commodity, with negligible risk attached.

Questions driving your outsourcing exit strategy should concentrate on the following key areas:

- Is the outsourced function a core competency for your business model or your products or services?

- Have you matured in the outsourcing stages to the level that it is no longer a competitive advantage, or, alternatively, has the outsourced function turned into a commodity?

- Are your vendors likely to develop into your competitors in that product or service market segment?

- Have the cost of withdrawal and the geopolitical risk changed from the time you started outsourcing in a particular location?

- Can you can cash (sell) the now mature outsourcing process to leverage it for an alternate business growth strategy?

Core Competency as an Exit Strategy

Some companies, such as JPMorgan, withdraw from outsourcing relationships if the process they are outsourcing becomes a core competency. For example, retaining customers is central to a commercial bank's survival, so functions relating to customer service are core competencies, while employee payroll can be outsourced to a reliable vendor. In the technology industry, a high-tech company might outsource management of its help desk or call center to any vendor and exit from there but keep critical R&D functions.

In 2002, JPMorgan signed what was at one point its largest-ever contract, a seven-year year IT outsourcing agreement with IBM worth more than $5 billion. The idea was for JPMorgan to scale its computing needs with IBM's on-demand services. Following its merger with Bank One in July 2004, JPMorgan announced that it was canceling the remaining portion of its contract and rehiring the 4,000 workers who were transferred to IBM at the project's beginning.

The JPMorgan CIO officially stated, "We believe managing our own technology infrastructure is best for the long-term growth and success of our company as well as our shareholders. Our new capabilities will give us competitive advantages, accelerate innovation, and enable us to become more streamlined and efficient." From this statement, you might infer that JPMorgan was massively overspending on the IT outsourcing contract with IBM and thought insourcing would reduce its expenses.

In 2004, RBC Insurance announced that IBM would purchase Liberty Insurance Services, RBC's U.S. business process services operation. A spokesman for RBC indicated that the sale would allow the company to allot more time to its core insurance businesses, while IBM would gain a foothold in the fast-expanding area of life insurance processing, (expected to reach a market size of $2 billion by 2005) in which IBM hopes to become a major player.

Cost of Withdrawal Analysis

As an early adopter, investments in captive outsourcing units can appreciate significantly in some locations due to real estate valuation or increased outsourcing interest from other newcomers, as British Airways, GE, and Swissair learned. In situations like these, if the outsourcing unit has reached a high level of maturity, then you may be better off selling it to venture capitalists (or carving it for a management buyout) and looking for alternate, lower-priced new locations.

In 2004, GE sold a 60% stake in General Electric Capital International Services (Gecis), its global BPO operation, to two venture capital companies, General Atlantic Partners and Oak Hill Capital Partners, for $500 million. Before the sale, Gecis was the largest shared services environment in India, with 17,000 employees, but the captive center operation had grown too large and expensive to retain, especially in comparison to newer BPO players that had sprung up. In addition, Gecis did not align with GE's strategy of "creating products that make life better." GE will remain a client of Gecis under a multiyear contract.

Geopolitical Landscape Shifts

Similarly, greater unforeseen geopolitical risk may also drive you to exit from an outsourcing location. Delta Air Lines cancelled the Sykes call center planned in the Philippines, citing security reasons in the uncertain political environment as the reason for putting the call center on hold.[1]

Sometimes the costs rise rapidly in countries well-known for outsourcing, diminishing their attractiveness. Countries can experience higher subcontractor costs, increased wage pressure, elevated immigration and foreign travel costs, and greater general and administration expenses. All these expenses can cause companies to trigger their exit strategies.

Exit or Grow

Just like you decide clear measures of declaring outsourcing a success or a failure, you must write down criteria for timely exit for better business growth. Any exit strategy assumes that the outsourcing process or service has become a commodity, and, therefore, is available from others without operational risk.

Final Thoughts

Over the past decade, outsourcing as a business strategy has gained momentum. Companies have recognized the importance of "make-versus-buy-versus-lease" decisions when striving to meet corporate cost reduction and growth objectives.

Corporate boards and senior management are beginning to better understand the economics of onshore, nearshore, or offshore outsourcing.

They are investigating what their competitors are doing in this area and deciding what their own strategy should be.

In this succinct but detailed guide to global outsourcing, we provided an in-depth look at the onshore, nearshore, and offshore outsourcing processes, the benefits that companies may accrue from outsourcing strategies, and the path necessary to achieve them. Using best-practice case studies, we illustrated that outsourcing is not a nice-to-have strategy but a need-to-have strategy in some cases. Some of the critical success factors we emphasized throughout this book follow.

The first success factor: executive leadership. Executive leadership is critical for obtaining and maintaining organizational support for global outsourcing. Communication and strategy begins with top-level executives and flows downward. This flow of information is initiated when organizations start their efforts and should continue through the outsourcing process as new decisions are both considered and reached.

The following activities are examples of how executive leadership can be demonstrated:

- Keep the entire organization informed throughout the outsourcing initiative.

- Conduct regular peer-to-peer meetings at each level in the organization.

- Secure key executive support before eliciting organizational support.

- Establish a communications team to constantly communicate internally the business value of outsourcing.

The second success factor: partner alignment. Aligning client and provider objectives in a partnership helps build consensus and is imperative to establishing early trust among all stakeholders. For this alignment to occur, the client and provider must work together to establish common project goals beyond the objectives stated in the RFI and RFP. Both sides must recognize and understand each other's underlying motives and strive to exceed expectations.

The following activities are examples of how partnership alignment can be demonstrated:

- Enlist upper-management support from both sides for governance.

- Evolve with the provider to determine business direction and identify available technology and requirements for meeting end-user needs.

- Review with the provider's senior executives the performance of the outsourcing relationship.

The third success factor: operational execution. Day-to-day relationship management ensures daily communication and the resolution of issues. Relationship management goes beyond the structure of the contract. The client develops and employs standard processes to manage the relationship in areas such as resolving concerns and initiating or directing work. Responsibility is executed through control and management of the processes, people, and technology associated with the outsourced functions. The following activities are examples of how relationship management can be demonstrated:

- Client and provider management strategies are flexible enough to adapt to business changes.

- Senior managers from both sides handle lower-level client employees' resistance to change by holding periodic meetings to address it.

- Active lines of communication remain open between the client and provider throughout the process.

The key to global outsourcing success is a disciplined plan that minimizes risks. The market leaders that have benefited from outsourcing do not view it as a short-term fix for saving money and "getting rid" of noncore functions. They regard it as an integral part of their long-term foundation that can help lower operating costs, improve customer service, and generate top-line growth.

Appendix A

Request for Information

Here we provide an example of a request for information (RFI) from a large hardware company. The document originally spanned more than 40 pages. Due to the length, we have included only the table of contents and the vendor submittal list. The contents will give you an idea of the sections you need to include in your RFI. We have masked the company names and simply refer to the business that is outsourcing as Company and to the service provider as Vendor.

> An RFI is a method companies use to notify vendors that they may be interested in purchasing services and to gain knowledge about vendors.

Request for Information

Company invites informational responses from potential suppliers ("Suppliers") to provide information technology (IT) services, finance and accounting (F&A) business process services, and human resources (HR) business process services that complement Company's current IT, F&A, and HR service delivery strategy.

Company is evaluating alternatives that will expand and enhance its IT, F&A, and HR capabilities and will allow Company effective and efficient implementation of technology and business solutions and respond to changes in Company's business.

Company will determine at the conclusion of the RFI process whether to proceed with an RFP, and determine the scope of services for consideration of sourcing.

Table of Contents

II.   **Information Technology Services**

    A.   Objectives

    B.   Services description

III. **Finance and Administrative Services**

    A.   Objectives

    B.   Services description

        1. Accounts receivable

            a) Invoicing

            b) Cash application and manual adjustments

            c) Other A/R maintenance

            d) Collections

            e) Period-ending closing

            f) Internal and external end-user support

            g) Deduction resolution and management

            h) External audit support

            i) Document filing, storage, and retrieval

            j) Budget support

            k) Performance measurement

            l) Database administration

            m) Other A/R processes

        2. Accounts payable

            a) A/P processing including manage document receipt, verify and process invoices, resolve exceptions, process payments, and update vendor master file

            b) Respond to inquiries

             c) Provide internal and external reporting

            d) Performance measurement

            e) Other A/P processes

        3. Employee expenses

            a) Manage EE processing including document management, verify and process expense claims, resolve exceptions, process payments, and update vendor master file

            b) Respond to inquiries

             c) Provide internal and external reporting

            d) Performance measurement

            e) Other EE processes

        4. Fixed-asset management

            a) Fixed-asset accounting

            b) Special processes

            c) Performance measurement

5. Payroll
   a) Balancing, time, and attendance
   b) Pay calculation and check processing
   c) Research and resolution of end-user inquiries and issues
   d) Taxes and related compliance services
   e) Reporting
   f) Special processes
   g) Ad hoc projects and analyses
   h) External audit support
   i) Document filing, storage, and retrieval
   j) Performance measurement
6. Financial and cost accounting and reporting
   a) Cost accounting
   b) Financial accounting and reports

IV. Human Resources Services

A. Objectives
B. Services description
   1. Compensation, benefits, and rewards services
      a) Compensation services including surveys and analysis, job evaluations and benchmarking, salary administration for base pay plans, incentive plans, and communications and rollouts
      b) Benefits services
      c) Stock options services;
      d) Service awards services
   2. Organizational and employee development services and training
      a) Organizational development services
      b) Training services delivery
      c) Employee development services, including attitude and pulse surveys
      d) Succession planning services
   3. Employee data management services
      a) Employee records management services
      b) HRMS and payroll
      c) Employee and manager self-service services
      d) Workforce analytics services
      e) Data security services

4. Workforce planning and deployment services
   a) Staffing services including sourcing, candidate pool management, candidate assessment and selection, and contract and temporary staffing management
   b) Expatriate administration services
   c) Domestic relocation services
   d) Workforce deployment services
5. Human capital services
   a) Labor and employee relations services
   b) Vendor sourcing and management services
   c) Policy and legal compliance services
6. Cross-functional services
   a) Employee service center services
   b) Problem management services
   c) Change management services
   d) Documentation services
   e) Quality assurance services

V. RFI Process

A. Key dates and activities

B. Company primary contacts

C. Questions regarding RFI
   1. Process for submitting questions
   2. Question confidentiality
   3. Question file name format

D. RFI updates

E. Supplier capability presentation requirements
   1. If two or more Suppliers decide to respond to this RFI as part of a teaming arrangement, the capability presentation should be a combined response from all members of the "response team," as opposed to a set of responses from each Supplier in the team. This means that one combined capability presentation will be given for all "team" members.
   2. All presentation and handout material should be marked "Confidential."
   3. Company expects approximately 25 Company attendees. Bring handout material and one soft copy of your presentation on the assigned date.

F. Supplier evaluation criteria
   1. Processes
      a) Superior processes

       b)   Ability to integrate Supplier's business processes with Company's environment

       c)   Ability to integrate Supplier's support infrastructure with Company's environment

  2. Staffing and skills

       a)   Management qualifications of project team assigned to Company

       b)   Currency and depth of project team's technical skills

       c)   Human resources approach

  3. Service levels

       a)   Approach to managing service levels

       b)   Commitment to meeting or exceeding service level objectives

  4. Corporate culture

       a)   Corporate culture compatibility

       b)   Commitment to customer satisfaction

       c)   Commitment to relevant emerging technologies

  5. Supplier experience and reputation

       a)   Proven ability to provide end-to-end services management

       b)   Satisfaction of reference clients

       c)   Stability of supplier

       d)   Global capability and experience

G.   Response preparation costs

H.   News releases

I.   Termination of RFI process

VI. Supplier Qualifications

A.   Supplier company background

B.   Supplier customer base

C.   Supplier SEI capability

D.   Supplier ability to provide full scope of services

E.   Supplier commitment to compatible technology

F.   Description of supplier methodologies

G.   Supplier service delivery model and resource staffing process

H.   Governance

I.   Supplier BPO approach

J.   Supplier offshore and nearshore capability

VII. Legal Notification

Appendix A: Functional Categories — Scope

Appendix B: Company Employees by Location

Appendix C: Estimated Annual Spend by Function

Appendix B

Request for Proposal

This is an example of a request for proposal (RFP) one midsize company issued. Since the original document ran over 50 pages, we have included only the table of contents and the vendor submittal list. The abbreviated document should give you an idea of the sections you need to cover in your RFP. We have masked the company names and simply refer to the company who is outsourcing and the service provider as Company and Vendor, respectively.

An RFP, also known as a request for bid (RFB) or a request for quote (RFQ), is a formal method companies use to notify vendors they intend to purchase goods or services and to allow competing vendors to bid on projects. Organizations in need of outsourcing services typically use this standardized process for ease of vendor analysis and comparison.

Request for Proposal

The template shows you the different sections you should include in your RFP. The company section gives the vendors details about your company. The proposal specification section supplies the vendors with information about the proposal process. The project summary section details the project to be outsourced. The vendor questionnaire outlines the information you are requesting from the vendor.

Table of Contents

I.   General Company Information
    A.   Background
        1.   Business description, industry, market position, and revenue
        2.   Business and technical reasons for outsourcing
    B.   Outline of the RFP document

II.   **Proposal Specifications**
- A. Introduction
  1. Expected proposal format
  2. Proposal delivery and number of copies
- B. Acceptable section layout for all vendor proposals
- C. Contact information
  1. Decision makers and point of contact for questions
- D. Procedure for responding to vendor questions
- E. Schedule of events
  1. Date of the RFP release
  2. Proposal deadline
  3. Dates for vendor presentations
  4. Notification details
  5. Date of contract award
  6. Expected date to sign letter of intent
- F. Evaluation criteria
  1. Desired vendor qualifications
  2. Evaluation procedures and criteria
- G. Terms
  1. Standard contract terms
  2. Expected vendor service levels

III. **Project Summary**
- A. General considerations
  1. Geographic dispersion of current Company environment
  2. Company applications, software, and equipment
  3. Company security
  4. Company network infrastructure and management
  5. Company help desk
  6. Company process flows
  7. Company current service levels
- B. Goals
  1. Primary project goals
  2. Secondary project goals
- C. Project details
  1. Budget
  2. General scope
  3. Time line

    D.   Requirements
- 1.   Business requirements
- 2.   Design requirements
- 3.   Functional requirements
- 4.   Ongoing support and maintenance requirements

IV.   Vendor Questionnaire

This section includes any information the vendor will be required to complete. It's designed to provide a comprehensive understanding of each vendor's services.

    A.   General information
- 1.   Vendor name
- 2.   Vendor address, telephone, fax, and Web site
- 3.   Year vendor founded
- 4.   Vendor CEO and years with company
- 5.   Senior management team (names, titles, years with company)

    B.   Company information
- 1.   History
- 2.   Percentage of overall business dedicated to service requested by Company
- 3.   Overview of services and capabilities
- 4.   Key personnel bios

    C.   Employee information
- 1.   Total number of employees
- 2.   Employee numbers by function
  - a)   Sales
  - b)   Marketing
  - c)   Professional services
  - d)   Technical support
  - e)   Research and development
  - f)   G&A
  - g)   Other

    D.   Education
- 1.   Percent of application developers with formal IT education (B.S. or higher degrees in the computer sciences, MIS, or respective disciplines from foreign educational institutions)

    E.   Experience
- 1.   Application developer's experience (in years) in modern technologies (e.g., Java, XML, or .NET)

    2. Application developer's experience (in years) in legacy technologies (e.g., Power Builder, Delphi, or mainframe technology)

F. Certifications

    1. Percent of application developers with formal certification in major technologies (e.g., Sun Microsystems' Java certification, Microsoft's .NET certification, or Oracle's DBA certification)

G. Business domain expertise

    1. Experience in the fundamental business processes (e.g., enterprise resource planning, customer relationship management, or supply chain management)

    2. Experience in the financial services industry

    3. Experience in the United States

    4. Developers' experience in Vendor's own business (in years)

H. Contact information

    1. Proposal contact name

    2. Proposal contact title

    3. Proposal contact address, telephone, e-mail address, and mobile phone

I. Financials

    1. Public or private (if public, stock exchange and ticker symbol)

    2. Ownership structure

    3. Month in which fiscal year ends

    4. YTD results (2002–2004) revenue/profit

    5. Current balance sheet information

    6. Cash and cash equivalents

    7. Current assets and liabilities

    8. Quick ratio (current assets - current liabilities)

    9. Total amount of debt

    10. Litigation

        a) Litigation pending

        b) Number of lawsuits in history of company

J. Proposed solution

    1. Summary

    2. Methodology

        a) Execution plan

        b) List of tasks

        c) List of deliverables

        d) Time line

        e) Implementation time frame for new users

3. Details

4. Scalability

5. Features and functionality

6. Technical requirements

7. Project team
   a) Number of employees staffed on the project
   b) Qualifications
   c) Location

8. Budget

9. Cost of services

10. Required third-party costs

11. Support and maintenance costs

12. Ownership

K. Technical environment

1. Skills and experience with project software specifications

2. Skills and experience with project hardware specifications

3. Project management. methodology
   a) CMM or similar certification (e.g. ISO 15504) and level
   b) If not CMM certified, define rigor of project processes
   c) Role of project manager
   d) Experience with tools that support project management process: project portfolio management tools, modeling tools, version control, configuration management tools, or software quality tools

4. Change management
   a) Company expectations for change management
   b) How often are changes implemented?
   c) Description of vendor's back-out procedures

5. Performance management
   a) Company performance management requirements and reporting needs
   b) Vendor tools and processes for monitoring service levels

6. Security management
   a) Security procedures for people, process, and technology

L. Training

1. Description of training program

2. Classroom training
   a) Classes offered
   b) Schedule for upcoming classes
   c) Location where classes are held
   d) Maximum and minimum class size
   e) Instructor credentials
3. Media and activities employed in training
   a) Written materials
   b) Audio/visual
   c) Hyperlinked reference materials
   d) Hands-on workshops
   e) Online training available via the Web
4. Time an average developers spend in training

M. References
   1. Total number of customers
   2. Active number of customers
   3. Examples of previous work
   4. Client references (minimum of 3 active client references)
      a) Client reference contact name
      b) Client reference contact phone number and e-mail address
   5. List awards and special certifications

Appendix C

Master Services Agreement

Following is an example of a master services agreement between a large outsourcing company and a Fortune 500 company for human resources outsourcing. The document originally exceeded 100 pages. Due to the length, we have included only the table of contents and the schedule list. They will give you an idea of the sections you need to incorporate in your MSA. We have masked the company names and simply refer to the company that is outsourcing as Company and to the service provider as Vendor.

> The master services agreement functions as a broad agreement that establishes the high-level outsourcing relationship between two companies. The MSA provides an umbrella set of terms and procedures applicable to multiple outsourcing projects, each of which has separate statements of work or purchase orders. Large companies often use one MSA that covers all outsourcing projects with a preapproved vendor in order to reduce overhead.

Master Services Agreement

Table of Contents

Table of Schedules

Appendix D

Statement of Work

Following is an abbreviated example of a statement of work (SOW) between a large outsourcing company and a midsize application company. As the document was originally over 20 pages, we have included only the table of contents and tables list. This will give you an idea of the necessary sections for your SOW. For confidentiality reasons, we have masked the company names and simply refer to them as Company and Vendor.

> Developing a standardized statement of work is important when outsourcing. A SOW defines the scope of the project, the services definitions, and the types of services performed, as well as the deliverables, requirements, and roles of each party. Based on the size of the outsourcing agreement, a single SOW may cover the entire project or multiple SOWs may be drafted for individual projects. SOWs can be static, utilized throughout the outsourcing engagement, or dynamic, changing and terminating with different projects.

Statement of Work

This document is the Statement of Work (SOW) document prepared for services for Company. It will be used in conjunction with Company purchase orders and the master services agreement (MSA).

Conflict between the SOW and the MSA shall be resolved in favor of the MSA, except where the SOW expressly supersedes the MSA. Consultant has submitted a firm, fixed price for services and deliverables defined by this SOW.

Table of Contents

3.0: Requirements

4.0: Responsibilities and Ownership

5.0: Reports

6.0: Payments

7.0: General Terms and Conditions

List of Tables

Appendix E

Service Level Agreement

This is an example of a service level agreement between a small outsourcing company and a midsize telecommunications company for call center services. Due to the length of the original document, we have included only the table of contents and an addendum list. These items will give you an idea of the sections you need to include in your SLA. We have masked the company names and simply refer to the two parties as Company and Vendor.

> An SLA is an agreed upon objective document for measuring service levels. On a predetermined frequency such as quarterly or yearly, the company and vendor review the agreement to monitor service levels and negotiate changes. By having the service levels documented, this ensures that both parties use the same criteria to evaluate quality of service.

Service Level Agreement

This Service Level Agreement made as of the 10th day of January 2005 (the "Effective Date")

BETWEEN:

Vendor Inc., amalgamated under the laws of Canada with its principal office at address ("Vendor")

AND:

Company, a Georgia corporation having an office at address (the "Company")

FORMING part of a Services Agreement by and between the parties hereto with an effective date of the 3rd day of January 2005, and subject to its Terms and Conditions.

Table of Contents

Service Level Agreement Details

Addendums

Endnotes

Chapter One

1. For more examples of offshore outsourcing, see Marcia Robinson and Ravi Kalakota, *Offshore Outsourcing: Business Models, ROI and Best Practices* (Alpharetta: Mivar Press, 2005).

2. HCL Technologies, "HCL signs Software Development Agreement with Boeing for the 787 Dreamliner program," February 8, 2005, press release.

3. The leader of this school of thought, Oliver Williamson, developed the concept of asset specificity and built a theory of the firm based around the need for firms to economize on transaction costs.

4. The source was a presentation given by William Strauss, senior business economist and advisor, Federal Reserve Bank of Chicago, titled "Manufacturing in Long-Term Perspective," at a workshop held on September 30, 2003.

5. In *Crossing the Chasm* (New York: HarperBusiness, 1991), Geoffrey Moore popularized the concept of the technology adoption lifecycle. His model is based on the diffusion work of Everett Rogers.

6. These percentages are based on the classic normal distribution, or bell curve, which means statistically that a random sample of any given population of companies must contain: 2.5% innovators, 13.5% early adopters, 33.4% early majority, 33.4% late majority, and 16.0% laggards.

7. Michael Fitzgerald, "Big Savings Big Risk," *CSO* Magazine, November 2003.

8. Associated Press, "Dell Cancels Indian Tech Support," as released on the CNN Web site on November 25, 2003.

Chapter Two

1. Spencer E. Ante, "Savings Tip: Don't Do It Yourself," *BusinessWeek*, June 23, 2003.

2. Source: Patni Computer Systems Limited, IPO prospectus, February 10, 2004.

3. E-Business Strategies conducted an interview with Richard Swanson, director of BPO Services, Patni Computer Systems, on September 19, 2003.

4. For more information, read Dell's press release, "Dell Launches International Services in India," June 14, 2001.

5. Chitra Phadnis, "Dell Forays into Software — On Hiring Spree," *The Hindu Business Line* (Internet edition), June 14, 2002.

6. Associated Press, "Dell Cancels Indian Tech Support," as released on the CNN Web site on November 25, 2003.

7. J.R. Carter originally stated this in the June 19, 2002, LUXOFT press release, "DELL and LUXOFT Set up a Dedicated Software Development Center."

8. David Tzeng and Chou Hua-hsin, "Wistron Lands 1.1 Million PDA Contract from Dell, Due out for Christmas," Digitimes.com (www.digitimes.com) July 31, 2002.

9. Andrew Park, Faith Keenan, and Cliff Edwards, "Whose Lunch Will Dell Eat Next?" BusinessWeek Online, August 12, 2002.

10. Times News Network, "Tesco to hire 770 in Bangalore," January 7, 2005.

11. Sykes Enterprises, "Sykes Enterprises, Incorporated Selected by Procter & Gamble for 5-Year, $70 Million Global Customer Care Contract," June 30, 2003, press release.

12. Aviva, "Aviva announces offshoring plans for 2004," December 2, 2003, press release.

13. Unisys, "Blue Cross Blue Shield Association Awards Unisys a National Contract for Claims Outsourcing Services," February 17, 2005, press release.

14. Knowledge@Wharton, "What Works, What Doesn't: Lessons From Two Companies that Outsource Back-Office Tasks," publication date unknown.

15. This information originated from a presentation given by American Express at the NASSCOM India Leadership Forum, held on February 12, 2003.

16. See note 14.

17. Knowledge@Wharton, "Anatomy of an India Success Story," as released on CNET News.com on June 7, 2003.

Chapter Three

1. E-Business Strategies conducted an interview with Phaneesh Murthy, CEO, iGATE Global Solutions, on December 3, 2003.

2. E-Business Strategies conducted an interview with Sanjay Kumar, founder and CEO, vCustomer Corporation, on September 22, 2003.

3. Businesswire (via ClariNet news services, www.clari.net), "ICICI OneSource 4th Q Forecast: Financial Services Offshore Outsourcing Will Grow by 20%," September 24, 2003.

4. E-Business Strategies conducted an interview with Richard Swanson, director of BPO services, Patni Computer Systems, on September 19, 2003.

5. Jack McCarthy, "Redefining offshore outsourcing," *InfoWorld*, November 29, 2002.

6. E-Business Strategies met with Johnny Vega, CEO of IsThmus, on August 5, 2004.

7. E-Business Strategies conducted an interview with Tim Lavin, senior vice president for operations, Ambergris Solutions, on November 21, 2003.

Chapter Four

1. E-Business Strategies conducted an interview with Somshankar Das, chief executive officer and president of e4e, on October 23, 2003.

2. This information was based on a case study that TransWorks sent to E-Business Strategies on October 27, 2003.

3. This data was released at the 2002 annual conference of the Society for Human Resource Management.

4. This Coors case study written by EDS was posted on the EDS Web site, www.eds.com, as of December 9, 2003.

5. The information related to LexisNexis was pieced together from several sources. Two primary sources were the LexisNexis case study written by Datamatics and LexisNexis case study published by Microsoft.

6. Mylene Mangalindan, "Google to Open Center in India," *The Wall Street Journal*, December 11, 2003.

7. This information was released in the BT Outsourcing Case Study, "Outsourcing gives BT focus and adds value to bottom line," written by BT and available on the company's Web site, www.btglobalservices.com, as of December 11, 2003.

8. Accenture originally included this information in its case study "BT—Human Resources Outsourcing" available on the company's Web site, www.accenture.com, as of December 11, 2003.

9. Michael Sasso, "Accents To Cost Indian Call Center Jobs," *The Tampa Tribune*, January 21, 2005.

10. E-Business Strategies conducted an interview with 24/7 Customer on November 23, 2004.

Chapter Five

1. This information originally was released on one of GE's many Web sites, www.gecapitalindia.com/gecapital/factsheet.pdf.

2. Mr. Scott Bayman, president and CEO, GE India, included this information in a presentation titled "Return of the Big Bet: U.S. Business in India" given to the U.S.-India Business Council at its 27th annual meeting in Washington, D.C., on June 17, 2002.

3. This information was contained within the Nasscom (India's National Association of Software and Services Companies) and McKinsey 2002 report the two organizations coauthored.

4. In the area of IT offshore outsourcing, TCS pioneered many of the significant developments in the Indian IT services industry, including the offshore delivery model for IT services.

5. EDS released this information during its 2003 annual shareholders meeting held on May 20, 2003.

6. Same as note 2.

7. The source for this information was a 2003 LUXOFT white paper. See the LUXOFT Web site, www.luxoft.com, for more information.

8. Larry Greenemeier, "Offshore Outsourcing Grows to Global Proportions," *InformationWeek*, February 11, 2002.

9. December 3, 2003, Accenture press release titled "Accenture Set To Ramp Up India Headcount To 10,000," posted on the Financial Express Web site, www.financialexpress.com

10. Motorola and Affiliated Computer Services, "ACS and Motorola Sign 10-Year Contract for Human Resources Services Valued at $650 Million," December 19, 2002, press release.

11. Although GE sold a significant stake in Gecis, it will remain a prominent client of the service provider for several years.

Chapter Six

1. David Lazarus, "Lazarus at Large: A politician who reads the papers," *San Francisco Chronicle* (column), October 26, 2003.

2. For more on Delta Air Lines' offshore outsourcing project, see *Offshore Outsourcing: Business Models, ROI and Best Practices* by Marcia Robinson and Ravi Kalakota (Alpharetta: Mivar Press, 2005).

3. Kerry Massaro, "Managing the Offshore Relationship," *Wall Street & Technology* (part of the *InformationWeek* media network), October 3, 2003.

4. Ibid.

5. Ibid.

6. E-Business Strategies conducted an interview with David Burke, vice president sales and marketing, Bleum, on February 14, 2005.

Chapter Seven

1. E-Business Strategies conducted an interview with Vellayan Subbiah, vice president of sales and marketing at 24/7 Customer, on September 23, 2003.

2. Stephanie Overby, "The Hidden Costs of Offshore Outsourcing," *CIO*, September 1, 2003.

3. E-Business Strategies conducted an interview with Tim Lavin, senior vice president for operations, Ambergris Solutions, on November 21, 2003.

4. E-Business Strategies conducted an interview with Derek Holley, president of eTelecare, on October 10, 2003.

5. E-Business Strategies conducted an interview with Krishnaswamy Subrahmaniam, president and CEO of Covansys India, during November 2003.

6. E-Business Strategies conducted an interview with Deena Harapanahalli, founder of Opensegue Technology Partners, on February 8, 2005.

Chapter Eight

1. Source: Stanley Singh, the director of Exploits Centre for Information Technology Excellence (EXCITE) Corporation.

2. Canadian salary information from the 2004 Information Technology Toolbox, Inc. (ITtoolbox) Salary Survey.

3. E-Business Strategies conducted an interview with Gregg Scoresby, chief executive officer of Core3, and Van Hansen, vice president, sales and marketing at Core3, on December 13, 2004.

4. Salary information derived from Brendan B. Read's article "'Gracias por Llamar' (Thank You for Calling)," published in *CallCenter Magazine* on October 10, 2003.

5. Infrastructure data originated from Christian Stracke's excellent article, "Mexico—The Sick Man of NAFTA," published in the *World Policy Journal* in 2003.

6. Salary information came from the following Web site: www.offshoreitoutsourcing.com. The Web site of IDA Ireland, the Irish government agency responsible for the industrial development and investment of overseas companies Ireland, www.ida.ie, releases information on the number of graduates from Ireland's higher-education institutions.

7. E-Business Strategies met with Andy Hilliard, COO of IsThmus, on August 5, 2004.

8. E-Business Strategies interviewed several professionals in the Chinese IT services industry who provided this salary information.

9. Elizabeth C. Economy, "Asia Expert Says U.S.-China Relations Booming," interview by Bernard Gwertzman, posted on the Council on Foreign Relations Web site (www.cfr.org) September 12, 2003.

10. This information was originally released in a 2002 white paper written by the American Chamber of Commerce in the People's Republic of China.

11. U.S. salary information from the 2004 Information Technology Toolbox, Inc. (ITtoolbox) Salary Survey. Indian salary information from E-Business Strategies' contacts in the Indian IT services industry.

12. E-Business Strategies conducted an interview with Srinivas Koneru, founder and partner of Opensegue Technology Partners, on February 8, 2005.

13. E-Business Strategies conducted an interview with Charina Quizon, marketing manager, Ambergris Solutions, on September 19, 2003.

14. Source: Business Processing Association of the Philippines.

15. neoIT's "Mapping Offshore Markets" white paper published in April 2003.

16. ePerformax, a company that specializes in offering contact center solutions from the Philippines or the United States, released this information on its Web site, www.eperformax.com.

17. Stuart Grudgings, "Corruption Dogs Philippines as Elections Near," Reuters, September 26, 2003.

18. The source was the Russian Web site www.outsourcing-russia.com.

19. Vladimir Kitov's article, "Software firms aim to copy India's success," *The Russia Journal*, June 8, 2001, was a good source of salary information. The World Bank provided the numbers on Russia's technical employees.

20. "Whitepaper on Offshore Software Development in Russia" published by the American Chamber of Commerce in Russia, last modified February 21, 2003.

21. E-Business Strategies conducted an interview with Alison Jones, director of sales and operations Europe for Source One Communications, on September 10, 2003.

22. As of February 2005.

23. Salary information derived from the 2004 Information Technology Toolbox, Inc. (ITtoolbox) Salary Survey.

24. The Washington Post News Services "World in Brief: One-Fifth of S. African Military Has Aids Virus," October 8, 2003.

25. Ismail Al Naqi, director of the Dubai Outsourcing Zone, released this quote to Suresh Sharma on February 27, 2005.

26. Akash Arora's quote originated from an electronic communication with E-Business Strategies on February 25, 2005.

27. Andrew Bibby, "Outsourcing to Vietnam," *Financial Times*, August 20, 2003.

Chapter Nine

1. The Press Trust of India, "Wipro bags IT outsourcing contract from Shell," May 3, 2004.

2. This quote originated from an interview that E-Business Strategies conducted with Tim Barry, vice president of outsourcing at Keane, on October 14, 2003.

Chapter Ten

1. Larry Dignan, "Outsourcing: Slow and Steady," *Baseline*, July 29, 2004.

2. E-Business Strategies conducted an interview with Daniel Wittner, senior vice president at Zenta Group, on January 27, 2005.

3. Mary Hayes, "Doing Offshore Right," *InformationWeek*, August 4, 2003.

4. E-Business Strategies conducted an interview with Ilya Billig, former vice president of marketing at Luxoft, on November 11, 2003.

5. Stephanie Overby, "Inside Outsourcing in India," *CIO*, June 1, 2003.

6. E-Business Strategies corresponded with Shobhit Kumar, HCL marketing, on February 5, 2005.

7. The source for this information was an overview presentation written by Ambergris Solutions and released to E-Business Strategies on November 10, 2003.

8. E-Business Strategies communicated with Johanna Chapman of Atlanta Accent Management on February 3, 2005.

9. Same as note 3.

10. E-Business Strategies conducted an interview with Gregg Scoresby, CEO of Core3, and Van Hansen, vice president, sales and marketing at Core3, on December 13, 2004.

11. Paul McDougall, "Opportunity on the Line," *InformationWeek*, October 20, 2003.

12. E-Business Strategies conducted an interview with Eric Rongley, CEO of Bleum, on February 15, 2005.

13. Same as note 10.

Chapter Eleven

1. PMI: the Project Management Institute; SEI: the Software Engineering Institute at Carnegie Mellon University.

2. Paul McDougall, "Opportunity on the Line," *InformationWeek*, October 20, 2003.

3. Source: Unisys Web site, www.unisys.com.

4. E-Business Strategies conducted an interview with Sanjay Kumar, CEO of vCustomer, on September 22, 2003.

5. Jack McCarthy, "Redefining offshore outsourcing," *InfoWorld*, November 29, 2002.

6. Karl Schoenberger, "Outsource firm sues in India - Alleged code theft highlights foreign risk," *Mercury News*, August 26, 2004.

7. Karen Guglielmo, "Reading between the HIPAA guidelines," SearchCIO.com, December 13, 2003.

Chapter Twelve

1. This information originated from an overview presentation that ICICI OneSource sent to E-Business Strategies on November 23, 2003.

2. Stephanie Overby, "The Hidden Costs of Offshore Outsourcing," *CIO*, September 1, 2003.

3. Quantitative research methods were originally developed in the natural sciences to study natural phenomena. Examples of quantitative methods include survey methods, lab experiments, formal methods (for example, econometrics) and numerical methods such as mathematical modeling. Qualitative research methods were developed in the social sciences to enable researchers to study social and cultural phenomena. Examples of qualitative methods are action research, case study research, and ethnography. Qualitative data sources include observation and participant observation (fieldwork), interviews and questionnaires, documents and texts, and the researcher's impressions and reactions.

4. Eric Krell, "6 Ways to Maximize Contact Center Profitability," *CRM Magazine*, February 2005.

Final Thoughts

1. Paul McDougall, "Opportunity on the Line," *InformationWeek*, October 20, 2003.

Index